Praise for *The Other Side of Sadness*

"An intriguing and reassuring exploration . . . a useful correction to a lot of well-intentioned misinterpretation." —*NYTimes*.com

"Illuminating . . . while the popular and the professional literature on death and dying continue to surge, Bonanno's work manages to offer a clearly professed alternative way to understand grief that will be a refreshing new resource for professionals, as well as for the grieving."

—*Library Journal*

"Bonanno's thoughtful study of how different people grieve differently features tales of loss that resonate and give us hope."

—*AARP Magazine*

"Bonanno acknowledges that grief is sometimes extreme and requires treatment, much like post-traumatic stress disorder. But with this work, science and common sense come together in a thoughtful, kind-hearted way; stories of loss go far beyond striking a familiar chord—they give us hope." —*Publishers Weekly*

"Bonanno's new book offers to the reader a new insight with a lucid and pleasant . . . and very lively style." —Metapsychology Online

"*The Other Side of Sadness* is brilliant and moving. Bonanno turns our thinking about loss on its head. He reveals the subtle and myriad ways we are resilient, how we find new layers of meaning, why we laugh, and gain insight when loved ones pass. This inspiring book will fill you with wisdom about the other side of loss, and make life immeasurably richer."

—Dacher Keltner, Professor of Psychology, University of California, Berkeley, and author of *Born To Be Good*

"Bonanno, the most productive and influential bereavement researcher in America today, has changed the scientific landscape in the field of grief and bereavement."

—Camille Wortman, Professor of Psychology, Stony Brook University

"*The Other Side of Sadness* paints a refreshingly new and scientifically-grounded portrait of the grieving process, one infused with positivity, laughter, and enduring bonds. Anyone interested in the emotional nuances of the human condition will value this warm, engaging, and accessible book."

—Barbara L. Fredrickson, Ph.D., Kenan Distinguished Professor, University of North Carolina, Chapel Hill, and author of *Positivity*

"George Bonanno's groundbreaking research on grief illuminates mankind's profound capacity for resilience, and shows us how to find meaning in life after death."

—Jim Whitaker, Founder and Director, Project Rebirth

"Drawing on empirical research and the words of bereaved individuals, Bonanno presents an optimistic view of human resilience in the face of loss. *The Other Side of Sadness* is a welcome antidote to assumptions that have dominated the bereavement literature over many decades."

—Susan Folkman, Ph.D., Professor of Medicine Emeritus, University of California, San Francisco

"Bonanno has revolutionized our thinking about how people respond to loss and trauma. *The Other Side of Sadness* has tremendous implications for interventions and for how people see themselves."

—Susan Nolen-Hoeksema, Professor of Psychology, Yale University

"*The Other Side of Sadness* melds rigorous research and compelling case examples to inform, enlighten, and inspire. I highly recommend this book."

—Christopher Peterson, Professor of Psychology, University of Michigan

"*The Other Side of Sadness* is an excellent, emotionally moving account of how people overcome the pangs of grief."

—Richard J. McNally, Professor of Psychology, Harvard University, and author of *Remembering Trauma*

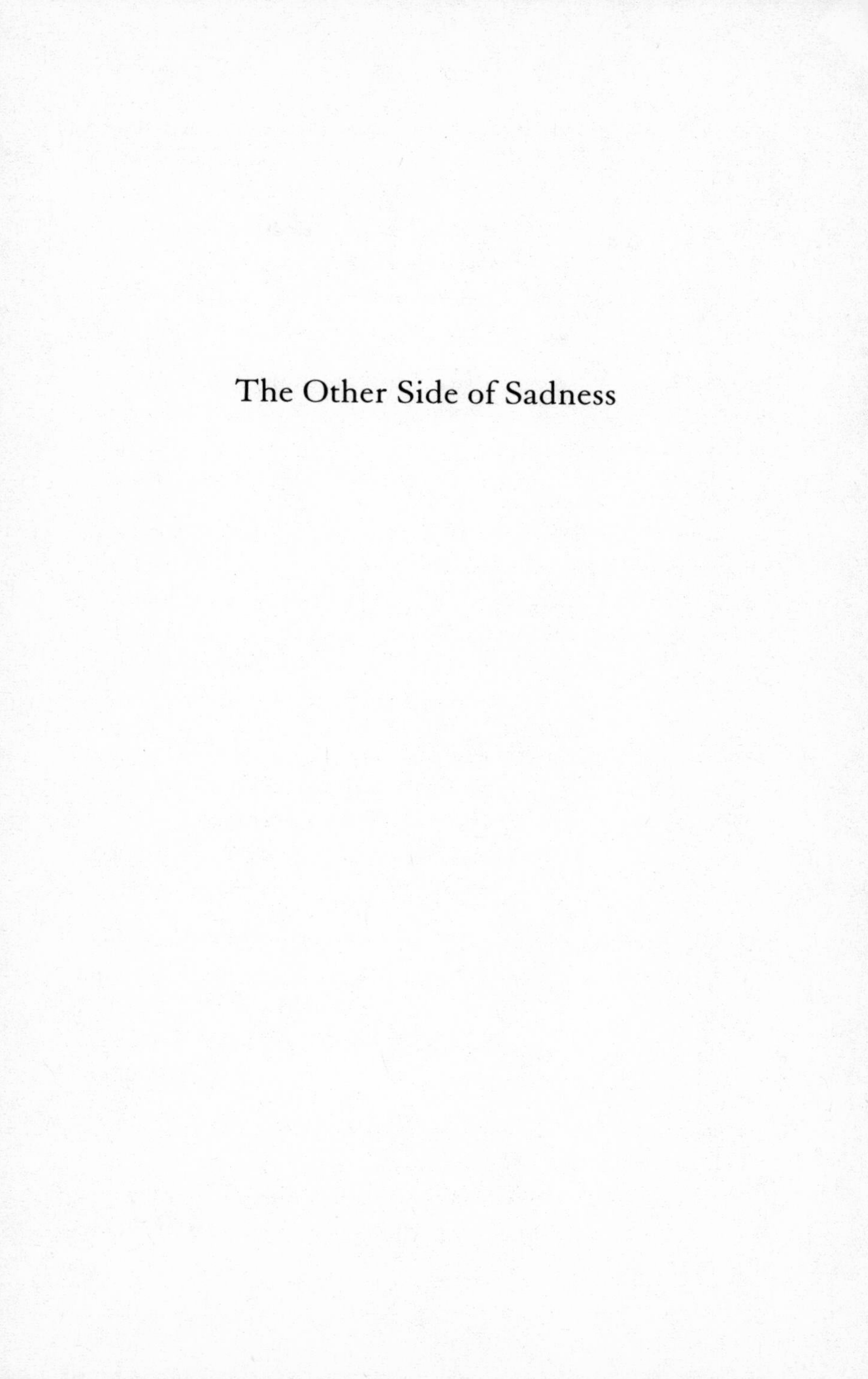

The Other Side of Sadness

Also by George A. Bonanno

Emotions

The Other Side of Sadness

What the New Science of Bereavement Tells Us About Life After Loss

GEORGE A. BONANNO

BASIC BOOKS
A Member of the Perseus Books Group
New York

For Maria Bonanno,
my mother, my friend, and my hero.

Hardcover first published in 2009 by Basic Books,
A Member of the Perseus Books Group
Paperback first published in 2010 by Basic Books

Designed by Trish Wilkinson
Set in Granjon

The Library of Congress has catalogued the hardcover as follows:
Bonanno, George A.
The other side of sadness : what the new science of bereavement tells us about life after loss / George A. Bonanno
p. cm.
ISBN 978-0-465-01360-9 (alk. paper)
1. Loss (Psychology) 2. Bereavement—Psychological aspects. I. Title.
BF575.D35B66 2009
155.9'37—dc22 2009019165

Paperback ISBN: 978-0-465-02190-1

10 9 8 7 6

Contents

Author's Note

With the exception of Sondra Singer Beaulieu, the names and personal details of the people described in this book have been changed to protect confidentiality.

CHAPTER 1

The Worst Thing That Could Ever Happen

Heather Lindquist was in the kitchen cleaning up after lunch when she heard a dull thud. It sounded as if it came from the hallway, and it was just a little too loud to ignore. "Boys!" she yelled. "What are you up to?" There was no answer. She found her two boys playing quietly on the couch in the living room. They giggled. "You jokers," she said with a smile. "What was that sound?" They shrugged. "Where is your father?" Without waiting for an answer, she ran toward the hallway. She cried out in fear when she found her husband, John, writhing on the floor. John had severe asthma. He was taking a new medication, and it had seemed to be working, but suddenly he had collapsed in the worst attack he'd ever had. Heather tried everything she could think of to save her husband's life. Then she called an ambulance. The rest was a blur. John died of cardiac arrest on the way to the hospital.

Heather was thirty-four years old. Her boys were five and seven. At that moment, John's death felt like the worst thing that could ever have happened to her.

Most of us are so fearful of harm coming to those we love that we find it difficult even to think about. With time, though, we have no choice. Surveys on stressful life events put the death of a loved one right at the top of the list.[1] We imagine grief to be a relentless shadow that can lock onto us and follow us everywhere. Grief, as we imagine it, turns light into dark and steals the joy out of everything it touches. It is overwhelming and unremitting.

Grief is undeniably difficult. But is it really always overwhelming?

Heather Lindquist had lived her entire life in the same quiet suburban community in northern New Jersey. She and John had been high school sweethearts. They married and purchased a small ranch-style house. They had children. They got a dog. The schools were good and the community was stable. Heather thought that the television was on more than it should be, but other than that, everything seemed in order.

Then John died and she had to rethink it all.

Now she was a single parent. She had to find new ways to earn money and also find extra time to be with her boys. And somehow she had to contain everyone's anguish. She found strength she didn't know she had. It was lonely and painful at times. But Heather found meaning and vigor and even joy in the idea that she was going to make it.

"I expected to collapse. I really did. That's what I wanted to do. That would have been the easiest thing to do," Heather explained. "But . . . I couldn't. Each day I got up and did what I had to. The days passed and somehow it was OK. The boys were great. They were upset in the beginning, of course. We all were. They hung in there. And we stayed together. I love those boys so much. John would have been proud of them."

* * *

Heather's story illustrates a curious irony in the way we think about grief and mourning. We can't help but know that the pain of loss is inevitable. Death and taxes, as the saying goes. Eventually, grief confronts everyone, and probably more than once in a lifetime. Yet, despite its ubiquity, most people know next to nothing about what to expect. Even people who have already suffered a major loss often do not know whether the grief they experienced was normal or whether they will experience anything remotely similar if they have to go through it again.

The questions we might ask are endless: What does it really mean to lose someone? Does grief feel the same each time? Is it the same for everyone? Is it always dominated by pain and anguish? How long does it last? How long should it last? What if someone doesn't appear to grieve enough? What if someone talks about having an ongoing connection to the person who died? Is that normal? These are big and important questions. If we understand the different ways people react to loss, we understand something about what it means to be human, something about the way we experience life and death, love and meaning, sadness and joy.

There is no shortage of books on grief and bereavement. Most take a surprisingly narrow perspective, avoiding the bigger questions. One reason is that many of the books on grief are written by medical practitioners or therapists. This is not surprising, but it does create a bit of a problem when we try to understand grief in broader terms. Grief therapists are apt to see only those bereaved people whose lives have already been consumed by suffering, people for whom professional help is the only chance of survival. These human dramas may be compelling, but they do not tell us much about what grief is like for most people.

Self-help books tend toward the same end of the spectrum. They portray grief as a paralyzing sadness, an anguish that removes us from the normal path of life and makes it difficult to function as we once did. The bereaved, in these books, can hope only to gradually wrench themselves from half-conscious despair. Self-help books embody this dramatic representation in titles like *Returning to Life* or *Awakening from Grief*.[2]

Overwhelming grief experiences are not trivial, to be sure, especially for the people who suffer them. But they are not the experiences most people have when they lose a loved one. While researching bereavement, my colleagues and I have interviewed hundreds of people. As part of our research, we ask people to explain their personal story, how they have experienced loss and what their grief was like. Many who volunteer for our studies make the point that they tried to read up on bereavement. They quickly add, however, that they couldn't seem to find anything in their reading that matched their own experience. They often tell us, in fact, that they wanted to participate in our research just to have the chance to show the so-called experts what grief looks like on the inside.

* * *

Not long after obtaining my PhD in clinical psychology in 1991, I received a curious job offer: a chance to direct a research study on grieving at the University of California in San Francisco. I say it was curious because at the time I knew almost nothing about bereavement, either professionally or personally. I had experienced only one major loss: My father had died a few years earlier, and I had explored our relationship as part of my training to become a therapist. But since then, I hadn't given much thought to my own grief reactions. I confess that I found the idea of studying bereavement a bit unsettling. I wondered if it might be too depressing a topic to study. I wondered if I might become depressed.

Delving into books and papers on grief, however, quickly piqued my interest. Although bereavement is part of the fabric of life, something almost everyone must deal with, it had received surprisingly little systematic study or attention.

At the time I got interested, though, that lack of attention was just beginning to change.

The Vietnam War had generated a great deal of interest in the idea of psychological trauma. Initially, most of the research had been limited to war trauma. Then, gradually, the scope widened to other types of adversity, like natural disasters, rape or physical assault, and, eventually, bereavement.

Surprisingly, those early bereavement studies provided only modest support for the traditional picture of mourning. Some of the research even seemed to suggest that the accepted ideas about bereavement were actually wrong. Even more intriguing, two prominent scholars, Camille Wortman and Roxanne Silver, published a paper in 1989 with the bold title "The Myths of Coping with Loss."[3] They argued that many of the core assumptions about bereavement were, in fact, wrong. The more I looked into the subject, the more I tended to agree. The "state-of-the-art knowledge" about bereavement, it seemed, was woefully outdated. How interesting, and how inviting, for a new researcher! In spite of my reluctance because it seemed a capricious thing to do, I decided to take the job offer. I moved to San Francisco.

I assumed I would study bereavement for only a few years at most, moving on eventually to bigger and better things. To my surprise almost two decades later, bereavement is still the focus of my career. The reason is simple: So little was known about bereavement that every new study and every new question seemed to unearth something. Often the discoveries that my colleagues and I made were unexpected, simply because we had asked questions about bereavement that had not been asked before.

Our approach was straightforward. The originality, if there was any, was that we simply applied standard methods from other areas of psychology to the topic of bereavement. Grief experts had assumed, for example, that it was essential to express one's pain after a loss. Yet they had never actually tested this idea. Mainstream psychology offered us myriad possible tests. We used experimental paradigms, for example, in which we asked recently bereaved people to tell us about their loss and about other important events in their life, and then we compared the two. As our subjects talked, we recorded their facial expressions and their autonomic nervous system activity as a way of measuring their emotional responses. We also transcribed what our subjects said so that we could measure how often they talked about the loss and how much they described their emotional reactions when they did so. None of these techniques was innovative in itself, but none of them had ever been used before to study the grieving process.

The fact that I knew so little about bereavement turned out to be a big advantage. Although my naïveté could have been a problem, and sometimes it was, for the most part it gave me a fresh perspective. I had few preconceived notions about what we should expect to find, and for that reason I tended to ask simple questions that had not yet been addressed.

I wondered, for example, what the typical course of grief looked like. Until recently, most theories about grief and bereavement viewed grief as a kind of progressive work that takes a long time to complete. Bereavement experts have, in fact, used the phrase "grief work" to describe the extensive process that they assume all bereaved people must go through before they can successfully resolve a loss. They have fleshed out this idea in elaborate detail. Books and journals on bereavement often include charts and lists showing the various tasks and stages that comprise the normal mourning process. "Successful" grieving, it is often argued, depends on these tasks and stages, and failure to complete them will lead to more pain.

Inherent in the lists and charts is also the assumption that grief is more or less the same for everybody and that there is something wrong when people overcome their grief quickly or when they appear to have skipped some of the "stages" of mourning. Armed with these ideas, it is easy to become suspicious when a bereaved person seems too happy or at ease. "Is this some sort of denial?" we might wonder. Or worse, maybe the person never really cared about the loved one in the first place? Or maybe, without help to get in touch with the grief, she or he will suffer some sort of delayed reaction years from now.

Remarkably, though, after many years of studying bereavement, I've found no evidence to support any of these ideas. A good deal of what my colleagues and I have found, in fact, suggests a completely different picture of grieving.

One of the most consistent findings is that bereavement is not a one-dimensional experience. It's not the same for everyone and there do not appear to be specific stages that everyone must go through. Rather, bereaved people show different patterns or trajectories of grief reactions across time. I've depicted the three most common patterns in Figure 1. Some bereaved people suffer from *chronic grief* reactions. The pain of loss simply overwhelms them, and they find it all but impossible to return to their normal daily routine. Unfortunately, for some, this kind of struggle can endure for years. Others experience a more gradual

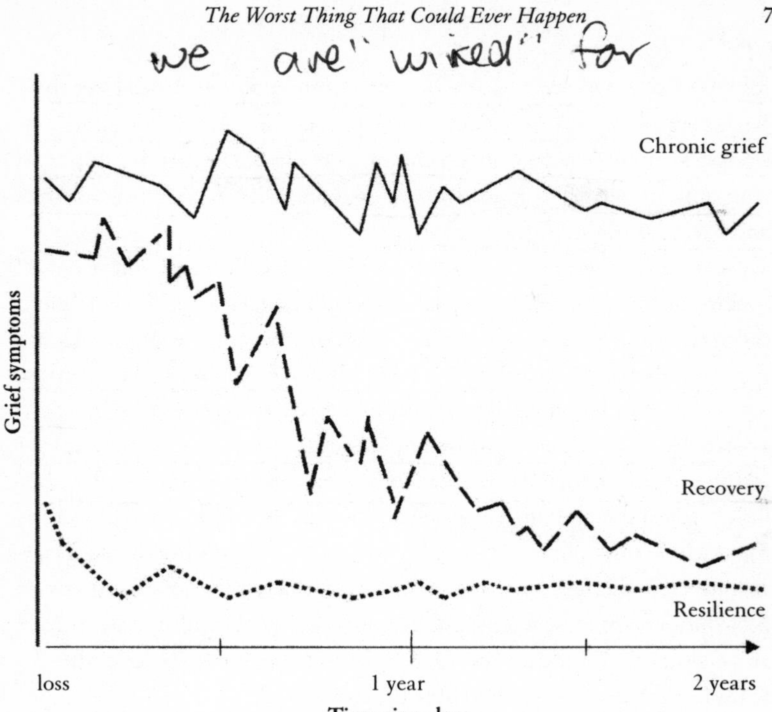

FIGURE 1.—The three most common patterns of grief reactions. Adapted from G. A. Bonanno, "Loss, Trauma, and Human Resilience: Have We Underestimated the Human Capacity to Thrive After Extremely Adverse Events?" *American Psychologist* 59: 20–28.

recovery. They suffer acutely but then slowly pick up the pieces and begin putting their lives back together.

The good news is that for most of us, grief is not overwhelming or unending. As frightening as the pain of loss can be, most of us are *resilient*. Some of us cope so effectively, in fact, we hardly seem to miss a beat in our day-to-day lives. We may be shocked, even wounded, by a loss, but we still manage to regain our equilibrium and move on. That there is anguish and sadness during bereavement cannot be denied. But there is much more. Above all, it is a human experience. It is something we are wired for, and it is certainly not meant to overwhelm us. Rather, our reactions to grief seem designed to help us accept and accommodate losses relatively quickly so that we can continue to live productive lives. Resilience doesn't mean, of course, that everyone fully resolves a loss, or finds a state of "closure." Even the most resilient seem to hold onto at least a bit of wistful sadness. But we are able to keep on living our lives and loving those still present around us.

Another thing my research has shown is that bereavement is not all Sturm und Drang. Sadness is, of course, a big part of grief. I'll explore sadness in some detail in Chapter 3. For example, I'll explain why we may experience it so profoundly during bereavement and what purpose it may serve in helping us deal with loss. I will also show that bereaved people are able to have genuinely pleasurable experiences, to laugh or indulge in moments of joy, even in the earliest days and weeks after loss. Most of the early literature about bereavement tended to gloss over these kinds of positive experience, which were often dismissed as examples of avoidance or denial. My research has suggested the opposite. Not only are positive experiences common, but they also tend to have an affirmative impact on other people and may actually help the bereaved recover more quickly after the loss.

I will focus most of this book on the natural resilience of bereaved people, but I don't want to minimize the great suffering some people experience after a loss. Actually, by taking a perspective that includes both severe pain and healthy resilience, we see these extreme reactions in even starker contrast, and we are better able to examine why some people suffer more than others and what, if anything, can be done about it.

When we put the full range of grief reactions on the table, we also see that there is usually more to grief than simply getting over it and moving on. Bereavement is a powerful experience, even for the most resilient among us, and it sometimes dramatically shifts our perspective on life. Under normal circumstances, most of us cruise through our busy days without the slightest thought of life and death and those other annoying existential questions, like where we came from and where we stand in the grand scheme of the universe. The death of a loved one tends to peel back the curtain on those existential questions, at least temporarily, and begs us to take a larger view of the world and our place in it.

Bereaved people often find themselves wondering where their deceased loved ones have gone. Have they simply vanished, or is it possible that they still exist elsewhere in a different form? Many bereaved people actually experience a strong, perceptible connection with deceased loved ones, something like an enduring bond, as if the person were still alive and communicating from an alternative reality. Such experiences can be comforting, even wondrous, but Western cultural norms about scientific objectivity may also make them deeply unsettling.

We don't see this kind of confusion in parts of the world where an ongoing relationship with a deceased loved one is commonplace, if not part of the very fabric of the culture itself. In some parts of Africa and in Mexico, for example, bereaved people participate in centuries-old rituals through which dead loved ones are allowed to return and walk among the living. In Chinese and other Asian cultures, ceremonies based on ritual communication with dead ancestors have endured for millennia and persist even to this day despite the wear of political upheaval and economic and cultural globalization.

What happens if we try to mix some of these cultural elements? Add a bit of the old in with the new? In Chapters 10 and 11, I ask the reader to accompany me in a bit of globe-trotting to explore these kinds of questions.

Before we do that, though, we need to start at the beginning. We need first to take a closer look at what happens in Western culture when someone important to us dies.

CHAPTER 2

A Bit of History

The death of a child is an unthinkable loss, an inversion of the natural order. Children are supposed to outlive their parents, not the other way around. Karen Everly had no reason to suspect that it would be any different for her. She and her husband had been good parents, and their children seemed to have turned out well. Their teenage son, Bradley, was studying art. He was confident and talented and would soon enter college. Their daughter, Claire, had finished college several years earlier and was well on her way to a successful career in finance. And then, in a flash, Claire was gone.

The day Claire died turned out to be a nightmare, not just for Karen Everly, but for thousands of people. The day was September 11, 2001. Karen Everly was on her way to work in Manhattan when she heard the news. Claire worked on one of the upper floors in the South Tower of the World Trade Center, the tower hit by the first plane. It was excruciatingly obvious, right from the beginning, that there was little chance she had survived.

The violent nature of Claire's death stunned Karen. She felt her heart sink. She heard the life rush out of her, and then, only silence. The emptiness of what had happened left her dazed and uncertain, unsure about what was real and what wasn't. She told me that one day, in the weeks after 9/11, she was alone on the terrace of a friend's eighteenth-floor apartment. As she looked out over the city, she felt something like the presence of God all around her. She was struck at that moment by a plainly obvious idea; all she had to do was leap from that terrace, allowing herself to free-fall to the ground below, and God would allow her daughter to come back. God was telling her this, she was certain. She could repair the tear in the universe, just like that, by taking her daughter's place. She felt her heart race and her face flush. Then she backed away from the edge of the balcony.

Karen Everly didn't listen to that voice. In fact, she did almost nothing irrational. Quite the opposite; she was the picture of responsibility.

When I first met Karen, I was impressed by her poise. This is obviously a person who gets things done, I thought. She was well dressed and confident, and even though she was beset by grief, there was something clear and to-the-point about the way she talked. Karen was also personable. And she held a managerial position in a large company. She was a hands-on kind of boss, taking pride in having good relations with the people who worked under her. None of that changed after September 11. Despite the anguish of losing her daughter in a violent terrorist attack, Karen was back on the job in less than a week. "This is what I do," she told me. "People at work needed me."

After Claire's death, Karen kept herself busy. She found it comforting to handle the details of the funeral services. She arranged a private memorial for family and friends and also organized a public event in Claire's name so that her life would be honored and remembered within the community she had grown up in. There was a steady stream of family and friends in the Everly household. Karen welcomed them. She welcomed the role of hostess, too. It helped her push aside the pain and reaffirmed her sense of belonging and purpose.

Above all Karen was determined not to let grief stop her from carrying on with her own sense of purpose in life. "Well, I don't see great changes in our lives—in my life. I think my life will be as near as possible to what it would have been. Claire loved dogs. It was something we shared, and we were planning to open a small breeding kennel. I am still going to do that. I have had feelings that maybe I shouldn't because I don't have Claire to share it with. 'Cause she—you see, she was so good with animals, all animals, especially dogs. But I'm sure that, you know, if I had died first, before her, she wouldn't have hesitated to go on with the kennel. And she would have told her family how much her mother loved dogs. So, I'm sure we will—I'll still do that."

She described other things in her life that were continuous, still part of her sense of purpose. She had lost her only daughter, but she still had a husband and a son, and her son was just beginning college. She talked about making sure she could continue to take care of her family, and she spoke about her future with joy. "Our lives are tremendously changed—of course they are. And they will never be the same. But in a way, I think I'm probably going to be a better person than I would have been had I not lost our daughter. And I guess that's because you become more aware of how you deal with others, and how you think about others."

Is there any reason we should doubt Karen's words? Maybe this was all just some kind of denial: a rosy veneer to mask her deeply hidden pain. Karen returned to work remarkably soon after Claire's death, but was she truly there to work? Perhaps what she really wanted was to hide from her anguish. What about her sense of purpose, the flurry of activity? Did they mean a genuine embrace of life, or perhaps a desperate attempt to avoid dealing with the inevitable emptiness caused by Claire's death?

Entertaining these kinds of suspicions when there has been a tragic death is not unreasonable. It is difficult to imagine the depth of pain someone has to endure after such a loss, let alone the possibility that they might actually push it aside and move on with life in short order.

But if Karen was in denial, it wasn't a very effective denial. When I first interviewed her, a little over three months after Claire's death, the sting of her loss was still obvious. She cried deeply and openly. Yet she was still able to talk at length about Claire and about her death, and she never seemed to shy away from my questions, no matter how difficult or penetrating they were. Even more important, when I administered a detailed clinical assessment, all the evidence pointed to only one conclusion: Karen was undeniably healthy and well adjusted.

Freud was once asked what he thought a normal, healthy person should be able to do well. His famous and often-quoted reply was

"Lieben und arbeiten" (To love and to work).[1] Karen could do both. Even in the early months of bereavement she was able to concentrate, to do her job; she could control her emotional reactions, she slept and ate normally; and she still enjoyed mutually satisfying relationships with friends and neighbors, with her coworkers, and especially with her husband and son. Of course, she still thought about Claire and still continued to experience sadness from time to time, but it was always measured. She let those feelings bubble up for the most part only when she could afford to, at the end of the day when talking with her husband or when she was alone and had time for quiet reflection. But when she needed to get things done, Karen was almost always able to put Claire's death out of her mind. In other words, although she had been deeply pained by her daughter's untimely death, she had coped extremely well. There were occasional disruptions and emotional upheavals, especially in the first few weeks after Claire's death, but Karen kept living her life pretty much as she always had, and she was moving beyond the tragedy of her loss.

End of story? Well, not exactly. No matter how well adjusted the bereaved might seem to be, no matter how quickly they might restart their normal routine, we still want to doubt them. Bereavement experts have turned this kind of misgiving into a fine art. It is almost as if we have inverted the "burden of proof." Criminals are innocent until proved guilty, but bereaved people are suffering until proved healthy.

Why so much suspicion? Where did it all come from?

The Curious Notion of Grief Work

In 1917, Sigmund Freud published a paper comparing grief and depression.[2] He was interested in the obvious parallels between these two afflictions. Both depression and bereavement, he observed, involve a longing for something that is lost.[3] Yet they differ in important ways. Although both grief and depression involve suffering, we usually don't consider bereavement a pathological condition. Therefore, Freud surmised, suffering must be a normal part of the grieving process, part of "the work of mourning." That deceptively simple phrase, "the work of mourning," was destined to have an enormous impact on how future generations viewed the grieving process.

In Freud's view, grief work involved reclaiming the psychological energy that we'd invested in the deceased loved one, or, as he somewhat unpoetically put it, the "non-existent object."[4] He thought that when we form a psychological bond with another person, we do so with a kind of primitive emotional glue, what he referred to as the "libido." This is the same motivational force that drives our reactions to everything else we care about, including, of course, sex. But the libido is more than sex, and it comes in a limited supply. Each of us has only so much psychological energy to invest, and we have to use it economically; what we invest in one person isn't available for anything else. In Freud's mechanics, the death of a loved one causes suffering because not only does the mind function poorly when it's running on less psychic fuel, but we also find ourselves in a state of constant longing for someone who is no longer there. This state continues, Freud believed, until we do the necessary grief work and reclaim the energy that was bound up with that person.

Freud could have called it "the routine of mourning" or "the task of mourning," or even "the resignation of mourning," but he chose the metaphor of work because he believed that once we bond with something—a person or an idea—by investing our psychological energy, it really does act like glue. We find it difficult to let go. When a loved one dies, Freud observed, bereaved people cling to the memory of that person so intensely that "a turning away from reality ensues."[5] This reaction has an almost hallucinatory quality, as if the bereaved cannot and will not accept that the person is gone, as if the person can be willed back into existence. Joan Didion described this desire in her best-selling memoir *The Year of Magical Thinking:* "I was thinking as small children think, as if my thoughts or wishes had the power to reverse the narrative, change the outcome."[6]

The only way, in Freud's view, to be free of the desire to have the deceased back, to reclaim that psychological energy, is to engage in an effortful review of "each single one of the memories and hopes which bound the libido to the object."[7] Freud believed it necessary to review all memories of, all hopes in, all thoughts of, and all longings for the lost loved one, "bit by bit." He understood that this process was time-consuming and "extraordinarily painful," but he felt it was the only way to break the bond with the deceased, detach the libido, and move forward.

If Freud was correct, any suspicions we might have about Karen Everly's mental health would be valid. Her seemingly picture-perfect health would have to be only a facade. She could not possibly have completed the "work of mourning" in such a short time and could be exhibiting only a kind of hidden grief. Sooner or later, she will have to complete the grieving processing and move on to a genuine resolution. She might not do so for a long period of time—one or two years, maybe longer—but eventually she will have to face it.

Although the language is archaic, the grief work idea does have a certain commonsense appeal. Bereaved people often painfully long for lost loved ones. Quasi-hallucinatory experiences are also not uncommon, like catching a glimpse of someone and, for a moment, thinking she is one's deceased wife, or hearing footsteps in a hallway and temporarily forgetting that a recently deceased husband is not actually coming home. There is some truth also to the idea that we have only so much energy to invest in intimate relationships. We can't go around forming close personal ties to every person we meet. That would be exhausting. So we limit our emotional investments, usually to family and chosen friends and lovers.[8]

But there is a surprising incongruity to Freud's ideas about mourning. For all the controversy his theories generated, Freud was quite a careful theorist, except when it came to bereavement. Freud's writings about grief work are uncharacteristically unformed, almost casual. And he was the first to admit it. When he introduced the grief work concept, Freud added several disclaimers about the speculative nature of his ideas.[9] Indeed, Freud never specified how his emotional glue was supposed to work, or why it had to be unglued during bereavement. The idea of the "work of mourning" is vague and idealistic. It would be nice to be able to regain the psychological energy we have invested in someone simply by going through all the memories and thoughts associated with that person, as if people were like drawers of old papers: Clean them out, file them away, and be done with it. The only problem is that our mental life is almost limitless; there would be a lot of cleaning out to do.

We've come a long way in our understanding of memory and emotional bonding since Freud's day. From where we stand now, it seems that the kind of process Freud attributed to normal mourning would probably achieve the opposite aim; it would actually tend to *strengthen* the emotional bond with a deceased loved one. Memories of people and places are not objects in our heads. They are clusters of snakelike neurons, arranged in branching pathways throughout the brain. The strength of a memory has to do with the connections of the neurons, their links to other ideas and other memories. The more elaborated the memory, the easier it is to find its neural address.

Although we can't undo or erase a memory, we can weaken it.[10] The way to do that, however, would be *not* to think about it, literally, to forget about it until it no longer circulates in our consciousness. When we don't think about something for a long time, traces of its neural pathway will still exist, but other memories and associations tend to obscure it, and to interfere with its retrieval. Its address becomes harder to find. The problem in applying this kind of process to bereavement, though, is that not thinking about something important or emotionally evocative, like a recently deceased loved one, is very hard to do. In actuality, the gradual obscuring of memories takes years, and for the kind of powerful, branched memories we have of our loved ones, even a lifetime is probably not enough to do the trick. We can't speed up the process either. When we intentionally try not to think about something, we usually end up making the memory easier to find, so that it becomes more likely to pop into our minds.[11]

And what if we think hard about something, or think about it repeatedly, as prescribed in the "work" of mourning? This, too, would make our memories of a deceased loved one more accessible, more likely to dominate our consciousness. The more something is on our minds, the more we tend to strengthen its neural pathway. And when we think about different ideas together, we strengthen their connections to each other, the paths of association between them. The most likely outcome, then, of going through "each single one of the memories and hopes" tied up with a deceased loved one is that it will actually make those connections stronger.

Freud never expanded his preliminary statements about grief work. In fact, he never again considered bereavement in any detail. But despite his brief treatment, the grief work idea caught on. Only it wasn't Freud who made that happen. It was his followers.[12]

The Even More Curious Notion of Absent Grief

About twenty years after Freud first mused about the work of mourning, one of his psychoanalytic descendants, Helene Deutsch, published a paper bearing the odd title "The Absence of Grief."[13] Deutsch described her observations of four patients in therapy. Each suffered from seemingly mysterious symptoms that had no obvious cause or antecedent. For example, one patient was troubled by "compulsive weeping which occurred from time to time without adequate provocation," while another had come to therapy "without apparent neurotic difficulties" but was unable to experience emotion or to show even the slightest interest in any aspect of his life. From her analysis of the patients, Deutsch concluded that the symptoms could be explained only as "absent grief." Although she had no concrete evidence for the link, Deutsch believed that her patients had never finished the work of mourning and that the problems that had brought them into therapy must have been delayed expressions of unresolved grief reactions.

This general idea stems from a common element of the classic psychoanalytic approach. The unconscious mind is seen as primitive but, paradoxically, also autonomous and intelligent, like a clever but childish beast within us. If we deny the unconscious, it will get the best of us. It will find a way to express its needs, even if it has to be in cloaked form. When this view of the unconscious is combined with the idea that mourning is work, then grief becomes a kind of inner psychological need with a will of its own and the power to make itself heard.

At first blush, it seems unlikely that Deutsch's account would have much of a lasting impact. Four patients is a small number to base such a provocative theory on. Perhaps Deutsch was only fishing. Perhaps she was hard-pressed for an explanation of what might otherwise be viewed as failed therapy cases. The loss of loved ones is a fact of life. It would not be uncommon to find bereavement lurking somewhere in almost any patient's past. Linking these earlier losses to a patient's current unexplained symptoms offered a convenient way to explain the case and provided a rationale for the analytic treatment. But this link was also highly subjective and couldn't be verified. This small detail didn't seem to matter. In fact, Deutsch's paper became something of a classic. By the time of its publication, the mental health world generally regarded psychoanalysis as the preferred method for penetrating the deeper recesses of the human mind. And no research was yet available to refute Deutsch's claims.

Nonetheless, the idea of absent grief might still have vanished into the scholarly waste bin if it wasn't for another paper that appeared just a few years later. In 1944, American psychiatrist Eric Lindemann published what is generally considered the first study on bereavement and a landmark exploration of the topic.[14] Not only did Lindemann work with a much broader group of bereaved people, but many were survivors of the infamous Coconut Grove nightclub fire that had taken place in Boston in 1942. On the night of the fire, the club had been packed with boisterous celebrants from a Harvard–Yale football game, and nearly five hundred people lost their lives. It was a horrendous event, and it gave Lindemann's work a bit of notoriety.

Lindemann was firmly anchored to the conceptual limitations of his era. He viewed grief primarily as a medical problem, and he championed the concept of absent grief that Deutsch had first introduced. But Lindemann took the idea a step further. Not only did he believe that psychological problems could be traced back to an earlier, unresolved grief reaction, but he also argued that even outwardly healthy responses to loss were suspect. Lindemann believed that no matter how healthy bereaved people might appear, or how much they might seem to have moved on, or even how long ago the loss occurred, a hidden, unresolved grief might still be lurking somewhere in their unconscious.

So what was the evidence for this bold speculation? Surprisingly, there was none. What Lindemann did was gather a group of bereaved people together, interview them, and then summarize his "psychological observations." There was nothing particularly objective about his approach, and there was no way to substantiate his conclusions.

This is *not* how we do investigative research these days. The reason we rely so heavily on research evidence in developing psychological theories is that it provides a relatively objective picture, a glimpse of the "psychological truth" of whatever it is we are observing. Researchers today go to great lengths to demonstrate that the measurements they use and the observations they make are reliable, that is, that they will be the same each time, no matter who uses those measurements. It is also crucial that the methods used in a research study be described in great detail, so that other researchers can evaluate the quality of the study and replicate the findings to ensure they are valid. Lindemann followed none of these rules, and consequently we have no way of knowing whether his observations were accurate.

It was another fifty years before researchers got around to examining the issue of delayed grief. By this time, however, the standards of evidence had changed, and the newer studies that looked into the question of delayed grief, using reliable and valid measurements, found absolutely no support for its existence.[15] People who were well adjusted after a loss were almost always healthy years later. Delayed grief simply did not occur.

Stages of Mourning

Despite the evidence, or I should say lack of evidence, the idea that not grieving enough will lead to delayed grief has somehow become a cultural given. Not only do most professionals still endorse the idea, but almost everyone else believes it as well. And although modern theories of bereavement are more detailed and broader in scope than the original writings of Freud, Deutsch, and Lindemann, they have nonetheless retained the idea that grief is work—work that is time-consuming and must be done before full recovery can take place. Modern conceptions of bereavement have simply filled in the spaces of Freud's grief work idea. The work of mourning is now commonly viewed as requiring a series of tasks or stages.

Perhaps the most well-known stage model of mourning is that of Elisabeth Kübler-Ross.[16] She believed that bereaved people pass through five distinct stages of mourning: denial, anger, bargaining, depression, and finally acceptance. Kübler-Ross assumed that each stage was an essential component of the mourning process and that most bereaved people work through the struggles inherent in each stage before moving on to the next one.

Kübler-Ross's model was actually inspired by an earlier theory of British psychiatrist John Bowlby.[17] The peculiar thing about both Kübler-Ross's and Bowlby's stage theories is that neither was derived primarily from work with bereaved people. Kübler-Ross devoted her career to helping terminal patients confront their own death. Her idea about stages of grief was developed largely from observations of her dying patients. But grieving over the death of a loved one is not the same as facing your own death. There are some commonalities between dying and grieving to be sure, and we'll get into that a bit later. For the most part, though, it seems that facing one's own death is not the best experience upon which to model how people cope with the loss of a loved one.

Bowlby's beliefs evolved out of his own detailed observations of the attachment patterns of children and their caregivers. In the first half of the twentieth century, when Bowlby was developing these ideas, it was not uncommon for women in Western industrialized countries to be hospitalized for a week or longer following childbirth. Since most women had more than one child, a mother had to be separated from her other children while giving birth to a new baby. Bowlby observed that infant reactions to separation seemed to progress through a series of stages, beginning with a protest reaction, followed by anger, then sadness, despair, withdrawal, and disorganization. He then modified these observations to fit what he presumed were similar reactions in bereaved adults. But again, the way infants react to separation from their mothers is not necessarily the same as the reaction of an adult trying to come to terms with the death of a loved one.

There is something else rather curious about the "stages" idea: Like much of the conventional wisdom on bereavement, there is not much in the way of empirical evidence to support it. Admittedly, the stages concept has its appealing features. It serves as a neat and tidy way to think about grieving. It provides a comforting outline of what people might expect while they are going through difficult times. But one could argue that if the stages aren't accurate, then such an idea may be dangerous. Perhaps it does more harm than good.

The major problem with these ideas is that they tend to create rigid parameters for "proper" behavior that do not match what most people go through. As a result, they foster doubt and suspicion about successful coping, and when we cast suspicion on a bereaved person just because we think she coped with death too well or got on with her life too quickly, we only make her loss more difficult to bear. I've heard innumerable stories of well-meaning family and friends who've pressured otherwise healthy people to seek professional help so that they'll "get in touch" with their hidden grief. The fact is that most of the time, there is no hidden grief. There may be lingering questions about the relationship, or changes wrought by the death may have to be dealt with, but usually when grief has come and gone, that's it. Even if the anguish was short-lived, most of the time all that means is that the person has managed her or his grief effectively and is moving on with life.

"Maybe You Should See a Grief Counselor"

Julia Martinez's story shows the kind of unwarranted suspicion that often occurs when a bereaved person doesn't conform to common expectations about working through grief. Julia was home from college for the winter break. Her mother was in the kitchen preparing dinner. Julia heard the phone ring, then her mother's cry of anguish. Her father had been hit by a car while bicycling home from work. He was in critical condition in the hospital's intensive care unit. Julia and her mother arrived just in time to witness the hospital staff struggling, but ultimately failing, to revive him. They were stunned.

"I don't remember much after that," Julia told me, "other than crying a lot." In the days that followed, she withdrew from her mother and spent long hours alone in her room. She worried about the future and what might happen to her family, and she had trouble sleeping. When her brother came home from college, his presence made everything a lot easier for Julia. She and her brother were close, and they spent most of the few weeks after their father's death together. They were quiet at times but found that they could go out, laugh, and forget about their troubles, at least for a little while. Finally, it was time to return to school. Other relatives were around to help their mother, and everyone agreed that it was best for Julia and her brother to maintain their grades.

Once back at college, Julia launched herself into her studies. She spent time with her friends. When they asked her if she wanted to talk about her father's death, she said that she preferred not to, that she would rather enjoy their companionship just as before. Things seemed to go pretty well for the next few months. Julia said that during this time she tried not to think too much about her father's death. There were occasions when she felt sad and confused, and sometimes she cried, but at these times, she said, "I was mostly worrying about my mother, and my brother, too. He was having a difficult time at school."

That summer, back at home, Julia got an internship at the local newspaper. She was excited about trying something new: "I thought everything was going to be OK." Then one night, Julia's mother said that she was worried because Julia seemed to have completely forgotten her father. She wondered if maybe Julia had denied her grief.

"Maybe you should see a grief counselor," said Julia's mom, looking hesitant and worried.

"At first, I didn't think she was serious." Julia told me, "but she kept at it. Then I knew I was in trouble. Once my mother sets her sights on something, it gets done." Rather than fight her mother, Julia agreed to see a counselor. The sessions with her therapist lasted eight weeks, and Julia hated every moment of that time. "He kept asking me about my

father, what our relationship was like, and stuff like that. I mean, I've had some psychology in school, you know. I'm not stupid. I could see what he was getting at." Julia told me she tried to "play along" but mostly felt bored and annoyed. She said there was no question in her mind that she had loved her father, but she resisted the therapist's attempts to examine the relationship. The insurance coverage for the sessions eventually expired, and Julia's mother agreed she could stop going.

Julia was probably wise to question a therapy that didn't feel right to her, and her mother was probably wise to acquiesce in Julia's stopping the therapy. Psychotherapy is helpful when it is used for the right kind of problem, but in my experience, someone's not grieving "enough" is rarely a problem demanding psychotherapy, and in fact, it is rarely even a problem.

Like Julia Martinez, many people who suffer difficult losses exhibit a natural resilience. They hurt deeply, but the hurt passes, and relatively soon after the loss they can resume functioning and enjoying life. This is not true of everyone, of course. Not all bereaved people are lucky enough to cope so well. We'll come back to this serious issue later. For now, though, we'll stay focused on the empirical fact that most bereaved people get better on their own, without any kind of professional help. They may be deeply saddened, they may feel adrift for some time, but their life eventually finds its way again, often more easily than they thought possible. This is the nature of grief. This is human nature.

CHAPTER 3

Sadness and Laughter

If grief is not work, then what is it?

Robert Ewing thought he knew. Robert was in his late fifties, when I met him. A successful advertising executive, he dressed well but was slightly overweight and a bit disheveled. This gave him a casual air. It seemed to suit him. He was friendly and easy to talk to and, as I eventually learned, enjoyed his leisure time.

A few years before I interviewed him, Robert had lost both his parents. His father died first. He had lived a full life but his heart gave out. Although Robert saw it coming, it was the first major loss he had ever experienced. He was pinched by sadness and a bit frightened of what might lie ahead. But the grief did not last long. There were too many other things to think about. For starters, his mother was in her eighties and now lived alone. She was going to need help. Robert's wife looked in on her when she could, but most of the burden fell to Robert. There were also his three children to think about. Each had finished college and was living independently. They all seemed to be doing fine, but ever the dutiful father, Robert felt compelled to stay in close touch with them. He also stayed close to his sister, Kate; he was especially fond of her two young sons.

Three years later, Robert's mother died. With both parents gone, he began to think more about his own mortality. Still, the grief was not overwhelming. "You expect your parents to die someday. We all know it's going to happen," he told me. "I felt very sad at times, but it seemed more that I was feeling sorry for myself because they were both gone. I knew I would get over it. I knew I would have to," he explained. "I still had my wife, and the children seemed to be doing fine. And there was my sister, Kate, her family, those boys of hers. We all got along so well, spent a lot of time together, at family events and the like. And you know, everyone was healthy. We were lucky that way."

Then the luck ran out. A little over a year after their mother passed away, Kate was diagnosed with a malignant brain tumor. The news came as a shock, but Robert vowed to help in any way he could. He threw himself into the fight, making phone calls, researching alternative cures. If there was a way to beat the cancer, Robert would find it. But nothing worked—and within six months Kate was dead.

At first, Robert was stunned. "You know, it was just impossible to make sense of it. Kate had such a presence. She was a real dynamo. When she came into a room, everything changed. She was that magnetic. To watch her wither away, the life draining out of her like that, it made no sense . . . I couldn't believe it."

Over the few days following Kate's death, it began to sink in. Kate was gone. She would never again pester him with late-night phone calls. He would never again watch in quiet admiration the flawless way she orchestrated family gatherings, never again tease her, never again share a laugh with her. Those experiences were now memories, and already growing distant.

What Robert Ewing found out was that one of the key components of grief is intense sadness. Most of us know, of course, that people feel sad when they grieve. But we know this as an abstract fact, a bit of information. It is not until we actually experience a profound loss that we really know how intensely sadness can penetrate our being, how all-encompassing and bottomless it can seem. Robert had never felt this kind of sadness before. Not when his father died, and not when his mother died. He had been sad about their death, but he had known each loss was coming, and he managed the pain well. When Kate died,

Robert felt as if the dam broke. All he could think about was "Kate's soft face" and "that kind twinkle she always had in her eyes." He felt as if he was "drowning in sadness." At first, it was unbearable: "I thought my heart had shattered. . . . I didn't know anything could hurt that much."

Theologians have likened the sadness of grief to an "inward desolation."[1] When Karen Everly's daughter died on 9/11, Karen's sadness was strangely noiseless, as if her heart were "silently" tearing in two. Heather Lindquist's sadness after losing her husband felt weighty. She kept herself busy, and if she sat with the sadness too much, it would crush her. Julia Martinez wasn't able to find words to do justice to the anguish she experienced when her father died. When I pressed her, she simply shook her head and said, "It was sad. Just plain sad."

* * *

Everybody seems to agree that grief is dominated by sadness, but why? Why do we become sad? Why would nature have given us these reactions? What good do they do? These questions were percolating in my head when I arrived in San Francisco to begin my work on bereavement. They might be floating in my head to this day, if serendipity had not come into play. When I left for San Francisco, a colleague gave me the name of a friend, Dacher Keltner, who lived in the area. She thought Dacher and I might have something in common. Like me, he was beginning a career as a research psychologist. I called him and we arranged to get together. It turned out to be one of the most important meetings of my life.

Dacher didn't look much like a scientist. When I met him, he had longish blond hair and a friendly, casual demeanor. He seemed as though he'd be more at home in the ocean with a surfboard than in a classroom or laboratory. I soon discovered that not only was he enormously charming, but he also possessed one of the most probing and thoughtful minds I have ever encountered.

At the time, Dacher was working with Paul Ekman, the pioneer of modern research on emotion. Ekman's research had changed the way psychologists think about emotion. For most of its brief history, psychology had placed emotions in the background. They were considered primitive, a vestige of our ancient animal brain that we needed to control. Ekman's research changed all that. He showed that emotions are more than just a primitive annoyance. They are varied, they are complex, and above all they are useful. The ability to understand and communicate emotional nuance, Ekman argued, is something we are born with, and the different emotional reactions we have play a key role in almost every aspect of our behavior.[2]

As Dacher and I got to know each other, we discovered a wealth of shared interest and began to discuss collaborative research projects. Eventually, the focus of our conversation shifted to the topic of bereavement. I explained the dominant theories on facing the loss in various stages and on working through the painful emotions of grief. I described the reservations I had about these theories: To me, they just didn't seem to make sense. For his part, Dacher began teaching me about emotion. He helped me understand how emotions work, what various methods researchers had been using to study emotion, and where the field was headed. There seemed to be so much we could do, so many angles to explore. Almost nothing was known about how emotion worked during bereavement, and there were so many questions that at first we didn't know where to begin. We decided to start with the basics.

* * *

Emotions are seen in all humans in all cultures. They seem to have spread along the evolutionary tree. We can't ask animals about their feelings, but as Darwin pointed out over 150 years ago, and as many pet owners today will attest, animals often exhibit behaviors that, at least on the surface, appear similar to human emotional responses.[3] We will probably never know for sure whether animals have emotions, but we can say with some certainty that during the course of our evolutionary development, we seem to have expanded on these same basic animal propensities and developed an exceptionally rich and complex emotional repertoire.

Psychologists who study emotional behavior believe that the evolution of emotions was crucial for human survival.[4] As difficult as our lives might seem today, the modern world is a veritable piece of cake compared to what our ancient ancestors faced. Tens of thousands of years ago, every day was a potentially life-threatening ordeal. Food was almost always scarce, and if disease or the elements didn't pose enough of a threat, predators did. Emotions very likely came about because they helped early humans deal with these demanding circumstances.

We continue to confront some of the same challenges today: getting along socially with others, competing for resources, avoiding physical danger, defending ourselves from aggression, taking care of those we love, and, of course, dealing with loss.

Emotions help us manage these situations in two main ways. The first is that we "feel" emotion. This might seem obvious, but most of us take this simple fact for granted. Emotions come and go. Sometimes they are pleasant and sometimes unpleasant, and most of the time we are not sure exactly why. But if we pay attention to our emotional reactions, we quickly learn that they tell us a great deal about what is going on in the world around us, and they help us to understand how we are reacting to it. Take anger, for example. Anger is one of the most powerful emotions we have. It probably evolved as a useful response when we felt someone was trying to cheat us or take what was rightfully ours, or when we were threatened or demeaned. But the crucial component—what generates anger—is the perception that another person is deliberately trying to cause us harm.[5] When we get angry, we tell ourselves who, or what, we think is responsible for the threat. Along with the feeling of anger, our body initiates a chain of physiological responses that prepares us to defend ourselves. As a result, we focus our thoughts and consolidate our resources. Our heart beats faster. We tense our muscles and flare our nostrils. We breathe deeply. We take in more oxygen. In short, we ready ourselves to take action.

Nonetheless, as useful as our own feelings may be, there is more to emotion than what goes on inside us. The fact that we show emotion to others is also of great use. We all express emotions in a number of different ways, but the most prominent and most well-developed expressions occur in the face. We have developed a remarkably sophisticated set of facial expressions, involving literally hundreds of individual muscle actions. For evolution to have resulted in such an elaborate system, the facial display of emotion must have carried great survival value. But what is that value?

For anger, the function of emotional expression seems obvious. An angry expression indicates to other people, quickly and efficiently, that we are feeling threatened and, more important, that we are willing to respond to that threat. It is especially telling that when we are angry we often grit our teeth, usually with our mouths closed. This component of the expression is probably a modification of the more primitive animal response often seen in dogs and our closest primate relatives: showing the teeth as a threatening gesture. An angry expression may be provocative, but it may also prevent as many confrontations as it provokes. Sometimes just showing another person that we have been angered by his or her actions goes a long way toward resolving the problem.[6]

Another salient example is the facial expression of disgust. When we encounter something truly revolting, like a noxious taste or a horrible smell, we experience the potent feeling of being disgusted. We also tend to look disgusted. Our face typically contorts into a grimace that nearly everybody instantly recognizes as disgust. We literally look as though we are trying to expel something: The skin of our nose wrinkles, our eyebrows lower, and the corners of our upper lip pull back. Usually our mouths are open, and sometimes we stick out our tongue as if to voice the "blecch" sound. Out of context, the grimace of disgust is almost humorous, but in fact it may convey information of life-or-death importance. Consider, for example, our protohuman ancestors as they explored the world around them and tried to determine what they could safely touch or ingest, whether some strange object they had come across was diseased or poisonous. The expression of disgust instantly captures the attention of others and warns of possible toxicity. Although by comparison our world today is relatively free of such dangers, there are still plenty of noxious substances floating around: Just try finding a clean seat on a New York City bus! And experimental studies have demonstrated that the expression of disgust still readily captures our attention.[7]

The Function of Sadness

The emotion of sadness occurs when we know we've lost someone or something important and there is nothing we can do about it.[8] Of course, we sometimes blame someone or something for a loss. In those moments, we experience both sadness and anger, but sadness in its purest form is essentially about resignation.

Sadness turns our attention inward so that we can take stock and adjust.[9] When people are made to feel temporarily sad—for example, if they are shown depressing films or are exposed to heartrending music—they become more detail-oriented.[10] One study found that people exposed to a somber piece of orchestral music by Gustav Mahler were less likely than others to make false memory errors. Such errors are not uncommon, and most of the time we have no idea we are making them. For example, in general, when people are exposed to a list of related words, such as *bed, pillow, rest, awake,* and *dream,* and are later tested for their memory of those words, they are likely to falsely remember having seen words suggested by the category, such as *sleep,* that were not actually presented. Sad people are less likely to make these kinds of errors, which the researchers concluded indicates that "with sadness comes accuracy."[11] People made to feel sad are also more accurate in the way they view their own abilities and performance and are also more thoughtful and less biased in their perceptions of other people. For example, compared to angry people, sad people show greater resistance to stereotypes when they make judgments about others.[12] In general then, sadness helps us focus and promotes deeper and more effective reflection.

During bereavement, when we are trying to adjust to the death of a loved one, the functions of sadness become essential tools that help us accept and accommodate to the loss. As his sadness about his sister's death set in, Robert Ewing began to reflect on the many ways she had been a part of his life, and on the fact that he would never have those experiences again. The pain of this realization forced him to come to terms with the ways his life would be different without her. Sadness helps us make these kinds of adjustments by giving us a forced "time-out."[13] In this way, sadness is almost the opposite of anger: Whereas anger prepares us to fight, sadness dampens our biological systems so that we can pull back. Sadness slows us down and, by doing so, seems to slow the world down. Sometimes bereaved people even say that living with the sadness of loss is like living in slow motion. There seems to be less need to pay attention to the world around us, so we are able to put aside normal, everyday concerns and turn our attention inward.[14]

There is still more to sadness. When we are feeling sad, we can become lost in reflection, so occupied with the sobering reality of what we have lost that we may temporarily forget about our own immediate needs and responsibilities or the needs of those around us. If unchecked, this kind of preoccupation could be dangerous, but sadness comes equipped with a built-in safety mechanism. When we feel sad, we also tend to look sad, especially during bereavement.[15] The face literally sags. The eyebrows pinch together and raise upward, forming a triangle; the eyelids narrow, the jaw slackens, and the lower lip is drawn out and down to form a kind of pout. Whether we are aware of it or not, this expression is a compelling signal to others that we may need help. And as it turns out, sad facial expressions are very effective in eliciting sympathy, understanding, and often the help of other people.[16]

We are wired to react to each other this way: When we see other people looking sad, we tend to feel sad, for example, when we come across a photo of someone in dire straits or when we watch a sad scene in a movie. Somber film segments are so effective in eliciting sadness in viewers that they have become standard tools for researchers who study the emotion .[17] Neuroscience has recently confirmed that when people view photos or films of others in sorrowful circumstances, including scenes of grieving, activity increases in the amygdala, a brain structure that is intricately associated with emotional experience.[18]

Even newborn infants can distinguish between an audiotape of their own cry and a tape of another baby's cry, and another newborn's cry often provokes visible signs of distress.[19] When children view sad films, their heart rate slows.[20] In adults, a reduced heart rate and other signs of sympathy, such as oblique eyebrows, in response to another's distress predict the likelihood of altruistic behavior. [21]

I've always found room for optimism in these observations. Sure, we can list the horrors humans have inflicted on each other: war, holocaust, torture, and the like. It's a sobering résumé. But it's a hopeful sign that we seem to be wired, from the cradle to the grave, to respond with sympathy when others suffer. It suggests that as much as we are capable of damage and harm, we are equally capable of tempering those urges with compassion and concern

Not by Sadness Alone

The grief work process as Freud described it is lengthy and time-consuming. It is relentless and involves "each single one of the memories and hopes which bound the libido to the object." Sadness is nothing like this. Although when we feel sad, it may seem as if our sadness will last forever, in actuality, by definition, all emotions are ephemeral—that is, they are short-term reactions to the immediate demands on us, usually lasting only a few seconds and at the most a few hours. A little later we'll get to the interesting phenomenon of emotions almost always seeming as if they are going to last forever, but the short-term nature of emotion is important, and it highlights some crucial implications for the grieving process.

First, bereavement is a complex experience, and if sadness is ephemeral, it is probably not the only emotion bereaved people will have. A lot can happen when someone dies: Personal circumstances may change. Financial circumstances may change. Relationships change. The ordering of the social world shifts. Sometimes the change is for the better, sometimes for the worse, but each of these changes is likely to produce a variety of emotional reactions.

Robert Ewing's sister had always managed the family's interactions. It seemed effortless for her and was something everyone took for granted. After her death, it was apparent that the family would be different. "The saddest thing about the funeral," Robert told me, "was that, well, you know, this sounds odd, but it was that Kate was not there to organize it. Everyone seemed to be looking for her to run the show, to run her own show."

This was only one of many indications that Robert's family was going to change. Family relations are often described as a system: Change one part of the system and everything else changes.[22] People take on new roles, lose old ones, find new sides to their relationships, and revitalize old sides. Change can be good, but it can also be extremely taxing. It can generate friction and misunderstanding, and it can produce strong emotion.

Bereaved people sometimes experience anger along with sadness. In one of the first studies Dacher Keltner and I carried out, Dacher coded facial expressions of emotion from videotapes of bereaved people who were talking about the recent death of their spouse. Sadness was the most frequent emotion and also the most long lasting, but anger and the related emotion of contempt were prevalent, as were expressions of some other emotions.[23]

As a general rule, the usefulness of any emotion depends on its context, that is, where and when it occurs. Emotions tend to be most useful to us in situations they seem to be designed to address. Social psychologists have provided a compelling demonstration of how useful anger can be, for example, when we are faced with what seems like unwarranted or unfair aggression by another person.[24] In one study, researchers asked a group of volunteers to complete several simple but challenging tasks, such as a standard task psychologists use when they want to induce stress in a research study: asking people to count backward in increments of 7 beginning with the number 9,095. Most people can complete this task, but they have to concentrate. To make the conditions more ripe for angered responses, the researchers told their subjects that the speed and accuracy of the subjects' performance was a measure of their level of intelligence, which of course was not really true. The researchers also told the participants that their scores would be compared so that the most and the least intelligent people could be identified. Then, as if all this weren't intimidating enough, the study included a "harassing experimenter" who informed the participants each time they made an error and continually reminded them that they needed to work faster.

Not surprisingly, the research subjects' faces were more likely to express indignation—a combination of anger and disgust—during the stressful tasks than just before the assignment. Facial expressions usually occur only briefly, however, and during the assignment, some of the subjects also expressed fear, which demonstrated that this kind of harassing situation evokes a range of emotional responses. But the important result was that only the degree to which the subjects expressed indignation led to a reduction in stress in the situation, and this reduction was apparent not only in what the volunteers said but also in their bodily responses. People who showed indignation during the harassment had lower levels of stress hormones and a weaker cardiovascular response to the task than other subjects. By contrast, the more subjects expressed fear (deduced from facial expression), the more likely they were to show the opposite response: higher levels of stress hormones and a stronger cardiovascular reaction.

The logical explanation for the different consequences of these emotions is that anger is useful because it originally evolved to help us deal with threat from others. Fear, which I will discuss in more detail in Chapter 4, is generally thought to have evolved for situations that involve higher levels of uncertainty and dread. We experience fear when we think we might be in great danger but we are not exactly sure what will happen. In situations like the one with the harassing experimenter, the source of the threat is localized and manageable. We know the experimenter is not going to harm us, just annoy us for a while. In this case, fear is not really appropriate and does little to relieve the stress.

During bereavement, anger usually arises when we believe that another person has threatened us in some way, said or done something insensitive or unfair. Anger in this case may help us negotiate shifting social relations in the wake of the loss, deal with an ongoing battle with the medical bureaucracy, stand up to an insensitive friend, or hold our own in changing relations with friends and family. Anger is sometimes directed at a higher being, for allowing the death, or for failing to heed constant prayers. Sometimes expressions of anger are even directed at the deceased loved one. It is not uncommon, for example, for bereaved people to feel anger at lost loved ones for not caring for themselves better when they were alive. Sometimes bereaved people feel that by dying, the loved one has abandoned them. I have often heard angry survivors say things like "He had to know this would happen. He never seemed to care about his own health. He always said, 'Life's too short to worry.' But he didn't consider what it would be like for me when he died. He never thought about how hard it would be for me to be alone."

These reactions are personal and raw, but in measured doses they are also useful. Because anger's dominant function is to help us to prepare to defend ourselves, a bereaved person who feels vulnerable due to the emotional upheaval of grief might use anger to fortify herself for the upcoming struggle. Anger in this case might help her develop a sense that she will be able to survive on her own.

Laughing in the Face of Death

Probably the biggest insight into emotion and bereavement comes from positive emotions. There is something counterintuitive about putting positive emotion and grief in the same sentence. Historically, positive emotions received almost no attention in the bereavement literature and when they were mentioned it was almost always in the context of denial. It was assumed that a joyous emotion during grieving could only interfere with or suppress the normal process of working through the loss.[25] As it turns out, this is more folk wisdom than science. Positive emotions do more than simply indicate that we are feeling good, and they occur in almost every kind of situation, even in situations as difficult as bereavement.[26]

Our key to recognizing positive emotions is facial expression. The face can tell us when people are genuinely happy through a set of crescent-shaped muscles, nestled above and below the eyes, known as the *orbicularis oculi*. These muscles are involved in eyeblinks, so they are well developed and contract automatically. Much to the chagrin of beauty-conscious people everywhere, these are also the muscles that cause those branchlike wrinkles in the corners of the eyes commonly known as crow's-feet. In the mid-nineteenth century, French anatomist Guillaume-Benjamin Duchenne discovered something remarkable about the orbicularis oculi muscles: They tend to contract when we experience good feelings. These muscles help the eyes smile.

However, there are different kinds of smiles. Most of the time, when we smile we are not *really* feeling happy.[27] The most common smiles are intentional smiles. We deliberately smile in situations that require a polite gesture, a cordial assent, a grin for the camera. Sometimes these smiles serve other purposes. For example, they may cover up feelings that we want to hide from others. When we smile without an internal feeling of happiness, we make the familiar smile shape with our mouths, but there is usually not a visible contraction of the muscles around the eyes. In fact, it's quite difficult to fully contract the eye muscles intentionally. But when we experience a spontaneous burst of genuine happiness, when we make a true smile or laugh, the orbicularis oculi muscles contract involuntarily and visibly. Although this response is quick and most of the time we are only vaguely aware of it, research clearly shows that people respond differently to positive expressions when they involve the orbicularis muscles and when they do not. There is evidence also that different brain pathways are involved when we spontaneously smile or laugh compared to when our smiles are deliberate.[28]

In honor of the discoverer, emotion researchers have come to refer to genuine laughs and smiles, those that involve the contraction of the orbicularis oculi muscles, as *Duchenne expressions*. Research has shown that Duchenne expressions serve a variety of purposes.[29] One is that our happy feeling spreads to the people around us. Sincere laughing and smiling are contagious.[30] (Think of all that canned laughter that accompanies situation comedies on television. It's not there by accident; even when we know it's fake, it still works and it makes us feel more like laughing ourselves.) Duchenne expressions make people feel more valued, more like a part of the group, and therefore more inclined to be helpful and cooperative.[31] In one study, for example, people taking part in an economics game that used actual monetary payoffs were more cooperative with their partners if, before the game, they were shown a photo of the partner smiling.[32]

With all this infectious happiness, it should not be surprising that people who show a lot of Duchenne expressions tend to be healthier and better adjusted. A striking example comes from one of Dacher Keltner's studies. He and his colleagues found that women who had genuine smiles in their college yearbook photos had better relationships with other people, were more satisfied in their marriages, and were generally more successful in their lives over the next thirty years than those who had not shown Duchenne smiles.[33]

In a related study, Anthony Papa and I found that college students who responded with Duchenne smiles when we asked them to talk about their life were better adjusted and had larger networks of friends and acquaintances over the next several years of college than students who had not spontaneously smiled.[34] But there was more: We added a slight experimental twist to this study. Before we measured the smiles, we made some of students sad by showing them an extremely sad film clip. The other students watched a segment of an amusing comedy. It turned out that whether the students smiled or not after the comedy didn't matter much; the link between smiling and long-term health was evident only after the sad film. In other words, being able to smile at something funny is well and good, but it doesn't tell us much about how healthy a person is. What really matters, in terms of our long-term health, is the ability to crack a grin when the chips are down.

If genuine laughter and smiling are adaptive in everyday situations and especially adaptive when people are feeling down, then we should see a similar benefit during bereavement. In fact, Duchenne laughing and smiling are common during bereavement.[35] Most bereaved people can show at least one genuine laugh or smile as they talk about their loss, even in the early months after the loss. When we actually observe bereaved people, the prevalence of these joyful expressions is striking. In a typical example, a bereaved person is talking, with a somber expression, about the past or what the loss has been like. He may be crying, and then suddenly he shows a sincere smile. Just as often it's a robust laugh. In my experience, these expressions rarely seem odd or out of place. Quite the contrary. They punctuate the ebb and flow of a conversation, rendering it more natural.

But these expressions don't just *seem* right; they are adaptive. In the research I did with Dacher Keltner, we found that the more widows and widowers laughed and smiled during the early months after their spouse's death, the better their mental health was over the first two years of bereavement.[36] In other words, people who showed genuine smiling or laughter when they talked about their loss coped better over time. Part of the reason for this health bonus is that laughing and smiling give us a break, a temporary respite from the pain of loss; they allow us to come up for air, to breathe.[37] Another reason is the comforting effect these expressions of joy have on other people. It is not easy to be around someone who is grieving. But it is less taxing when that person is able to experience or express a genuine positive emotion.

This brings us back again to sadness. When we are with someone who feels terribly sad, we are also likely to feel sad. When a person's heart aches, that pain fills the room and seeps into our own heart. It's much less taxing and much more rewarding to spend time with someone else's pain when that person can let it go, even if only for a few brief moments, giving everyone a chance to breathe. Our research shows, in fact, that bereaved people who are able to laugh or smile while discussing their loss evoke more positive emotion and less frustration in others then do bereaved people who cannot laugh or smile.[38]

Oscillation

How can grief be dominated by sadness and longing, on the one hand, and include frequent smiles and laughter, on the other? If we think of grief only as work, then the back-and-forth pattern is unexpected. Indeed, many bereaved people who experience the coming and going of intense grief for the first time find it confusing.

Robert Ewing was stunned by the level of anguish he felt at his sister's death, but he was equally surprised by how suddenly the pain often vanished: "One moment, I felt so sad I thought it was going to crush me; then a moment later, I was talking with someone about some silly little thing, laughing as if nothing had happened. It was odd."

Robert's isn't an unusual case. Bereavement is essentially a stress reaction, an attempt by our minds and bodies to deal with the perception of a threat to our well-being. And like any stress reaction, it is not uniform or static. Relentless grief would be overwhelming. Grief is tolerable, actually, only because it comes and goes in a kind of oscillation. We move back and forth emotionally. We focus on the pain of the loss, its implications, its meanings, and then our minds swing back toward the immediate world, other people, and what is going on in the present. We temporarily lighten up and reconnect with those around us. Then we dive back down to continue the process of mourning.

That grief reactions work this way should not be startling. The same kind of back-and-forth fluctuation is apparent in just about every other mind and body function we know. Everything inside us oscillates, literally. We breath in, we breath out. Muscle fibers tighten, muscle fibers relax. We fall asleep, we become alert. Our body temperature rises and falls. Fluctuation is adaptive because it allows us to engage in contrasting activities. We can't inhale and exhale at the same time, so we breathe in cycles. We can't rest and be alert at the same time, so we sleep in cycles. Even as we sleep, we cycle through deeper and shallower sleep phases. It is the same with grief. We can't reflect on the reality of a loss and engage with the world around us at the same time, so we do that in cycles, too.

Probably the most striking implication of the oscillation of mourning is that it bears so little resemblance to the conventional idea that grief unfolds in a predictable sequence of stages. Inherent in stage models is the idea that each phase of mourning runs to completion before the next stage can begin. According to Kübler-Ross, bereaved people are initially immersed in nearly complete denial. Then, once denial is no longer possible, they move on to the anger phase. This, too, must run its course fully before the next phase, bargaining, can begin, and so on down the line through depression and, finally, acceptance.

Not everyone needs to go through the stages in exactly the same way, of course. But for most people, the pattern is thought to be uniform. And that uniformity makes it difficult to see where laughter and smiling would fit in. Kübler-Ross occasionally wrote about memorable episodes of laughter in her patients. But these stood out because they were rare. There is no stage for positive emotions, which is perhaps why traditionally positive emotion has been equated with denial. But in our research we have seen positive emotion at all points in bereavement, not just in the early months when denial is thought to occur.

Other theorists have observed that grief comes about in waves rather than in sequential stages. Robert Kastenbaum, one of the first social scientists to consider how humans adapt to death and loss, wrote in 1977 that "distress does not end with the first wave of shock and grief. After the realization that a loved one is dead often comes the realization that life is supposed to go on."[39] More recently, researchers have begun to theorize about the wavelike nature of grief. One theory, aptly named the dual process model of coping with bereavement, proposes that when we cope with loss effectively, we oscillate between two separate processes.[40] Similar to what we've observed in sadness, one of these processes is "loss-oriented" and involves focusing on "some aspect of the loss experience itself, most particularly, with respect to the deceased person."[41] The other process, however, is "restoration-oriented" and goes beyond the loss to focus on the tasks and demands of life without the deceased and on what needs to be done to restore normal functioning. The key, again, is that grieving is not static but involves a regular oscillation.

But even these wavelike models seem to underestimate the degree of fluctuation involved in bereavement. Indeed, when we look more closely at the emotional experiences of bereaved people over time, the level of fluctuation is nothing short of spectacular. In one study, bereaved people rated their emotional well-being on a daily basis over the course of the first several months after their spouses died.[42] Daily ratings over a long period of time produce a lot of information, so the researchers plotted the ratings from each participant across time. If grieving occurred in distinct stages, the resulting graphs should have revealed a clustering of

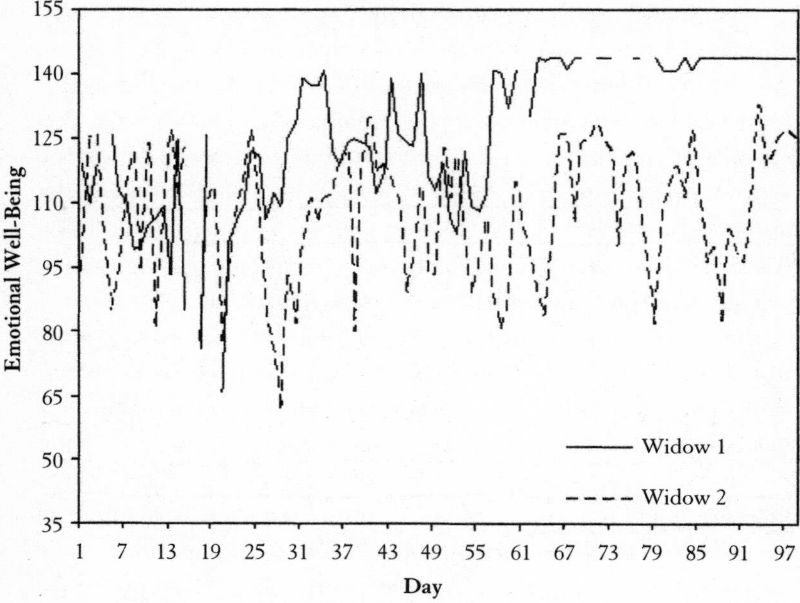

FIGURE 2.—Daily ratings of emotional well-being reported by two widows across the first several months of bereavement. Higher scores indicate better well-being. The figure is reproduced from Toni L. Bisconti, Cindy S. Bergman, and Steven M. Boker, "Social Support as a Predictor of Variability: An Examination of the Adjustment Trajectories of Recent Widows," *Psychology and Aging* 21, no. 3 (2006): 590–599.

flat lines at different points in time, something like a set of connected plateaus. Each plateau would represent a different stage of bereavement. As you can see in Figure 2, the ratings actually look quite random, more like the rapidly etched back-and-forth lines of an electrocardiogram or a seismograph. The lines zip up and down and begin to level out only after several months. This pattern was true even for resilient people (Widow 1 in the figure) and again suggests that oscillation is a normal part of grieving.

* * *

In his famous memoir, *A Grief Observed,* C. S. Lewis wrote, "The mind always has some power of evasion. At worst, the unbearable thought only comes back and back."[43] As his wife was dying of cancer, Lewis found it "incredible how much happiness, even how much gaiety" they "sometimes had together after all hope was gone." When his wife died, Lewis's grief felt relentless. Yet he reminded himself that it was not as constant, not as demanding, as he imagined his wife's physical pain must have been. "Physical pain," he said, "can be absolutely continuous . . . like the steady barrage on a trench in World War One, hours of it with no let-up for a moment," but "grief is like a bomber circling round and dropping its bombs each time the circle brings it overhead." It is that respite from the trench of sadness that makes grief bearable. It is the marvelous human capacity to squeeze in brief moments of happiness and joy that allows us to see that we may once again begin moving forward.

Love this

CHAPTER 4

Resilience

Daniel Levy's wife died sooner than she should have. Daniel and Janet had been together for eight years. They had had, in Daniel's words, an "easy relationship," one they had both thought would last the rest of their lives. They had met when they were both employed by a small housewares design company. Daniel worked on the creative side of the business. Janet had an administrative position. Both were in their early forties and neither had had much success in previous romantic relationships.

Daniel was a wiry man. He dressed neatly but plainly, as if he would rather not stand out in a crowd. He was slightly awkward when I first interviewed him, but he gradually became more comfortable as we talked. Daniel was thoughtful and had interesting things to say, I discovered, but most of the time he seemed content to keep things to himself.

When Daniel and Janet met, everything just seemed to click. "Being around Janet was the easiest thing in the world for me." Daniel told me. "It was as if I had known her all my life, instantly." Initially, Daniel decided that it would be best to keep his romantic feelings to himself and to restrict his relationship with Janet to professional exchanges.

That plan didn't last long.

After a few weeks, Daniel and Janet began dating. Soon, they were spending all their free time together. Before they knew it, they were living together. Then they began scheming about starting up a new furniture business. Janet had the financial resources, and Daniel had the artistic and professional background to make it work. The more they talked about their idea, the more irresistible it became. They took the leap, quit their jobs, and launched the new company.

There were a few rough spots and slow periods, mostly at the beginning. But for the most part, Daniel and Janet's joint venture was a success. The same was true of their relationship. Everything seemed to be going well.

At first, they didn't talk about marriage. Then their friends began to bring it up. People in the neighborhood began asking. One day the letter carrier mentioned it. "Well," Daniel told me, "I thought, 'Why not?'" He and Janet were driving one day and Daniel mentioned that they "ought to think about getting married." Janet turned to look at him, held his gaze for a brief moment, and then agreed. It was as easy as that.

For the next seven years, their lives charted more or less the same course. They seemed happy together and the work continued to go well. Then, as quickly as Janet had come into Daniel's life, she was gone.

She had gone out of town on a business trip. She could easily have flown, but she had always enjoyed long drives, especially alone in the early morning hours, when the roads were usually quiet. Janet decided to head back from the trip at dawn. It began to rain. An oncoming car spun out of control and struck Janet's vehicle. She was killed instantly.

I saw Daniel several months after Janet's death. It was obvious that he had loved her dearly, and that he had endured a period of pain and loneliness when she died. But there was almost no indication that he was openly grieving when I interviewed him. It appeared that Daniel was continuing to live his life more or less as he had before his wife's death. Daniel and Janet had a broad circle of friends and acquaintances. He continued to enjoy those relationships. He also continued the business that he and Janet had started together.

"Basically," Daniel told us, "the only thing that's missing, that's changed, is she's not there. I am still the same person I was before she died. Nothing else is different. Other than, you know, now I know what loss means." He continued, "There were times when I was terribly lonely. I still do experience that kind of loneliness at times, but those moments get further and further apart." Everyone on our research team agreed that Daniel exhibited healthy resilience. He loved his wife and had mourned her passing. But like the others in this book, he had found a way to move on.

Although resilience is common, resilient people are not a homogeneous group. Their stories give flesh to some of the myriad experiences of grieving, and they show that even when we cope effectively with loss, we have diverse reactions and find different ways to get past it.

Examples are not enough, however. Individual stories do not demonstrate how prevalent resilience is. Even hundreds of stories would show only that those particular hundreds of people are resilient. This chapter demonstrates that resilience is the norm rather than the exception, and not only during bereavement.[1]

What is perhaps most intriguing about resilience is not how prevalent it is; rather, it is that we are consistently surprised by it. I have to admit that sometimes even I am amazed by how resilient humans are, and I have been working with loss and trauma survivors for years. I must also confess that I am not entirely sure where the astonishment comes from. But I can make some educated guesses.

For starters, let's assume that at least part of the explanation is cultural. In other words, skepticism about resilience is almost certainly a product primarily of the industrialized nations that comprise most of Europe and North America. Those who live in these Western countries—especially Americans—place great value on individualism. We care about autonomy and personal freedom. And because we care about autonomy and personal freedom, we care a lot about what's going on in people's heads. We pay attention to feelings. We want to know what other people are feeling. We want other people to know what we are feeling. Caring about feelings means that when somebody loses a loved one, we tend to closely monitor how that person is feeling and what his or her experience of loss is. And because we know that bereavement is painful, we expect bereaved persons to feel constant sadness and grief. When they do not, we tend to be surprised.

There is nothing strange about caring about individual people and their feelings, of course, and nothing wrong in being surprised by how resilient people are. The important point here is simply that these reactions are not the same everywhere around the world. People in other cultures have different experiences of grief, as well as different reactions to the resilience of bereaved people. When we go beyond the Western industrialized world—for now, I'll put this huge portion of the globe in the uncomplicated category of "non-Western culture"—we find that people don't experience life quite the same way. The big difference is that people in non-Western cultures don't pay as much attention to individuals and their feelings. They care more about the interactions between people than about what is going on in any one person's head. Owing to this difference, bereavement in non-Western cultures is less about sadness and grief and more about what people do, whether they behave the way mourning people are supposed to behave. The idea of personal resilience has less meaning in non-Western cultures because what counts is not what people feel but whether they enact the rituals properly.

Another reason why people in Western industrial countries may be surprised by resilience is that we have a great deal of cultural knowledge about emotions. We know that people are devastated by loss, and if we should somehow fail to notice this fact, there are poignant cultural reminders to ensure that we get the idea.

Just a few years ago *The Year of Magical Thinking* served as just such a reminder. In the memoir, Joan Didion described in vivid prose just how stunned she was by her husband's death and how disorienting the experience was for her. The shock of grief she felt, and what it means for the rest of us, came through even more clearly a few years later when she adapted the memoir into a stage play. The show opens with Didion's character standing alone and withered before her audience, a harbinger of grief to come. She quietly gives her audience the sobering information: Her husband died on December 30, 2003. "That may seem a while ago, but it won't when it happens to you." Then, the clincher, "And it will happen to you. The details will be different, but it will happen to you. That's what I am here to tell you."

But as much as we might take notice when Joan Didion warns us, the truth is that most bereaved people are not debilitated by grief. In the next chapter, we'll examine why. But before we do that, we will spend a bit more time getting used to the idea that resilience is prevalent, not only during bereavement but in response to a host of potentially traumatic life events.

Durable Children

The very nature of childhood suggests fragility and dependence. We come into this world almost completely helpless, primarily because our brains are still relatively underdeveloped. As human intelligence evolved over time, human brain size expanded at a remarkable rate, so that it was increasingly difficult for our heads to fit through the birthing canal. When the human brain "reached the physical constraint of pelvic size,"[2] aspects of our brain development began to occur outside the womb. And as human intelligence has evolved over millennia, we've come to require a longer period of development and growth to maturity after birth.

Development and brain growth require nutritious food and adequate sleep. Imagine the child who goes hungry or subsists on junk food because it's cheap and readily available, or because no one is around to monitor what the child is eating. It goes without saying that children need more than just food and shelter. They need to be nurtured and guided so that they develop the moral sense to determine right from wrong, and so that their mental abilities will mature to allow them to negotiate the complex and competitive world around them. Imagine the child who is told to "shut up" and "be quiet" every time he or she expresses an opinion. Imagine the child constantly left alone to deal with emotional upsets and wounded feelings because no parent or adult is around to talk it out with them, or to help them find their way to a workable solution.

Children need nurturing and patience that foster in them the kind of trust and compassion they will require later in life when dealing with friendships or the demands of marriage. They need devotion and care that they can pass on to their own children. Getting along with other people is difficult even under the best of circumstances. Imagine what it would be like to be raised in fear, constantly subjected to the hatred and anger of your caretakers, or to be beaten and violated by those who are supposed to be your protectors.

There is no shortage of evidence to illustrate the damaging impact that poverty and maltreatment have on developing children. Beginning in the first half of the twentieth century, systematic reports emerged documenting class and income disparities in the United States and the cyclical and self-perpetuating quagmire they seem to create.[3] Poverty and poor nutrition contribute to dropping out of school early and to drug use. These factors, in turn, limit job opportunities and feed the ongoing cycle of poverty. Maltreatment and abuse can devastate a young child's self-esteem and trust in others, leading to withdrawal and often violent and reckless behavior, and resulting in further victimization and self-harm later in life.[4]

But as debilitating as these cycles may be, not all disadvantaged children are seriously harmed. Surprisingly large numbers of at-risk children manage to thrive. Think of folktale characters like Cinderella, Snow White, and Hansel and Gretel. In each of these stories, the hero struggles through exhausting periods of hard work and abuse before eventually making his or her way to riches and fulfillment. These characters originally evolved in oral tales, where they were refined through hundreds of years of telling and retelling to gradually capture compelling elements of the human condition.[5] Perhaps it's not surprising that they are still relevant today and very much alive in our contemporary imagination.

In the nineteenth century, Horatio Alger published wildly popular rags-to-riches novels. These stories became part of the fabric of American myth, but they were fed by the real-life narratives of early American industrialist giants like Andrew Carnegie, Cornelius Vanderbilt, and John D. Rockefeller, who began their careers in the obscurity of poverty before rising to untold and almost unimaginable wealth. A recent article in *Forbes* magazine pointed out that almost two-thirds of the world's billionaires had "made their fortunes from scratch, relying on grit and determination."[6]

Yet, as inspiring as these stories may be, they are also misleading, not because they depict a hero who comes out on top despite overwhelming odds, but because they encourage the same fallacy we saw in the bereavement literature: They imply that only the truly remarkable can succeed. When reports of resilience among disadvantaged children first began to emerge in the 1970s and 1980s, the media tended to describe these children as "invincible" and "invulnerable," or as a rare species of ghetto "superkids."[7] I don't mean to take anything away from these children. It goes without saying that anyone who overcomes an impoverished or abusive upbringing deserves all the credit he or she receives. But when we look at the numbers, it is quite obvious that more than just a few superkids beat the odds. No matter what the challenge—poverty, a chaotic family life, chronic maltreatment—many children endure and go on to meet normal developmental expectations for healthy adjustment.[8]

Bereavement experts have long doubted the resilience of people who endure the death of a loved one. Might there also be reason to question the resilience of disadvantaged children? If development is so complex and childhood so demanding, as we have seen, could these children truly be resilient? Most of what we know about the hardiness of disadvantaged children comes from studies of harsh and unfavorable environments. Often, it is difficult to untangle all the different factors that come into play. Harsh environments influence a developing child on so many different levels. It's not easy to define exactly what resilience should look like. Sometimes a child appears to be healthy in one aspect of his or her life, such as school performance, while failing in another area, like maintaining close friendships.[9]

Regardless of these kinds of variations, however, research has continually shown that many children cope extremely well with adversity. Even if we narrow our definition of resilience so that it includes only those at-risk children who turned out healthy in all the important areas of adjustment, on balance we still find unexpectedly high numbers.[10] No matter how we view the data, there are great numbers of children who beat the odds.

The durability of children becomes even more obvious when we look at isolated events. Most people would expect children confronted with the untimely death of a parent to be devastated. Some are, but bereaved children tend to show about the same frequency of resilience as bereaved adults.[11] The same is true of children exposed to extreme events that are likely to result in psychological trauma, such as natural disasters, serious accidents, abuse, assault, or the violent death of a loved one. Trauma researchers call these PTEs, or potentially traumatic events.[12] One of the best examples of resilience to PTEs comes from an ambitious study of over 1,400 children. The children in this study were initially interviewed during middle childhood, around the ages of nine to eleven years, and then reinterviewed annually until they reached age sixteen. More than two-thirds of these kids had been exposed to at least one PTE, yet very few were affected in any serious way. Only a small percentage of the children had diagnosable trauma reactions. And the vast majority of the children in the study showed no indication of any trauma reaction at all.[13] As much as we might expect otherwise, most of the children simply got on with their lives.

Durable Adults

Adults are no less resilient than children. If anything, they are more resilient. Yet many adults find this simple fact hard to believe. One likely reason is that enduring a potentially tragic event with equanimity might make us think that the event was not as severe as we thought. We stop thinking about it, and as long as we are unharmed, the event seems to quickly recede into the past. Over the years, I have seen countless examples of this phenomenon. In the normal course of an interview, I typically ask people whether they have experienced any potentially traumatic events in their lifetime. I do this by reading a list of such events, like being robbed or assaulted with a deadly weapon or suffering a life-threatening illness. Many people cruise down the list, absolutely sure that they have never experienced any of the events: "No . . . no . . . no . . . nope . . . no, never happened to me . . . no . . . no . . . no, not that either . . . no . . . nope." But later in the interview, as they talk about their past, their memories are jogged and suddenly they say, "Oh, wait, wait. Now I remember. I was assaulted. I remember now, with a gun. A guy once pulled a gun on me in a gas station."

A few years ago, my research team and I decided to investigate this intriguing tendency to forget. We asked a group of college students to log on each week to an Internet Web site where they would find a list of life events. The list included many of the things that typically happen to college students, like financial troubles or breaking up with a boyfriend or girlfriend, along with many of the potentially traumatic events that adults encounter across their lifetimes. We asked the students to indicate only the events that they had experienced during the past week, or if they missed a week, since they had last logged on. Most important, we asked them to continue doing this for their entire four-year college career so that by the end of the study we had a fairly accurate picture of how frequently such events had actually occurred.

Even though I expected that using a weekly Internet survey would capture a greater number of potentially traumatic events than people normally remember, even I didn't anticipate just how many we did capture. The average number of such events that each student reported over the course of four years was six; that's one or two per year. Granted, these were New York students, and potentially traumatic events do tend to happen with greater frequency in a large urban context. But one or two a year was considerably higher than most surveys led us to expect.

The most likely reason for the discrepancy was that life event surveys typically ask people to think back and recall the events they experienced over a number of years. We had already seen how easily people can forget even the most disturbing life events, so the one-time surveys probably failed to capture many of the events people were confronted with. By contrast, our "online" survey asked students about the past week or two, so they recorded these events more or less as they happened.

To better test this idea that we tend to forget disturbing life events, at the end of the four years we asked all the students who were in our study to try to recall how often they had experienced each event in the survey. Almost all the participants underremembered the potentially traumatic events they had reported earlier. We can't say for certain why

this happened, but the results certainly seemed to jibe with the idea that because most people cope effectively with potentially traumatic events, they simply stop thinking about them.

But not all potentially traumatic events are easily forgotten. Some are so frightening and impact our lives so fully that they become indelible. Some events change our lives forever, and some events change the world around us to such an extent that they become part of our shared cultural identity.

Unthinkable and Unforgettable

For most of World War II, London was spared from direct attack by Germany. Yet, as the war dragged on a nervous anxiety set in; it became increasingly apparent that Germany was planning a relentless aerial bombardment and that London would be the primary target. Everyone knew it was going to be a rough ride and that it would probably go on for quite a long time. Although the anticipation was nerve-wracking, the British government did what it could to begin preparing for the attacks. Children were sent to live with relatives, sometimes even with strangers, in the British countryside as a protection against the pending onslaught. The British mental health establishment began to prepare for widespread panic. Although little was known at the time about psychological trauma, London hospitals and clinics made room for the anticipated emotional casualities. Then the sirens began and soon after the awful roar of airplanes.

Several years later, and halfway across the globe, the citizenry of Hiroshima, Japan, was growing anxious. American B-29 airplanes or *B-san* as the Japanese had come to call them, had already bombed most major Japanese cities. But they had not yet hit Hiroshima. Why? It was unlikely that Hiroshima would remain untouched. That much seemed certain, and so the city had been busy preparing for an attack. A portion of the populace had been evacuated. Emergency sites had been readied, shelters had been constructed, and fire lanes had been widened. Daily air raid sirens, indicating the approach of enemy planes, had become a nervous routine.

On the morning of August 6, 1945, the sun was shining brightly in the sky over Hiroshima. At 7 a.m. an air raid siren was sounded, and people began their familiar routine of walking to the shelters.[14] But that morning, the Japanese radar had detected only three American aircraft. Assuming these were part of a reconnaissance mission and not a threat, the "all-clear" signal was given by 8 a.m. It was an odd moment of calm before the world turned upside down.

A little more than half a century later, on another bright, sunny day, New Yorkers were making their way to work. Some were ascending from the subway. Others were already at their desks, drinking coffee or preparing for the day. The tallest buildings in the city, the twin towers of the World Trade Center in lower Manhattan, were like a city onto themselves. As many as 50,000 people worked there on any given day.

The view from the upper floors of the towers was breathtaking, but also a bit frightening. Some worried that the towers were vulnerable to attack. Several years earlier, a car bomb had detonated in the parking garage beneath Tower One in a terrorist attack intended to bring the building down. The attack had failed, but many feared that some day the towers might be attacked again, and that the next time the terrorists might succeed.

* * *

The emotion most closely associated with psychological trauma is fear. We experience the emotion of fear when we sense the imminent possibility of danger and personal harm. Dangerous situations evoke a range of emotions—anger, disgust, and perhaps sadness being the most common—but what generates fear is not only pending danger but a sense of uncertainty, of not knowing what form the harm may take and what, if anything, we can do to stop it.[15] It is natural to experience fear in these circumstances, and it also is adaptive. Fear elicits the fight-or-flight response. Our eyes open wide, our muscles tighten, we breath rapidly, and our heart pumps violently; our newly oxygenated blood is withdrawn from the viscera and travels to the large muscle groups in our limbs so that we can strike out more effectively or make a run for it.

There was plenty of reason to be frightened in London when the bombs began to fall. Germany's explicit intention was to attack with such ferocity and over such an intensified period that the British would be demoralized into surrendering. Those attacks came to be known as the Blitzkrieg, a German word meaning "lightning war." But although Germany's aim was never achieved, the death and destruction took their toll. In less than a year, tens of thousands of Londoners had perished and countless homes and landmark buildings were damaged or destroyed.

When the first atomic bomb exploded over Hiroshima, there was a spectacular burst of light and 40,000 people were killed instantly. Although the bomb made a thunderous roar twenty miles away, survivors near the point of detonation described it as "a blinding noiseless flash."[16] People were frozen in their tracks. Then, after a brief but surreal pause, came the explosion's incredible impact. Those closest to the center of the detonation were killed instantly by the searing heat. Many were burned beyond recognition. Further from the center, clothing was torn from bodies. Eyeglasses, tools, household utensils were flung into the melee. People, objects, buildings—anything and everything, it seemed—was simply lifted and thrown. Many people were buried beneath the rubble.

Shortly after, as the stunned citizens of Hiroshima began digging themselves out, fires began to sprout up around the city. At first, there were only a few patches of flame, but the heat and air movement caused by the explosion whipped up a blaze that engulfed much of the city. Those who survived the blast, who could walk or be carried, struggled to safer ground. Many were trapped and had to be left to die.

The loss of life was inconceivable. Ninety five percent of the people within a half mile of the bomb's detonation had been killed. Over the days that followed, thousands more perished. Of those lucky enough to survive the initial blast, large numbers sustained nightmarish injuries: burns, bleeding, ulceration, and internal hemorrhaging. It was many days before even a cursory medical response could be mustered, and in many cases survivors could do nothing but watch helplessly as others died in agony. Many of those not immediately affected eventually succumbed to the ghastly consequences of radiation sickness, and the anguish continued.[17]

Compounding the misery was the total newness of atomic weaponry. The citizens of Hiroshima could not fathom what had happened to their city. Many survivors believed at first that they had been victims of a direct hit by a conventional bomb. But as the scope of the damage was ascertained, it became obvious that a greater force had been at work. Speculation ran wild. Had it been a cluster bomb? Perhaps gasoline or other highly volatile chemicals had been spread over the city and ignited? At the beginning, these conjectures remained unimportant. Survival was all that mattered. As the long-term effects of radiation poisoning began to appear, several weeks after the attack, fear and uncertainty about the nature of the bomb began to spread.

The horror of September 11, 2001, was different. The scope of the damage was more contained. But there were elements of the September 11 attacks that were similar to the attack on Hiroshima. Nothing like it had ever happened before, and the uncertainty and fear dragged on for months. Vertiginous buildings had become a common sight in most modern cities, and they had just kept getting taller. Occasionally, an older structure had had to be removed to make room for new construction, usually by controlled implosion. Nobody had figured out how to take down a structure as tall as the twin towers. Then a small group of terrorists demonstrated how easily it could be done.

Because it was still early in the day when the planes struck, the buildings were not yet full. A good many people managed to evacuate to safety. Few thought the towers would actually come down, and when they did, anyone still inside or in the immediate vicinity perished. All told, some 3,000 people died as a result of the attacks. Hospitals and medical clinics throughout the New York area freed up beds for what they assumed would be a flood of casualties, and in the days that followed, a massive rescue effort was organized to comb the rubble and dig out survivors. Sadly, there were few.

* * *

Bombs, radiation, and terrorism: horrific acts, planned and executed against masses of innocent civilians. How could anyone endure it?

The simple facts are that history is replete with such acts. The form may change and technology may differ, but mass violence has always been a part of human behavior.

Somehow we manage to endure it. Fear does its job and we get by. The struggle may last anywhere from a few hours to a few days to a few weeks, sometimes longer, but most of us find a way to regain equilibrium and get on with our lives.

Although Londoners were initially fearful at the onset of the Blitzkrieg, they quickly grew accustomed to the constant threat.[18] There were remarkably few cases of psychological disturbance and even fewer incidents of psychiatric disorders or requests for treatment for psychological problems in medical clinics. In the areas hit with the heaviest frequency, there was greater incidence of "transient emotional shock" and acute anxiety. However, most of these cases "recovered spontaneously or were responsive to the simplest forms of psychiatric first aid," typically requiring nothing more than rest and sympathy.[19] In the end, the official reports on the civilian reaction to the bombing simply emphasized the unexpected resilience that had been witnessed.[20]

Despite the carnage and the misery in Hiroshima, the available accounts again provide clear evidence of abundant resilience.[21] Of course, there was acute fear and anxiety soon after the attack. How could there not be? And there were plenty of opportunities for sadness in the aftermath; for many, the devastation and loss were simply unending. Yet many survivors evidenced a tenacious buoyancy. Hideko Tamura Snider, a child of ten who lived through the Hiroshima bombing, described feeling both terror and resignation as she struggled to find her family after the attack. She witnessed sights no child should see: bodies burned beyond recognition, walking corpses, and countless friends and strangers grieving for their lost loved ones. Alone and helpless, she literally willed herself to move on. "Out of nowhere," she recounted, "something inside of me started to say, 'You are on your own now. Get up Hideko, only you can make it happen.'"[22]

In his account of the days after the bombing, John Hersey reported "a curious kind of elated community spirit, something like that of the Londoners after their blitz—a pride in the way they and their fellow survivors had stood up to a dreadful ordeal."[23] Some experienced a wondrous sense of calm, even serenity, and many managed to keep their spirits up through the age-old use of humor and lighthearted banter.

As is almost always the case, children were ready and willing to make a game of it all. The Nakamura family had two children, both of whom suffered from what appeared to be radiation poisoning. Yet they remained fascinated by all that was happening around them and were "delighted when one of the gas-storage tanks went up in a tremendous burst of flame. Toshio, the boy, shouted to the others to look at the reflection in the river."[24] Not long after the event, Toshio "talked freely, even gaily about the experience." Months later he remembered the disaster as if it were a kind of "exhilarating adventure."[25]

Adults also found moments of relief. Father Kleinsorge, a German priest living in Hiroshima, was wounded in the attack but capable of dragging himself around the city to care for others. At a park designated for evacuees, he made repeated excursions to bring water to throngs of badly burned survivors. Amid this appalling scene, "he saw a young woman with a needle and thread mending her kimono, which had been slightly torn. 'My but you're a dandy!' he said. And in response, she laughed."[26]

In a memoir of the bombing of Nagasaki, Japan, the only other city to suffer atomic attack (on August 9, 1945), Dr. Takashi Nagai described an arduous trek he had shared with a small group of colleagues as they went from village to village tending the wounded. "Exhausted, overcome with pain, and ready to collapse," they nonetheless found humor in their own behavior "and then with a laugh, and without even noticing the distance," continued on their way. Dr. Nagai related the story of a nurse who made repeated trips to carry the wounded to safety after the attack. The task filled her "with a deep joy such as she had never experienced before. It was a noble joy accompanied by profound happiness." She had realized that if the people she helped survived, they would never know that she had saved their lives, "and as she reflected on this, a smile vibrated through her cheeks."[27]

Probably the most salient testimony to human resilience was how quickly people in Hiroshima and Nagasaki began to rebuild. Less than two weeks after the bombing, banks reopened in Hiroshima to reinstate commerce in the city. Within a month, when it was determined that the city itself was not radioactive, residents began streaming back to start life anew. Shanties and huts sprang up. Many survivors returned to the sites of their former homes and began planting gardens amid the wreckage. Within three months of the attack, the population had swelled back to more than a third of its previous level.

The same was true of Nagasaki. American military journalist George Weller made this firsthand observations only twenty-eight days after the bombing: "Trains coming from both Honshu and southern Kyushu were so jammed with returning human beings that the writer was able only to fight his way into the baggage cars. Some refugees rode the locomotives' cowcatchers. . . . But they are coming back. By the hundreds they streamed along the concrete platforms which alone remain of Nagasaki's station, their belongings tied in big silk scarves or shoulder rucksacks."[28] As is common in any tragedy, many people experienced acute emotional stress right after the attack, but these reactions typically lasted no more than a few days, and at most only a few weeks.[29] Only a small percentage of those who had endured the devastation remained depressed or exhibited other types of enduring psychiatric symptoms.

To assess the broader psychological impact, about three months after the attacks on Hiroshima and Nagasaki, the U.S. military conducted a survey of residents throughout Japan. Despite the crushing devastation, instances of lasting psychiatric disorders were relatively rare. Moreover, the level of morale among the survivors in and around Hiroshima and Nagasaki was not much different from that in other areas of Japan that had not been exposed to the bombing. There was relatively little hostility toward the United States or hopelessness about the future.[30]

In our own era, the 9/11 attacks on the World Trade Center stunned the American public, if not the world. For some time it seemed that they were all anyone could talk about. It was soon apparent, however, that New Yorkers had coped extremely well. A large-scale random household survey conducted six weeks after September 11 indicated that only a very small percentage of Manhattan residents had had trauma reactions that were severe enough to meet the definition of posttraumatic stress disorder (PTSD).[31] Even more surprising, however, was how quickly that low level of trauma declined. Four months after the attack, the prevalence of PTSD in the New York area had dropped to just a few percentage points, and by six months it was almost nonexistent.[32]

The absence of PTSD or some other psychiatric diagnosis is one thing, but how many people in New York City were able to maintain steady levels of good mental health after 9/11? To answer that question, I teamed up with the researchers who had conducted the original survey, and we examined their results from the entire New York City area, including the five boroughs of the city as well as the contiguous parts of New Jersey and Connecticut. We found that a large majority of residents had had no trauma symptoms at any point in the first six months after the attack, nor were they more likely to experience other types of psychological problems. If we narrowed our focus to only the people who had lived close to the attack, those living in downtown Manhattan near the World Trade Center site, the proportion showing resilience dropped only slightly. If we focused on people who had been directly exposed to the attack, those inside the World Trade Center at the time of the attack, we still found that the majority showed no significant signs of trauma.[33]

What about people who lost friends or relatives on September 11? Probably the most wrenching consequence of the attack was the uncertainty it wrought for those whose loved ones failed to return home that day. Although it was clear that few had survived the towers' collapse, there was always the possibility that a person had been injured or become disoriented after the attack and was somehow still alive. Many held onto whatever sliver of hope they could muster. Downtown New York City was literally plastered with photos of those still missing. But over time, hope gave way to somber resignation.

The survey data, as well as another more intensive interview study my research team had conducted, showed that people who lost loved ones in the 9/11 attack were every bit as resilient as other survivors. More than half of those in this category had no measurable trauma reactions, no depression, and, compared to others in the study, the lowest levels of other types of psychological problems.[34]

There was one small group of bereaved people, though, for whom 9/11 was especially difficult. These were people who had lost loved ones *and* had witnessed some part of the attack in person. In essence, these were traumatic losses because they involved the intense sadness of grief and also the intrusive flashbacks and the anxiety that are associated with trauma. Typically, this kind of reaction occurs when a loved one dies through violent means.[35] When these horrible things happen, not only must surviving friends and relatives contend with the normal emptiness of loss, but they are also left with disturbing and graphic images of their loved one's final moments.

For many who witnessed the 9/11 attacks firsthand, the loss of a loved one was excruciating. Some remembered looking on helplessly as the sky filled with smoke, while knowing, or perhaps finding out later, that people they loved were trapped inside. With the seemingly ubiquitous media repetition, the images sealed themselves into our collective memory, and it was nearly impossible not to dwell on them. The people who experienced this kind of bereavement had the greatest proportion of severe trauma reactions. Just under one-third met the criteria for PTSD. That is about the highest proportion of PTSD that any event will produce. And yet just as many people who had experienced this same horror—one in three—had no trauma reaction at all.

Epidemic

As difficult and demanding as war and terrorist attack are, these are not the only forms of extreme adversity we may face. There are natural disasters, for example, and throughout history there has been the potentially devastating threat of larger-scale biological epidemic. Almost unfathomable death tolls rose during the Middle Ages, for example, when bubonic plague swept through Europe. Closer to our own era, there have been malarial plagues and, in the early part of the twentieth century, the sweeping yellow fever epidemic.

One of the scariest biological epidemics in history, and one that threatened to spread throughout the globe, happened only a few short years ago. Severe acute respiratory syndrome, or SARS, first appeared in China late in 2002. Most people understood that SARS was a respiratory problem, but few knew anything beyond that. No one was sure where it came from, or what caused it, or most important, how to stop it.

The initial symptoms were flulike and included fever, lethargy, gastrointestinal problems, a cough, and a sore throat. More severe respiratory problems often followed. Overall, SARS proved fatal for about 7 percent to 15 percent of those infected. Mortality rates were lowest in young people and considerably higher in the upper age brackets. A staggering 50 percent of those infected who were over sixty-five eventually died from the syndrome.[36]

One of the places hardest hit by SARS was Hong Kong. Approximately 1,800 people were infected, and almost 300 died. I spent two summers there shortly after the epidemic. I was working at the time with my good friend and colleague Samuel Ho at the University of Hong Kong, and I was also having long discussions with Cecelia Chan, director of the University's Center on Behavioral Health. From Sam and Cecelia and others I learned more about the near panic SARS had induced in the city.

SARS was especially frightening because there was no known treatment. The only available remedies were fever-reducing medications and containment. Typically, those infected were quarantined to keep the spread in check. But quarantine is not a comfort to someone facing the possibility of severe illness or even death. The idea of treatment by containment was particularly terrifying in Hong Kong, as the city is built on a small island. Part of greater Hong Kong, called the New Territories, extends onto the Chinese mainland. But until 1997, when the United Kingdom returned Hong Kong to the Chinese, the New Territories were politically separate from the People's Republic of China (PRC) and the border between Hong Kong and the PRC was tightly controlled. At the time of the SARS epidemic, access between Hong Kong and the PRC was still regulated, and Hong Kong residents knew how easy it would be to close the boundary once again.

As the epidemic progressed, Hong Kong residents began to fear that the entire city might be sealed off, and they'd be left to die. Those hospitalized for SARS learned about the panic from the streets. Friends and relatives, prohibited from visiting, often positioned themselves near hospitals and communicated by holding up signs. If their loved ones managed to look out their hospital windows, they saw a remarkable sight: crowds of people wearing protective masks waving posters and signs of encouragement saying, "We love you." "We won't abandon you."

Sam Ho and I decided to take a look at how Hong Kong survivors had handled the epidemic.[37] Because the hospital system in Hong Kong is run by a central government agency, it was possible to track the mental health of about 1,000 Hong Kong residents who had been infected, hospitalized, and eventually released. We charted the overall mental health of these survivors at several different times during the first year and a half after they had been released from the hospital.

Because SARS was so stressful, we anticipated that a large proportion of the survivors would have suffered chronic psychological problems. Our survey indicated that the suffering was even worse than we had anticipated. Over 40 percent of the survivors had very poor psychological functioning each time we assessed them. At first I was troubled by these numbers.

Yet, as we've now seen many times, there was also abundant evidence of resilience. As overwhelming as the epidemic had been for some, an equally large number of survivors had maintained near perfect psychological health. Despite having been hospitalized with a life-threatening and mysterious respiratory illness; despite their knowledge that there was no known cure; and despite the panic and rumors of abandonment that seemed to spread throughout the city, these people had picked up where they left off. As a city, Hong Kong was changed, and no doubt those hospitalized for SARS were changed as a result of the experience. But many had quickly resumed their previous routines, albeit a bit more cautiously, and continued to live healthy and productive lives.

* * *

Why is it that when people are exposed to similar events, the same type of loss, or the same category of potentially devastating tragedy, some are so obviously devastated and others emerge, for all intents and purposes, unscathed? This is obviously a complicated question and not likely to yield a simple answer. But science has begun to put together a number of pieces of the puzzle.

CHAPTER 5

Whatever Gets You Through the Night

When we lose someone important to us, all we have is memory. Our heart wants the person back. Our mind does, too. We know the person is dead, but the memory persists. The memory of a lost loved one can be so strong, in fact, that it plays tricks on us. Occasionally the sheer habit of memory overrides all other systems, and we temporarily forget that the person is actually gone.

Heather Lindquist was standing in her driveway talking with her neighbor when she heard the phone ring inside the house. "I should get that," she told her neighbor. "It's John. He always calls this time of day." Heather's neighbor looked at her oddly, and then Heather realized how strange her words must have sounded. John had already been dead for months.

The tenacious grip of the memories of a dead loved one suggests that a good place to begin looking for clues about resilience is in the quality of the relationship that was lost. According to traditional bereavement theories, how we got along with someone when that person was alive should shape how we deal with grief for that person when she or he is gone. Thus, the emphasis on the painful work of mourning contains the belief that people who are not debilitated by grief must be emotionally distant and therefore must have had either a superficial or a conflicted relationship with the person they had lost.[1] This is a simple enough idea, but we could just as easily assume the opposite, that resilient people are exceptionally healthy and therefore must have had an exceptionally healthy relationship.

In reality, most important relationships are complex and idiosyncratic, and thus there is lots of room for variation. Karen Everly's relationship with her daughter, Claire, is a perfect case in point. Karen loved Claire with all her heart, but when Claire was young, Karen told me, they had often fought. Sometimes, the fights were volatile. "Claire always had a temper, even when she was a little girl. I remember her throwing these magnificent fits. She must have been no more than seven or eight at the time," Karen remembered. "I had to close the windows. Now it's laughable, but it didn't feel like that at the time. You know, I mean, the neighbors must have wondered what on earth was going on." Eventually Claire settled down, and ultimately the fights stopped. But she never lost her spunk. For Karen, this was a definite plus. "Claire had a soft, girlie side. But I liked that she could also be tough. I think I secretly encouraged it. I had a business career and I knew what it was like for a woman to make something of herself in this world."

As she grew older, Claire seemed to come to terms with her mother's good intentions. Just before she left home for the first time to attend college, Claire asked her mother if they could take a walk together. At first, they strolled along in silence. Claire seemed pensive. Then she began to speak. "She told me she had been thinking about mothers and daughters," Karen said. Claire had observed her friends with their mothers and had reflected on her relationship with hers. She had thought about the kind of person she hoped to become. Claire chose her words carefully. But when she finally got it out, Karen couldn't help but cry. "She told me basically that I had done all right, that I was about as good a mother as she could have had. She said that this was the reason why she was excited about her future. I can't tell you what an effect that had on me."

Heather Lindquist's relationship with her husband John was also far from simple. Heather admired John: "He was a good man. I think that's the truth of it. John was a generous soul, a good, solid husband, and a loving father." When I asked her about disagreements, Heather had a hard time coming up with examples: "I won't say we never had problems, but our life together was pretty good. We didn't fight much. Never had those knockdown arguments."

But Heather also had doubts at times. She wondered if they had been too independent of each other: "Ever so often it occurred to me that maybe we were living together apart, if you know what I mean, like we were just passing time in the same relationship." She thought for a minute and then grew pensive. "The independence seemed like a good thing, because we could develop—we could become different people. I always thought it one of the main reasons we got along so well. But I wonder now if maybe there was something missing. I don't know exactly what that would be—maybe a spark. We had been a couple for so long that I can't, I couldn't, remember what it was like to be alone," she explained. "It doesn't make sense to worry about it, but I find myself asking: Did we really have such a good relationship? Did we love each other? We cared deeply for each other, and I think we were a good, solid couple, but I wonder sometimes if we might have been living out the relationship everyone expected of us—you know, the happy couple. I don't know what the past was anymore. I wish I could see John's face again, how he would react when I talk with him."

I have interviewed more bereaved people than I can count. Most coped extremely well with the pain of grief. Yet there seemed to be no clear pattern, no emergent theme in the way they described the past, that might account for their resilience. Very few of the relationships seemed superficial or shallow, as the traditional theories would lead us to expect, but by the same token, the stories did not seem to describe uniformly healthy relationships, either.

If there is one constant, it is that most bereaved people idealize the lost loved one. This is only natural. The pain of grief serves as a constant reminder of what lost loved ones meant to us and what their presence brought to our lives. Their gifts, whatever they may have been, loom larger because we can no longer have them. Studies have consistently documented this kind of veneration, and it turns out that it is not

unique to resilience. Almost all of us remember those we have lost with at least a little bit of a positive spin.

What, then, can the quality of the lost relationship tell us about successful coping with loss? A few years ago, I had a chance to find out. I was invited by Camille Wortman and her colleagues at the University of Michigan to help them understand the results of a one-of-a-kind long-term research project. The project was called the Changing Lives of Older Couples study, or CLOC for short. What Camille and her colleagues did was interview about 1,500 married people and then follow them for close to a decade.[2] Along the way, the spouses of some of the people died, and Camille and her colleagues interviewed the bereaved survivor at regular intervals afterward. These interviews gave them a snapshot of the person's life at multiple points in time, both before and after the loss.

When I joined the CLOC team, my first goal was to identify the bereaved people who were resilient, that is, those who had no signs of depression at any point before or after the spouse's death and almost no grief at any point during bereavement. As should not be surprising by now, a lot of bereaved people in this study fit the bill, in fact, close to half. What about their marriages? What had they been like? Just as I had seen in interviews with other bereaved persons, the quality of the marriages of the resilient people were not much different from anybody else's. In other words, the relationship itself was simply not a factor in determining who would cope well after the loss. It was not that the quality of the marriage didn't matter: Some negative characteristics of the marriage clearly foretold more severe grief reactions. But that is another story that I'll get to in Chapter 7. The crucial point here is that there was no general rule about the kinds of relationships that promoted the healthiest forms of grieving.

There were also no rules about the resilient people themselves. Everyone had been interviewed at the onset of the study, years before any spouses had died. The people who eventually lost a spouse but coped well, the resilient group, were rated by the interviewers about the same as everyone else. They were not seen as cold and unsympathetic, as had long been predicted by traditional bereavement theorists, nor were they exceptionally warm and sociable.

These were important findings. They showed that the relationships  we have with others will not necessarily determine whether we will cope well if they die, and that one doesn't have to be an exceptional per- 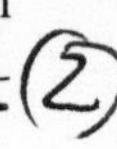 son to deal well with loss.[3]

Finding Comfort in Memory

The quality of the relationship is less important than expected in a grief reaction because we don't grieve the facts. We don't grieve the actual details of the relationship. We grieve only what we remember of the relationship. And the accuracy of our memories does not determine how we grieve; that is determined by what we do with our memories, how we experience them, and what we take from them during bereavement.

After Janet's death, Daniel Levy came to appreciate how much she had helped him find an inner calm. This realization helped him cope with his grief over her loss. "Often," Daniel told me, "especially in that first year after her death, I would seek out quiet moments when I could conjure her up, when, I could be with her. I wrapped her memory around me. It reminded me of the warmth and love she gave me."

Karen Everly thought often about Claire and felt that in many ways Claire was still with her. Karen was able to summon calming and soothing recollections: reminiscences from Claire's childhood, images of her accomplishments, or simply memories of daily life together, at the dinner table, walking in a park, or caring for their dogs. She seemed to have an endless variety of memories that she could call up to help her feel that Claire was still with her.

Julia Martinez used photos to help remind her of her father. There was something remarkably purposeful, almost precocious, in the way she did this. She would decide on a good time to remember her father, a time when she was unlikely to be interrupted. She would close the door to her room, carefully get out the photos, and let her eyes and her mind roam over them: "It was like visiting him, in a way. You know, it made me sad sometimes, when I remembered him. But usually it made me feel better. It helped me remember how lucky I'd been when he was alive. It was a little bit like he was still there."

Heather Lindquist made a deliberate effort to keep alive the positive memories of her husband, John. She felt she owed it to her sons. She thought they should have a strong image of their father. She kept photos of John in prominent places around the house. She talked about him often and made sure that John's friends remained a part of her family's life. She found that positive memories came to her in private moments, and without much effort: "We had so many good years together. I couldn't forget that. There is no way those memories were going to fade."

Robert Ewing found that summoning up comforting memories of his sister, Kate, required no special effort. In fact, most of the time he didn't need to search. Kate had been such a big part of his life and his family's life that the reminders were everywhere. And more often than not, the reminders brought back feelings of the warmth and care that was Kate's presence.

We are not accustomed to thinking of grief as a process of finding comfort. The idea seems a bit odd, but this is precisely what resilient people tend to do. Regardless of what the relationship was actually like, resilient people are generally better able to gain a feeling of comfort from remembering the relationship during bereavement. They are also more likely to find comfort in talking about or thinking about the deceased, which, they report, makes them feel happy or at peace.[4]

People confronted with the pain of loss need comfort. We see this same need in just about anyone faced with aversive circumstances. Children who survive poverty or abuse, for example, usually have someone in their life they can talk to, someone to lean on, someone they know will be there even when everything else seems to be falling apart. This person might be a close friend or confidant, or perhaps a positive adult figure.[5] The availability to a disadvantaged child of a caring and supportive helper has such a salubrious effect, in fact, that it may even cancel out a genetic risk for depression.[6] The same is true of adults exposed to potentially devastating events like war, assault, or natural disaster. They consistently fare better when they have other people to turn to.[7]

In this context, it is not surprising that the bereaved people who are able to deal with a loved one's death, and who are able to accept the finality of the loss, are also able to find comfort in memories of that person. They know their loved one is gone, but when they think and talk about the deceased, they find that they haven't lost everything. The *relationship* is not completely gone. They can still call to mind and find joy in the positive shared experiences. It is as if some part of the relationship is still alive.

In contrast, other bereaved people, those who are more debilitated by loss, find it harder to hold onto positive memories, as if they can no longer find the person they lost, as if the memories are hidden from them. The pain of grief, it seems, can block all memories of the good.

C. S. Lewis provided a poignant example of this kind of frustration in *A Grief Observed.* Lewis grieved intensely after the death of his wife, to whom he referred in his memoir as "H." During the time when his grief was most acute, he worried that he was losing her memory. He worried that what he could recall about her was fading and no longer a representation of what they had shared when she was alive. But just as Lewis's grief was beginning to subside, as he was beginning to recover from his wife's death, something "quite unexpected" happened: "Suddenly at the very moment when, so far, I mourned H least, I remembered her best. Indeed it was something (almost) better than memory; an instantaneous, unanswerable impression. To say it was like a meeting would be going too far. Yet there was that in it which tempts one to use those words. It was as if the lifting of the sorrow removed a barrier. . . . And the remarkable thing is that since I stopped bothering about it, she seems to meet me everywhere."[8]

There is power in these memories. Even when it seems as if we've lost someone forever, we find that there is still something to hold onto, something to nurture us, something that, as C. S. Lewis discovered, is almost better than memory.

Traditional bereavement theories tend to look askance at this sort of remembering. Grief has to be painful, these theories hold; resilience is an illusion and the comfort people claim to find in memories of lost loved ones is just another barrier to dealing with the reality of the loss.

From this traditional perspective, comforting memories are probably nothing more than a kind of fantasy substitution that masks the more painful facts of the loved one's death. They may be useful in the short term, but beyond that, they are unhealthy.

The science of bereavement strongly counters this idea. Resilient people are actually less likely than others to use avoidance and distraction as coping strategies. They are less inclined to evade thinking about the loss, or to deliberately occupy their minds to avoid confronting the pain.[9] It is important to remember that even those bereaved people who cope with loss the most effectively suffer at least some distress and confusion, and that most bereaved people continue to experience occasional intensely painful waves of longing for the lost loved one. So if comforting memories act as denial, it must not be a very effective denial.

I prefer to view the use of positive memories during bereavement as evidence of the flexibility of the human brain. We use positive memories and positive emotions to keep ourselves on an even keel, so that we can confront the pain of the loss at times when it is most tolerable, as in moments of quiet reflection. As time passes, we are able to go back and forth between positive memories and negative memories, and on our own terms. This kind of flexibility evolves from oscillation, the back-and-forth process, discussed in Chapter 3, that occurs naturally soon after the loss.[10] Shortly after a loss, most bereaved people experience intense sadness, along with periodic bursts of positive emotion. These brief swings provide a temporary respite from the pain and keep us connected to other people around us, and by doing so, they help us gradually adapt to the loss.

As times goes by, grief further subsides and the bereaved person moves closer to normality. The oscillating pattern evolves into a broader flexibility and a more stable balance as the pull of painful emotions and the yearning for the lost loved one gradually decrease. They may still be there, but the bereaved survivor gains some control over the grieving and is able to choose when to mourn, when to talk about the loss with close family or friends. By the same token, the reprieving swing toward positive emotions is enhanced, so that the comfort and solace they provide becomes a more established part of daily life.

Karen Everly gives us a compelling example of this kind of evolving balance. She had no shortage of painful memories. The relentless media coverage of the attacks that took her daughter's life on 9/11 provided a storehouse of searing thoughts and images. When Karen talked to me about Claire's death, several months after 9/11, it was obvious that the wound was still sore. But she was also able to pull back from the pain. Even when talking about that fateful day, her eyes still wet from tears, Karen was able to shift to more positive memories and beam with pride over her daughter's accomplishments or smile with contentment at the memory of a family gathering.

Is There a Resilient Type?

Not every bereaved person can muster comforting memories. Not every bereaved person copes so well with the pain of loss. Then can we say there is actually a resilient type, a kind of person who by disposition is especially good at dealing with extreme stress? Although the CLOC study did not reveal such a type, other studies I've conducted have confirmed, at least in part, the existence of a resilient type. I say in part because the issue is not as simple as it may sound. People who cope well usually have a number of positive factors going for them. For example, they tend to have better financial resources, better education, and fewer ongoing life stressors to worry about; they are also likely to be in better physical health and to have a broader network of friends and relatives on whom they can rely, both for emotional support and for helping with the details and demands of daily life.[11]

But even taking these factors into account, we can safely say that some people are, in fact, more resilient than others, and a growing body of evidence even suggests a genetic underpinning to a resilient type. We need to be very cautious here because the evidence for a genetic link is preliminary. It is also not quite as simple as it may sound. Advances in genetic research have shown us that genes do not create behavior in a simple one-to-one correspondence, like a blueprint. Rather, they seem to function more like a recipe or game plan that predisposes us to behave a certain way.[12] The researchers who study these effects describe them as "gene-by-environment interactions." The genes do their work only when turned on or "expressed" by a specific environmental trigger, in this case exposure to extreme stress. At this time, only a few genes have been researched in this connection, but the evidence that we have so far does indeed suggest that a person who possesses certain forms of these genes will fare better when exposed to serious adversity than someone who does not.[13] The genetic research has not yet examined whether these same genes help people to manage grief. However, there is indirect evidence to suggest that this is likely to be the case.[14]

Regardless of how cautious we might be about the genetic evidence, we can still talk about the psychological findings. Here the evidence is solid. We consistently find specific psychological characteristics among people who cope well during bereavement. One such characteristic is the ability to adjust to the shifting demands of different situations. This is a kind of behavioral flexibility not unlike the flexibility I described earlier in the use of positive memories. Every stress and adversity challenges us in particular ways. The types of struggles people confront when they lose a loved one to a graphic or violent death are different from the stresses that arise when a loved one succumbs to a prolonged illness. The demands of these losses also tend to change over time. And, of course, dealing with loss is different from coping with other types of violent or dangerous trauma, like surviving a hurricane or tsunami. By and large, the people who deal best with these different situations are those who can do what it takes to get through the event.

Part of this ability comes from the way we think about stressful circumstances. There is an advantage, the research shows us, in being optimistic. People who cope well tend to have an indelible belief that things will somehow turn out OK. They also tend to be confident. They believe that they will be able to exert at least some control over the outcome of even the most difficult life events. This is not to say that optimistic people believe they can undo the past or stop certain things from happening. Sometimes, even the hardiest of individuals are initially stunned after a tragedy. Nonetheless, fueled by their deep-rooted sense that they can and should be able to move on, they manage to gather their strength, regroup, and work toward restoring the balance in their lives.[15]

Along with these optimistic, self-confident beliefs, people who cope well also have a broader repertoire of behaviors. Simply put, they seem to have more tools in their toolboxes. One example is how resilient people express emotion. We think that, as a general rule, the more we show what we are feeling, the better off we will be. This is especially true when bad things happen to us, and it is actually a cornerstone of the traditional grief work idea.

Certainly there is some advantage in emotional expression, but there are also times when suppressing emotion, keeping one's feelings to oneself, may be adaptive. Imagine that you have been overcharged on a bill, you've already made several attempts to correct the problem, and you are speaking with a customer service person who might be able to adjust the bill. Of course, giving full vent to your frustration and anger might get the quickest results, but then again, as anyone who has ever dealt with a large bureaucracy knows, expressing anger sometimes only makes matters worse by hardening people to us and making them less likely to want to help. In our hypothetical situation, we may get the best results by hiding our anger and instead plying the customer service person with smiles and compliments.

The same may be true of the way we express sadness and other emotions during bereavement. As we've already discussed, the expression of sadness evokes sympathy and caring in other people. Yet, in some situations, we may be surrounded by people not very sympathetic to our pain. There are also times when the expression of sadness and grief is impractical, at least temporarily, as when we are caring for someone else or focusing on a necessary duty, on work, or on some other obligation. Because most of us find ourselves in a variety of circumstances, being flexible in expressing or suppressing sadness is adaptive. My research team has been able to demonstrate the advantage of this kind of expressive flexibility by using an experimental paradigm. In one study, for example, we examined emotional suppression and expression among New York City college students who had just recently lived through the September 11 terrorist attack. We found that students who were skilled in only one of these behaviors—either expressing emotion or suppressing emotion, but not both—fared about the same two years after the attack as other students in the study. However, the students who were flexible—that is, who could either express or suppress emotion as needed—were markedly less distressed two years later.[16]

Bereaved people who evidence a similar kind of emotional flexibility relatively soon after their loss also cope more effectively with the pain of grief. We have found this to be true even among the more depressed people in our studies. If they can evoke this kind of flexibility, they are more likely to recover from their grief.[17]

Coping Ugly

Flexibility is adaptive because different kinds of adversity create different kinds of demands. The better able we are to adapt ourselves to those demands, the more likely we are to survive. An intriguing implication of this idea is that in some circumstances, it is adaptive to think or behave in ways that we would normally think of as inappropriate or even unhealthy.

Imagine yourself among those seeking emergency shelter during Hurricane Katrina. You are stuck inside a domed football stadium for days along with thousand of other people, a gapping hole in the roof that allows rain to pour in, no bedding, no sanitation, very little food or clean water, human waste and rubbish piling up, and then the threat of rampant violence, gang fights, and a general state of disorganized chaos.[18] How would you deal with that situation? You would probably take whatever measures were necessary to get by, and you might not behave exactly as you would under normal circumstances. As long as your behavior helps you get through the ordeal, and you don't directly harm anybody, it is probably adaptive. I have come to call this kind of behavior "coping ugly."[19]

The phrase comes from baseball. In the mid-1970s, my home team, the Chicago White Sox, were winning baseball games with unexpected frequency. They were winning through a combination of gritty determination, cleverness, and the mistakes of their opponents. Sportswriters began referring to this particular brand of baseball as "winning ugly." It has since become a somewhat common phrase in sports and, ironically enough, politics.[20]

The phrase captures the kind of "whatever it takes" approach that we might use to deal with the unexpected adversities in our lives. Another phrase might be "pragmatic coping." John Lennon's famous song "Whatever Gets You Through the Night" also comes to mind.[21] When bad things happen, people often find the strength to do whatever is necessary to get back on track.

An example of coping ugly is what psychologists refer to as a *self-serving bias*, in which we distort or exaggerate our perception of something so that it works in our favor. Common instances of self-serving biases are taking credit for something we had little to do with and denying responsibility for something we did by blaming it on something or someone else.

I have a personal example of self-serving bias, though a rather silly one. I was once an avid yoga practitioner. Unfortunately, that was many years ago, when I was younger and considerably more pliable. A few years ago, my wife took up yoga. By that point, my body just didn't bend the way it used to. She, however, thought yoga would be good for anyone, including me. More than a little reluctant, I agreed to join her one day. We were both trying to do a standing pose called the Lord of the Dancer, also known by its Indian name as the Natarajasana. When it is done correctly, a person in the pose looks like a Hindu statue. One leg is extended backward, lifted well above the head, and then held at arm's length. The torso is bent forward and the other arm is extended out in front. My wife had done the pose perfectly. I, on the other hand, was wobbling and waving my arms just to keep my balance. I looked more like a traffic cop than a statue. And then, of course, I fell.

The key question is not why I fell but rather how I *explained* to myself and to my wife why I fell. Was it that I hadn't practiced yoga in years? Was it that I had aged and was no longer nimble? Or was it the floor's fault? It just so happens that we live in an old apartment with hardwood floors. The slats are somewhat uneven and have buckled here and there—the perfect excuse. I fell, I explained, because it was impossible to hold such a delicate pose on wobbly flooring. Of course, the explanation was a bit desperate, but it allowed me to accept the obvious limits of my performance without delving too deeply into nagging thoughts about my aging body.

At first, the idea that self-serving biases can be useful may seem counterintuitive. Aren't healthy people supposed to be realistic about their faults and limitations? It turns out that the average healthy person is not always completely realistic and unbiased. Actually, most of us tend toward slightly self-serving and distorted views of ourselves. Moreover, these mildly distorted views have been associated with a number of health-promoting qualities, such as happiness, confidence, and the ability to maintain higher levels of motivation and achievement.[22]

In his popular radio program *A Prairie Home Companion,* Garrison Keillor describes his fictitious hometown as a place where "all the women are strong, all the men are good looking, and all the children are above average."[23] It turns out that most of us believe we are "above average." Psychologists have come to call this belief the better-than-average effect,[24] and it is remarkably easy to demonstrate. Ask any group of people to rate themselves on any variety of traits and qualities, like intelligence, sense of humor, attractiveness, work ethic, friendliness, or community spirit. Most people will rate themselves as slightly above average, a statistical impossibility as we can't *all* be above average.

In connection with bereavement, self-serving biases have proved to be useful when people are dealing with extremely painful or difficult events, including the death of a loved one.[25] Thinking ourselves to be slightly better than average, for example, tends to bolster our confidence that we are going to be OK. In addition, self-serving biases can help us contend with the nagging thoughts we sometimes have that we could have done something to prevent the death. Of course, people die, and most of the time there isn't much we can do to prevent it. Yet in moments of weakness we may succumb to irrational self-blame and doubt. The self-serving tendency to assign blame to factors outside our control may keep self-blaming thoughts at bay.

Other forms of self-serving bias may also be useful, like finding benefits. We do this when we turn a bad event into a positive one by finding the silver lining inside the dark cloud. Benefit finding helps us maintain the idea that the world is basically a decent place and life is good. For example, people confronted with major illnesses like cancer often use benefit finding to help ameliorate an otherwise unfathomable reality.[26] Bereaved people also use this mechanism to help them cope with the pain of loss, as is seen in statements like "I never knew I could be so strong on my own," or "The loss has helped me become more focused on priorities," or "After she died I realized how many true friends I have." Another kind of benefit finding is counting our blessings by focusing on how much worse the loss could have been, as in "I am just thankful that I had the chance at least to say good-bye." People making these statements are not in denial; rather, they are accepting the reality of the loss. By finding some benefit, they are creating a different, and in many ways more tenable, way to look at an otherwise unendurable event.

* * *

Nobody wants bad things to happen. Nobody wants loved ones to die. But these things do happen and there is not much we can do about it. When I first began to study resilience, I assumed that at least some people would show a relatively consistent pattern of good health across time, in other words, that they would be reasonably healthy and happy before a loved one's death and then reasonably healthy and happy after it. As I learned more about how people manage to withstand extremely aversive events, it became all the more apparent to me that humans are wired to survive. Not everybody manages well, but most of us do. And some of us, it seems, can deal with just about anything. We adapt, we change gears, we smile and laugh and do what we need to do, we nurture our memories, we tell ourselves its not as bad as we thought, and before we know it, what once seemed bleak and bottomless has given way; the dark recedes and the sun once again peeks out from behind the clouds.

CHAPTER 6

Relief

Most people get over their losses. Many cope exceptionally well. Sometimes the quality of life is considerably *better* after a loved one's death.[1]

Kyle Wilkin battled colon cancer for three years. He died at the age of fifty-four. When his surviving wife, Adelle, came in to talk about her grief and the period leading up to Kyle's death, at first she found it hard to describe. "It's all kind of one big blur. I mean, everything in those last three years was colored by Kyle's illness, you know. I can't quite pinpoint particular moments in time, specific events. It's a mash of things." Those three years so dominated Adelle's existence that she came to mark the chronology of events in her life as being either before or after Kyle became ill: "Everything that happened before then seems more distant than I think it normally would seem. Everything before Kyle got sick feels as if it happened soooo long ago."

When Kyle was diagnosed, the cancer had already progressed. At first, he and Adelle were hopeful that he might survive, and it seemed as if he might, but then his overall health gradually deteriorated. Kyle's doctors estimated that he had about one year to live. Somehow he managed to hang on longer. Adelle considered his endurance a blessing, but it was also exhausting: "So we had three years together, which was so important to me. Then, when he was ill and getting more and more dependent, it made everything completely different, more a parent–child relationship than a husband-and-wife relationship, because, you know, he was—he needed everything done. I—you know, it colors things."

Despite the anguish and exhaustion of three years of caregiving, Adelle kept herself on as even a keel as possible. There were moments of deep sadness. Sometimes she thought she was becoming depressed. Sometimes, however, the strain made itself known in other ways: the imbalance of caregiving created resentment and conflict. When Kyle became ill, Adelle was negotiating a career change. Not long before Kyle's diagnosis, she had completed a master's degree that would have qualified her for a new job: "I had just finished my one year of school, which now seems as if it was eons ago. This was probably the biggest conflict because I was changing; as a person I was changing. It was hard for him to see that. Because of the illness, you know, Kyle couldn't really see that. The way it distanced things is, was, you know—I was tired a lot, too, and it wasn't the same kind of relationship it was before. I was going to be doing this new thing, but then I wasn't. The shift was hard, to become the one that was totally depended on, all the time, you know. I had to stop thinking about everything else."

When Kyle died, what Adelle felt most acutely was relief. Kyle's suffering was over. Her exhaustion and worry were over. Kyle was gone, and now she could finally move forward. Adelle exhibited almost no symptoms of grief. She was not distressed. She did not yearn to have him back: "I missed Kyle, of course. We had a decent relationship. But, you know, during those last three years, we kind of said our good-byes."

There were changes to be made. Adelle was going to have to rethink her life, now as a middle-aged single person, and sometimes she worried about what the future might hold. But for the most part, she was peaceful and reconciled. As she explained, "It's hard to know what would have happened if Kyle hadn't died. I was changing anyway. We had a good marriage and we were able to talk about the things that really mattered. When he was ill, we talked about what I would do when he wasn't there, what I should do and, you know, whether I should get remarried, which was good. So we were able to talk about the things that needed to be cleared up before he died. There weren't really any things left that weren't resolved fairly well."

In the year following Kyle's death, Adelle gradually acclimated to her changed life. She took time off to travel and visit old friends. Then she found a job in her new field, public health nursing, and eventually began dating again. She was busy, enthusiastic, and optimistic. "This is not what I would have thought my life would be like" she told me, "but it is good. Those were a rough couple of years there. I still miss Kyle. But I've come out of it OK. I have a new direction now. I think I can honestly say that I am happy."

Caregiving

Adelle's story exemplifies the relief pattern: exhaustion from caring for and anguishing over a loved one's suffering, and then relief, even calm, when the suffering is finally over. More often than not, there is a lengthy battle with physical illness or disease, sometimes lasting years. A close family member or spouse may have to tend to all of the sick person's needs, sometimes with no help: washing and bathing, helping with the toilet, shopping and running errands, discharging various duties and other obligations. Life becomes a demanding twenty-four-hour-a-day, seven-day-a-week job that may feel relentless.

Beyond the physical burden, there is the psychological pain of watching a loved one suffer. Sometimes this is the worst part. Sometimes there is conflict when caregivers like Adelle Wilkin have to put their lives on hold. This a tough row to hoe, and not surprisingly, people who exhibit relief at a loved one's death often say that during the loved one's illness, life felt unfair to them.

Another interesting characteristic of the relief pattern is that, in contrast to people showing a more straightforward kind of resilience, people who are relieved by a death do *not* tend to find comfort in memories of the deceased, at least not at first. However, their initial relief changes over time. Calm sets in, and it becomes easier to find comfort in the more joyous memories of the lost loved one.

What I find especially compelling about people who experience relief is that they are usually as surprised as anyone else by their good adjustment. When we asked people in our study who were showing the relief pattern how they were doing after the loss, many tended to endorse statements like, "I feel amazed by my strength," or "I am proud of how well I am managing."[2]

In retrospect, this pattern shouldn't have been surprising at all, even to the people who experienced it. In 1990, sociologist Blair Wheaton had suggested that in certain situations, what seems like an undesirable life change may be a change for the best and may actually prove beneficial for mental health.[3] Wheaton emphasized the importance of taking into consideration the context in which major life events take place. In situations where there is ongoing stress, he noted, another bad event may improve a person's lot by providing relief from the previous stress.[4] Marriages fail, children develop problems, jobs become dissatisfying, relationships sour, finances slip out of control, and loved ones grow ill. We adjust as best we can and eventually get so used to the situation that we forget it was not always there. And then even an undesirable event like divorce, a job loss, or the death of a loved one simply dissipate the burden we have grown so accustomed to.

When Death Opens New Doors

The death of a loved one may come as a relief even when caregiving is not involved. There are times when we can do nothing but lessen a loved one's suffering; their death comes as a relief mainly because it brings an end to their misery. A loved one's death may also bring changes to our lives that we couldn't have imagined. Sometimes a loved one's death opens new doors.

In his autobiography, the famous scientist Edward O. Wilson described a period in his life just after having graduated from college. Although he was passionate about science and on the verge of a promising career, he feared he might have to forestall his research endeavors just as they were getting off the ground. Wilson's father suffered from a number of chronic health ailments. He also had a serious drinking problem and was growing increasingly depressed and helpless. Then, early one morning, Wilson's father "wrote a calm note of apology to his family, drove his car to an empty section of Bloodgood Street near the Mobile River, seated himself by the side of the road, put his favorite target pistol to his right temple, and ended his pain."

How could such a tragic event not be devastating? To Wilson's surprise, he found that "after a few days the shock of grief was infiltrated by feelings of relief, for my father who was now released, for [my mother] Pearl whose desperate siege had been broken, and for myself—the filial obligation I had feared might tie me to a crumbling family was now forgiven. The impending tragedy took final form, and happened, and was over. I could now concentrate entirely on my new life."[5]

It would be neither fair nor accurate to say that Wilson had no difficult feelings related to his father's death. He tells us that he did experience sorrow for his father, as well as guilt over having felt relief about his death. But he did *not* grieve extensively, and whatever the lingering feelings he harbored, they did not impede his ability to live out his dreams. After his father's death, Wilson went on to a brilliant career and ultimately myriad achievements and awards, including the National Medal of Science. Over the years, too, he came to admire his father and to view his life not as failure but as a courageous struggle.

My own father struggled with health problems, and near the end of his life he was depressed. He had a heart condition and he did not take very good care of himself. His life was stressful and frustrating, and eventually it overwhelmed him. My father's stress also influenced my life in ways I didn't fully understand as I was growing up. And although his was a sad story, I, too, felt relief when my father died.

He came from tough stock. His parents had emigrated from southern Italy in the early 1900s. My grandfather worked with his hands. He made things. He fixed things. When he came to the United States, he found employment with the railroad in Chicago as a mechanic. He was a hardworking, stern man and, as my father told it, a tough disciplinarian.

You could see the toughness in my grandfather's tools. I still have some of those tools. One of my favorites is a handmade steel monkey wrench. I keep it on my desk. I had always assumed my grandfather made it himself. The handle had been twisted several times around, before the steel cooled, to give it a pretzel-like quality. It was an aesthetic detail, but it was also a boast. It showed that its maker could bend steel to his own will.

I also have a wide-angle group photo of my grandfather and his coworkers, the Erecting Department of the Chicago and Northwestern Railway. The photo was taken in the 1930s. The men posed for the photo with one of the gigantic steam engines they had worked on. They surround the locomotive like hunters with a subdued beast. Almost everyone was smiling in that photo, except my grandfather. He never smiled in any photo.

This was the culture my father was raised in.

When he was young, my father was strong and wiry. As a child, I remember being awed by the size of his wrists. His arms seemed to me to be as wide as other people's legs. Like his father, my dad also enjoyed working with his hands, and although he had a white-collar job, on weekends, more often than not, he could be found up a ladder somewhere, fixing something, or in the garage working on his car. He loved baseball, too, and as often as he could my father arranged his vacation time to coincide with the World Series. For my father, this was as good as life could be. He would work around the house during the morning and then in the afternoon settle in, still in his work clothes, to watch the Series on television, a beer in one hand and a cigar in the other.

Unfortunately, the rest of my father's life was not so comfortable. He had only a high school education, but slowly he worked his way up through the ranks to a managerial position in the midwestern distribution center for the Eastman Kodak Company. This meant more money and a better life for his family, but it was a strain for him. He felt out of place in a suit and tie. And I think he felt he had taken on more responsibility than he could competently manage.

My father did not read much, but it is telling that one of the few books I ever saw him spend any time with was *The Peter Principle*.[6] A best-seller in the late 1960s, this book had the basic thesis that in the modern workplace hierarchy, the typical employee rises through the ranks until he reaches "his level of incompetence." People are promoted, the author argued, primarily on their performance in their current position. The new, higher-ranking position is not necessarily more difficult, but it does often require a different set of work skills, which the employee frequently does not possess. Although he never said so directly, *The Peter Principle* seemed to perfectly describe my father's work experience—and the stress it caused him.

Stress in and of itself is not necessarily bad.[7] Stress reactions are closely linked with emotions, and together they form our natural ability to cope effectively with threats. When we feel endangered, our brains instigate a set of responses designed to maximize our ability to respond to the threat. Our hearts race. We breathe deeply. We temporarily stop longer-term bodily activities, like digesting food, which can be put on hold until the threat passes. The ways that our bodies and minds respond to stress appear to have evolved to help us deal with actual physical threats, like being chased by a predator. The parts of our brain that orchestrate the stress response are the oldest brain structures, which are similar to the corresponding structures in the brains of many animals. But other animals typically have stress reactions only when confronted by actual physical threats, whereas we humans also tend to experience threat in the abstract, as when we worry about our mortgage or whether another person likes us or not. Thus we feel stress in a wider range of situations, and we also are more vulnerable to chronic stress.

When stress is unremitting, not only does the quality of life plummet, but there is a serious physical cost as well. In the simplest terms, chronic stress wears us out: It breaks down our immune system. It makes us more susceptible to illness and infection. It contributes to the breakdown of bodily systems, like bone maintenance and weight control. It can even interfere with memory formation.[8]

The constant stress my father experienced in his job eventually took its toll. He suffered his first heart attack when he was only forty-three. As his career advanced, his health continued to deteriorate. He gained weight. He smoked. He drank. He found fewer and fewer opportunities for physical exercise. He had further heart troubles, and in his later years, he became diabetic. Gradually he became depressed.

Growing up, I felt close to my father. I was one of three boys, all born one year apart. These days we live dramatically different lives, but as children we were nearly inseparable. Although my brothers were also close to my father, my mother once confided in me that of all his sons my father considered me "the one he and my mother could depend on." I am not sure why he felt that way, but it probably had something to do with my acute awareness of his pain. I could see his frustration, his unfulfilled dreams, and I could see that they were killing him. I was the only one of his sons who attempted to speak to him about the situation.

I remember once finding him alone in my parents' bedroom. It was daytime but he had drawn the shades. I was perhaps ten years old at the time. I watched him from the doorway for a minute or two and then, hesitantly, ventured into the room. I stood by the foot of the bed. He looked at me. The room was dark, but I could see the gloom in his eyes. "Dad, are you OK?" He didn't respond right away. Then he let out a pained whisper, "George, don't try to talk to me." The frustration in his voice was palpable. I didn't know what to do. Slowly, I backed out of the room and closed the door.

Watching my dad suffer left an enormous impression on me. At an early age I vowed never to let the same thing happen to me. I promised myself that I was going to live my life as fully as I could. I was going to see the world, take chances.

My father had always wanted to travel, but he squelched the desire. He felt he had to. Given the culture in which he grew up, he was probably right. I once found a shoe box filled with mementos from his days in the military. He had been stationed in the southwestern United States for basic training near the end of World War II. People didn't travel nearly as much in those days as they do now, and this was the first time my father had ever been far from home. In that box, I found tourist postcards. I found photos of my father in the mountains, in the desert, photos of him with women, forgotten girlfriends, and clowning around with his buddies. These scenes fascinated me. It was a version of my father I had never seen; it was like discovering his long-lost brother. He looked happy, even carefree.

This period didn't last long.

When the war ended and my dad returned from the military, he found that his father's health had begun to fail. It was time for his father to retire and it was time for my father to take up the filial duty that was expected of him. He didn't question it. From that point forward, he would be the man of the family. Before World War II, he had worked in an entry-level position at Kodak. After the war, he returned to that company and never left. He worked there for the remainder of his life. His first job was to pack cameras for shipment to local shops. Gradually he was promoted through the ranks and took on more and more responsibilities. Like his own father, he worked hard, so hard in fact that there wasn't much time for anything else. Our family rarely took vacations. We rarely went anywhere, in fact, because my father was always working. He left early in the morning and often returned late at night. He was busy doing what he was supposed to do, supporting his family, making a few extra dollars in whatever way he could.

When I was an adolescent, the idea of free-form travel became something of an obsession for me. I even began sleeping without a pillow. "If I am going to have adventures," I reasoned, "I will probably not be able to plan where I sleep. I may have to sleep in open fields and I will probably not always have a pillow. I had better start getting used to it."

The passion continued to grow. When I finished high school, at the age of seventeen, I announced to my parents that I was leaving home. I should have been making concrete plans for the future. I should have been planning to go to college. I knew it and my father knew it, but I was hell-bent on going off on my own.

My father was not happy about it, and he forbade me to go. We began to argue, and then he threw down the gauntlet. "If you leave home, now," he stammered, "you are on your own. Don't come crawling back." The words stunned me. They sounded like a forecast of my pending failure, like a line drawn in the sand. I steeled myself, and then I crossed the line. I left home, and I vowed never to crawl back.

* * *

I was sleeping soundly when the phone rang. It was the middle of the night. I was twenty-three years old and living in a small apartment in Boulder, Colorado. For the past seven years—since leaving my parents' home—I had lived a more-or-less itinerant lifestyle. I had traveled much of the United States. I had been to other countries. I had slept on mountaintops and in fields, often as it turned out without a pillow. I had lived on farms and found temporary employment whenever I could. I had worked hard. It had been an exciting time for me, but also lonely and at times exhausting.

I didn't answer the phone.

Whoever it was would call back in the morning. But the phone kept ringing. I knew it had to be bad. I picked up the receiver and heard my older brother's voice: "George, I've got some awful news."

* * *

The next morning, I made plans to fly to Chicago for the funeral. I thought about how hard my father's life had been, about the relentless stress and the health problems he endured. It had seemed to wear him out. And now he was gone. These thoughts forced me to ponder my father's death. People sometimes say things like "It was probably for the best." They usually say these things when they don't know what else to say. But it's hard to think about death being a good thing when the loss is your loss. I let my mind try the thought on. No fire. No brimstone. Maybe it *was* for the best.

I turned on the radio. Then it popped into my head that perhaps I could request the local radio station to play a song in my father's honor. I called the station. I don't remember what song I asked for, but I do remember that the person I spoke with was very kind. Several minutes later, I heard his voice over the radio announcing, "The next song is for a young guy who just called because his father died." He dedicated the song to my father and me. It was a simple act, but it enveloped me. I knew other people were listening somewhere and that my name and my father's name had been spoken together on the radio. It felt like an apology of sorts, for the trouble I had caused him. I wanted to cry but no tears came. I felt gratitude. I felt relief, too. I wonder now if it was relief that my father's pain was over, or relief I had managed to do something right in that moment, or perhaps even relief that the pain of grief was not as horrible as I had feared it might be.

A week later, I was back in Colorado and back at work. I was glad to have my routine again. I noticed people were a bit hesitant around me, watching to see if I was OK. I wondered if I might break down at some point. But I never did.

In fact, my life opened up after my father's death.

It felt to me that I had been living my life as if in a stage play. I had been acting out a kind of duet with my father under bright lights in the center of the stage. The rest of the theater was dark. I could not see the faces in the audience. When my father died, it was as if the house lights had come on. To my surprise, I found that the theater was empty. Not only was I the only one left on the stage, but I was the only person in the entire theater. I had been acting out a play by myself. I could have stopped at any point, but I hadn't known it.

With time I came to appreciate the complexities of my father's life and how our hopes and dreams had become entangled. I came to understand that my father hadn't intended to issue such a draconian ultimatum. He had wanted me to understand the significance of the step I was taking when I left home. He had wanted me to understand that the consequences of my actions were serious. I had no clear plan and no particular means of supporting myself, and he knew that. It was reckless of me to cast everything to the wind.

But recklessness was part of the point, part of the adventure I was seeking. Unfortunately, my recklessness was what most irked my father. He had longed to do something just as capricious in his own life, but he had had to bury the desire. With hindsight I can see that I was trying to do that for him. I was trying to live out some of his fantasies. I wish I had understood that more fully when he was alive.

Two years after my father's death, I finally began attending college. I was twenty-six. It felt like a late start. At first I was tentative. I was not sure how I was going to pay for college, and I was not sure whether I would be able to handle the academic material after so many years. But that hesitance gradually abated, and soon I was thrilled to be on a new course. I made up for lost time. I felt like a sponge, soaking up any new ideas that came my way. To my great surprise, and relief, I found I could thrive in my new environment.

CHAPTER 7

When Grief Takes Over

I've emphasized resilience throughout this book, but we should not lose sight of the fact that not everybody copes so well. For some people, the death of a loved one is nothing short of devastating, and recovery from grief is a genuine struggle.

Rachel Tomasino was in her early sixties when she lost her husband, Frank. They had been married for over forty years. Frank had not been in great health. He was overweight. He didn't exercise, and he indulged himself regularly in his favorite unhealthy foods. But Rachel did not expect him to die—at least not as soon as he did: "We were married so long, you know, I just assumed he would be there, always. I always thought we'd grow old together. I never thought that he would just leave me like that."

Rachel and Frank had married young. They had no children, and over the years, Frank became a bigger and bigger part of Rachel's existence. Apart from occasional fishing trips with his buddies, Frank spent most of his free time with Rachel. She considered Frank her best friend in the world.

Then one day, Frank collapsed at work. His heart stopped. He died before Rachel could get to the hospital to say good-bye.

It was weeks before she could force herself to eat. She cried for hours at a time. She was unable to sleep. She lost weight. She grew pale and bleary-eyed. She did not even try to return to work for several months after Frank's death, and when she finally did she was unable to concentrate. She was fragile and lethargic and found herself sneaking off to cry in a back room. Her boss suggested she take a leave of absence, but this only seemed to make things worse. Rachel began to spend most of her time at home crying or lying in bed. A year later, she still had not returned to her job.

Prolonged Grief

It is only recently that the professional community has begun to understand extreme and prolonged grief. Ironically, this shift came about in part because of the greater attention paid to healthy adjustment. When we began to cast our net broadly, to capture the full range of grief patterns, including successful coping and mild grief reactions, we also began to move toward a greater appreciation of what it means to suffer. The focus on resilience made prolonged grief stand out in greater contrast.

Approximately 10 to 15 percent of bereaved people are likely to struggle with enduring grief reactions. In other words, one or two out of every ten people tends to have grief reactions that continue to interfere with their ability to function for several years or longer after the loved one's death.[1] In absolute terms, 10 to 15 percent is a relatively small proportion. However, when we recognize that almost everyone must confront the pain of loss at some time, 10 to 15 percent represents a lot of people, and makes it clear that prolonged grief is indeed a serious matter.

We saw earlier that we seem to be wired for sadness, that sadness is "functional," helping bereaved people reflect on their loss, take stock, and accept what cannot be undone. It helps people to recalibrate for life without the lost loved one. Our expressions of sadness also evoke sympathy and caring responses from other people. But when sadness becomes too strong, when it runs unchecked for long periods of time, it is no longer helpful. Rather, it becomes pernicious and dysfunctional. People who are overwhelmed by sadness get lost in themselves; they withdraw from the world and become mired in an endless preoccupation, an insatiable desire to have the deceased person back again. When that happens, grief has already begun to take over.

* * *

Rachel Tomasino's family and friends were worried about her, and for good reason. Well into the second year after Frank's death, she was still plagued by sorrow. She felt lost, aimless, and hopeless and was growing increasingly desperate: "When Frank died I was scared, really scared. I didn't know what I was going to do. I was afraid about what was going to become of me. I had a pretty good job, but then I couldn't get myself to go to work. It didn't matter, not anymore. I didn't know how to do anything else. I didn't know how to do anything, really. I was Frank's wife; that was it mostly. And he was gone. He's not here anymore. He's gone. And I am basically, I am, now—I am nobody."

Indeed, most bereaved people experience at least some temporary confusion about their identity; they lose track of who they are or what their life means. It is not uncommon to hear statements like "It feels like a piece of me is missing." People suffering from prolonged grief, by contrast, feel as if *everything* is missing. With prolonged grief, the loss of identity is profound.[2] Whatever life was about before the loss no longer seems to matter. Whatever goals or interests the bereaved survivor had, whatever were his or her sources of pleasure, are simply no longer important. In the simplest of terms, he or she has lost the focus in life.

As Rachel Tomasino's grief wore on, she became hopeless and eventually completely lost: "I just don't know what to do. I mean, what am I supposed to do now? We didn't have a fabulous life, but it was a good life. We were happy. We never had much money. But we always got by. It always seemed like enough. The days came and went. Every day was more or less OK. There was always plenty to do. I don't know what it was I did with my time. I worked. When I was home, when we were together at night and weekends, we were always doing something. Now I just sit there. Each day seems like forever. When I wake up in the morning, the minute I know I am awake, there is this awful moment when I realize that I am alive and Frank is dead. I wish to God I were back asleep. I can't even cry anymore. I stare out the window. I feel as if I live in a cave. I just sit there and watch the world go by my window. Everyone is out there in the sunshine. I sit here in the dark."

What causes this kind of emptiness and pain? What keeps people with prolonged grief in the dark, in their caves, apart from the rest of the world? These are riddles we have not yet fully solved, but fortunately some answers are beginning to emerge. One crucial insight is that prolonged grief is dominated by yearning, the repetitive and futile search for the lost loved one. People in this state can think only of the person they lost. They want nothing but to have that person back. They yearn for that person with their entire being.

This reaction is different from what we normally see in depressive states. The symptoms of depression have no object. They are global and undifferentiated and include such difficulties as a feeling of worthlessness, fatigue, the inability to concentrate, diminished interest or pleasure in activities that would normally be rewarding, reduced or exaggerated appetite, and difficulty maintaining normal sleep patterns. The yearning of prolonged grief, by contrast, is entirely focused on one thing: finding the lost loved one.

The paradox is that yearning brings no comfort, only deeper pain. Even when people suffering from prolonged grief manage to shut out the world and wrap themselves wholly in the past, they still feel only pain.[3] Their loved one is dead and cannot be found. Their search is endless, hopeless, and futile—a bit like chasing a ghost—and it brings only more and more pain.

This experience is almost the opposite of the daily experience of most of us. For most of us, thoughts of those we are closest to usually help us to feel safe and comforted. We call forth these images when we are frustrated or threatened or lonely, and often we feel better. This is how human emotional attachments normally work.[4] This pattern begins in the earliest moments of life[5] and continues as our brains slowly mature. As infants we become bonded with our caregivers, usually our mother, and this bond ensures that we remain close to her, where we can be protected. This kind of bonding also makes us pay close attention to our caregivers and makes possible all kinds of powerful social learning experiences. If all goes well, and it usually does, as we grow older we internalize these learning experiences. In other words, we create a kind of mental representation or image of the caring other. It is not a static image, like a photo. It's more like a kind of internal hologram, a prototype or template that encapsulates our history of experiences with the person. We tend to use this internalized hologram to understand most of the intimate relations we have as adults. When we bond with someone as an adult, we use this same internal template to create and understand that bond. It helps us feel safe. Of course, adults no longer require constant caregiving or the continual presence of a safe figure. But when we feel threatened, when things are not quite going our way, we want to be around those we are closest to and have attached to. Often, that's not possible, so we do the next best thing: We evoke our internalized hologram of that person.

Think about it a minute. Who are you closest to in your own life? Who is the person you can almost always count on, or the person you want to be with when you are feeling down or upset? Whom do you turn to for advice? For most of us, these questions are not difficult to answer. Parents or spouses usually come to mind; sometimes it is siblings or other relatives, often close friends.

I have asked these questions of many bereaved people. Almost everyone can name at least one and sometimes several people who serve these functions—everyone, that is, except those who suffer from prolonged grief. When prolonged grief sets in, all thoughts circle back to the lost loved one. Other people slowly drop out of the picture, and all needs for safety and comfort seem to become concentrated on the deceased. The more protracted the grief reaction, the more concentrated this focus seems to become. And a concentrated focus on the lost loved one only compounds the pain because that person is no longer here.

When grief persists, the bereaved survivor's desire to coax the lost loved one back begins to appear in dreams: "I saw him in a window. He looked right at me. He saw me. I knew it. But when I ran up to the window and peered in, it was dark. I could hardly see anything. I made out furniture and a door or something. It was hard to see. There were reflections on the glass from outside. I pounded on the window. I yelled. But I couldn't see him. I looked around, up the street. There were cars, but the street was empty. Then the window was gone. The wall was solid brick."

We saw in Chapter 5 that resilient people cope well, in part, because they are able to evoke comforting memories of the lost loved one. These memories provide relief and help make the loss more bearable. We also saw that longer periods of grief can make it difficult to hold onto those memories. C. S. Lewis worried that he was losing the memory of his deceased wife, that what he could recall was no longer a fair representation of the good things they shared. As he began to recover from the pain, he was surprised that his memories returned and that he once again found his wife, that when he mourned her the least he "remembered her best."

When grief persists for even longer periods of time, when it drags on for months and then years, the image of the deceased becomes elusive, fragmentary, and increasingly disturbing. Relentless suffering and yearning color everything. What was once a feeling of safety or happiness becomes mixed up with worry and fear and dread.[6] Memories fester and sour. They become, literally, haunting.

* * *

When Frank Tomasino was alive, Rachel never worried about infidelity: "Frank was a handsome man, but he was a good man. He would never have hurt me like that. Never." But then about a year after Frank's death, Rachel began having nightmares about catching Frank with other women: "I dreamed I walked into the room and there was Frank. He had his arm around this woman. He was laughing and talking with people. I don't know who she was. I never saw her before. She was young and pretty."

The most disturbing aspect of these dreams, though, was not the infidelity; it was the way Frank behaved toward Rachel: "He acted funny, different than I had ever seen him. He had this weird sneer, all cold and haughty, and he laughed at me. It made me feel so ashamed, just horrible. This was not my Frank. But it was him. He even had on that gray shirt he used to wear."

Rachel ruminated on the past. She returned over and over to the fact that she and Frank had been unable to have children. She blamed herself: "Frank wanted children. I knew it. He said it didn't matter. He said he didn't care. But I knew he wanted a child. We even applied for adoption, and when we were denied it made him very angry. I was upset, too. But it surprised me that Frank got so angry. The anger was because of me; it was because of me that we weren't going to get the child, the children. I should have done something, something else. I should have tried something else. He would have been happier. He might have lived longer. I was stupid."

Sometimes Frank appeared with a child in Rachel's dreams. For Rachel these were the worst dreams—far worse than the dreams about infidelity. They seemed to personify her emptiness: "He introduced me to the child. He called it 'his child,' as if he'd got the child somewhere else, without me. He seemed happy. He was happy without me, with a child." Frank was gone, and the child she'd never had was gone. Her losses had merged and had found each other, somewhere else, without her. In the dreams, Frank and the child were together. Only Rachel was alone.

* * *

Watching someone go through this kind of loneliness is heartbreaking, especially for other people in the bereaved person's life, like the well-intentioned family or friends who try to help draw the bereaved survivor back into a full life. Try as they may, these efforts are often futile. Others in the bereaved's life are repeatedly rebuffed, denied access, locked out.

This kind of frustration eventually takes a toll, and others begin to give up, adding further to the ongoing sense of loss. The downward spiral may begin in a remarkably short time. One study[7] revealed that it takes only about fifteen minutes of conversation with a depressed person for people to begin to feel an increase in their own levels of anxiety and depression and a hostility toward the depressed person. The people in this study also reported that they would be less willing to interact with the same depressed person in the future *and* that they would be willing to tell that person about their negative reactions. The depressed people, in turn, anticipated that they would be rejected, and they, too, were willing to express rejection of their counterparts. Close friends and relatives, of course, are generally more patient and tolerant, and for longer periods of time. But even their patience is not bottomless.

Dependency

Yearning, emptiness, and isolation—these are a thorny combination. In theory, each of these problems can be surmounted if it is dealt with separately. But separating these problems turns out to be easier said than done: The glue that seems to bind them together is dependency. There are no absolutes about bereavement because the process is too idiosyncratic. But the co-occurrence of the symptoms of prolonged grief with dependency is one of the most consistent patterns we have been able to identify.

The word *dependency* can mean many things. We say that two events are dependent when one is required for the other to occur. We say that a person who requires a particular chemical has a chemical dependency. Chemical dependency often has a psychological component, as is common in addiction and substance abuse. Sometimes we use the term *dependency* to describe a relationship in which one person is overly invested in or overly reliant on another person.

One common form of relationship dependency is economic dependency,[8] which occurs when one person in a relationship has almost complete control over the available financial resources, for example, when one person is the sole provider in the family. In some cases, one person controls the economic resources through bullying or intimidation. In others, the economic dependency may be more imagined than real.[9] For example, a person may come to believe that he is unable to earn a living, regardless of how capable he may actually be or how much work experience he may actually have.

Regardless of its source, economic dependency can cause serious problems during bereavement. Fortunately for Rachel Tomasino, economic dependency wasn't an issue, at least not initially. Rachel had almost always worked. She didn't earn a huge wage, but she made enough so that she felt she was contributing to her life with Frank. Their mortgage had long since been paid off, and together they had managed to put away enough for a reasonably comfortable retirement. Frank's death had also brought a sizable insurance settlement, so Rachel didn't have to worry about getting by financially despite her inability to work.

A more serious problem for Rachel was her emotional dependency. In the most general sense, emotional dependency is an exaggerated need for care, nurturance, and protection even when one is capable of functioning independently to meet normal everyday challenges. Emotionally dependent people—both men and women—tend to be submissive and clinging. They also tend to have a pronounced fear of separation.[10]

This kind of clinging and fear can strain a relationship. It can also be the basis of a painful and exaggerated grief reaction, should the spouse or partner die. When married people in the CLOC study were asked to think about what it might be like to lose their spouse, emotionally dependent people imagined that they would be "terrified" and "completely lost," that they would feel "hopeless" and "desperate." Unfortunately, their predictions held a measure of truth. Years later, when some of the people in this study did actually lose a spouse, those who had earlier revealed this kind of emotional dependency did, in fact, suffer complicated grief reactions.[11]

Rachel Tomasino had always felt anxious when Frank was not around, even when she knew he was safe: "Even though there was nothing really to fret about, I just couldn't shake the feeling. I always had this spooky feeling, like something bad was going to happen, and I thought about all the stuff that could happen to him. I'd get these terrible images. What if he didn't come back? I could get one of those phone calls saying something horrible had happened to him. I get gooseflesh now even thinking about it. The weird thing is that one day I did get one of those phone calls."

Rachel knew that her anxiety and clinginess bothered Frank. She did her best to keep them in check, but when he died, and her deepest fears were realized, she could no longer control those feelings. The dam broke. There was no adjustment, no recalibration. Frank was gone and Rachel was terrified. She was frozen in a relationship with someone who was no longer there. She couldn't let go, and she couldn't go back in time: "Everything came crashing in on me. All I could think about, can think about, is Frank. I don't know where to turn. What can I do? If I could only have my Frank back, it would be all right. I'd be all right, too. I could be like everyone else again, if I can have Frank back again, just for a few minutes, to put myself right again. Just a few minutes, my Frank. Just a few minutes."

Getting Help

As intractable as Rachel's suffering might seem, the situation is not hopeless. A great deal of progress has been made in recent years in finding ways to help people suffering from prolonged grief reactions. I mentioned earlier that therapy isn't always the best way to help a bereaved person. The reason, in the simplest terms, is that most bereaved people do not need treatment. But when the grief doesn't abate, when people find themselves in the same kind of depressing quagmire as Rachel Tomasino, then therapeutic interventions may be appropriate and effective.

In general, psychotherapy has proved to be a valuable tool for helping people deal with ongoing mental health problems.[12] One of the reasons is a general movement toward the use of what psychologists call empirically validated treatments.[13] When someone is not functioning well, the best way to help that person is to first determine as precisely as possible what the specific problem is and then apply a psychological treatment or intervention that has a proven track record for that problem. Of course, people are sometimes troubled in ways that elude understanding, in which case determining the appropriate treatment is much more complex. In addition, sometimes there is a clear psychological problem but not a well-established treatment for that problem. In general, however, first identifying the core problem and then applying a well-validated treatment has become a useful guiding principle for psychological interventions.

Although it has been a bit late in coming, this same logic has begun to influence the way we understand bereavement. Traditionally, people who had lost loved ones were almost always considered potential candidates for psychotherapy and were often referred for treatment whether they needed it or not. We saw an example of this practice in Chapter 2 with Julia Martinez. Julia's story illustrates that, to some extent, this kind of overprescription of grief counseling is still going on.

So what does it matter? If grief counseling can help people, what difference does it make if it is overprescribed? Someone who doesn't need treatment will probably be OK anyway, and providing therapy for as many bereaved people as possible should increase the chances of helping those who really need it, right? This has been more or less the attitude of most mental health professionals. Unfortunately, this kind of global, one-size-fits-all approach to grief counseling has, in fact, proved to be not only notoriously ineffective but sometimes even harmful.[14] In the language of empirically validated treatments, we would say that the problem has not been adequately defined. What can possibly be the effectiveness of a treatment that is not needed, as in Julia's case, or that is applied to people who are likely to get better on their own? And psychological interventions do sometimes actually make people worse, usually when the intervention is unwarranted and interferes with a natural recovery process.[15]

This kind of misuse of therapy has, unfortunately, become something of a common practice in the aftermath of collective traumatic events. If disaster strikes a community when someone carrying a gun opens fire on innocent victims in a crowd or a public institution, or when there is a high-profile terrorist attack, many people are affected, and not just those present at the time but also the friends and family of the victims, people who live nearby, and people who have some relation to the institution or community. The assumption over the last couple of decades has been that almost anyone even remotely involved in the event can benefit from a brief bit of therapy. These interventions have various names. Probably the most commonly used is critical incident stress debriefing or, for short, debriefing.[16]

When it was first developed, debriefing seemed like a good idea. It was originally intended as a prophylactic intervention for people in high-exposure professions, like emergency medical personnel. People in these professions are constantly exposed to horrific events. They are trained to deal with these kinds of situations, and generally they cope better than the average person. But at some point even the most highly trained individuals reach their limit and become overwhelmed. This is the situation debriefing was designed for, to provide a chance to take a step back and regain some perspective. On the surface, the idea seems to make sense, at least for emergency medical personnel.[17]

Problems arose when mental health professionals began to use debriefing more broadly as a preventive measure for everyone in the general public exposed to a potentially traumatic event. The logic seemed straightforward: If debriefing is helpful to those on the front lines of trauma, it should also be helpful to everyone else.

Unfortunately, that logic has a few serious flaws. For one thing, it fails to consider what the average person's experience of trauma is like. Emergency medical personnel are highly trained and thus already somewhat accustomed to traumatic events. They know what to expect. They know what a basic trauma reaction looks like. They know what it feels like. But most of us do not. Most people, in fact, have no idea what trauma looks like or feels like. It is not clear that teaching people about trauma immediately after they have experienced it for the first time is necessarily the correct approach.

Another crucial factor that was overlooked is that mental health professionals are experts and thus hold a position of authority with the lay public. To some extent, emergency medical personnel are already trauma experts, and thus debriefing for this group is essentially one expert helping other experts process what they have been through. But when debriefing is used with people outside professional circles, the dynamic is completely different. Untrained laypeople are not at all accustomed to trauma. They are often frightened and unsure and maybe a bit nervous. They are trying to make sense of the events they have just endured and are perhaps hoping that they will be all right. Just a therapist's belief that they need treatment may instigate a whole set of new worries.

And the consequences? Psychological debriefing has never been shown to be useful as a global intervention for the general public. Actually, virtually the same results have been observed as when grief counseling was used indiscriminately for all bereaved people. Global applications of psychological debriefing to anyone exposed to a potentially traumatic event proved to be not only ineffective but, all too often, harmful.[18]

In one well-known study, debriefing was tried with a group of people who had been hospitalized for injuries due to serious automobile accidents.[19] This was a good test because there was no question that the accidents were potentially traumatic: Auto accidents can be extremely frightening, and in this study, each person had been severely enough injured to require immediate hospitalization. In addition, the experimenters who conducted the study assumed that the debriefing would be helpful, so they were going to give it as honest a test as possible.

Each patient in the study was interviewed by the researchers as soon as possible after he or she arrived at the hospital. Most of these interviews took place within twenty-four hours of the accident. Then, by random selection, half the patients received a one-session debriefing, and the other half, the "control" group, received no intervention, just a plain interview.

I like this example because on the surface, the debriefing seemed innocuous. It lasted only one hour. All that was asked of each patient was that she or he review the accident in detail. The patients described the accident and how they had perceived what was happening to them as it unfolded. They were also encouraged by the researchers to express whatever emotional reactions they had. Each session ended with the researcher providing the patient "information about common emotional reactions to traumatic experience" and "stressing the value of talking about the experience rather than suppressing thoughts and feelings." Finally, the researchers gave the patients a pamphlet that summarized the principles of the study and encouraged them to seek support from family and friends. That's it; that's all there was to the debriefing.

It all seems harmless enough, but it wasn't. Actually, the results of this study were shocking. Three years after the accident, the patients who had received the simple one-hour debriefing session were doing more poorly in many different areas of their lives than the members of the control group. They had greater levels of distress, more severe physical pain, more physical problems, more impaired functioning in their daily lives, and greater financial problems, and they even reported less enjoyment as passengers when someone else was driving the car.

Could it really be the case that such a simple intervention harmed these patients? What about the most distressed patients? Did they, at least, benefit from the intervention? Actually, their reaction was even more decisively negative. For the most part, patients who were initially highly distressed but had *not* received the intervention recovered spontaneously within four months of the accident. By contrast, the initially distressed patients who had received the debriefing session were still distressed three years later. Indeed, they were almost as distressed three years after the accident as when they had first arrived at the hospital. The debriefing had interfered with their natural recovery process.

As a result of sobering findings like these, the mental health community has begun to drastically revise its policy on debriefing. In the weeks following the tsunami disaster of 2004, for example, volunteer therapists and paraprofessionals began flooding into Southeast Asia with the intention of providing debriefing to large swathes of the population. They were well intentioned but misguided, and the World Health Organization (WHO) decided to stop them before their mission got out of hand. The WHO issued a clear warning on its Web site: "Single-session Psychological Debriefing: Not recommended." The accompanying report acknowledged that single-session psychological debriefing had become "one of the most popular approaches" applied across the globe in the aftermath of conflicts or disasters. However, the report went on, "It is the technical opinion of the WHO's Department of Mental Hygiene and Substance Abuse—based on the available evidence—that it is not advisable to organize single-session debriefing to the general population as an early intervention after exposure to trauma." The reason, the report concluded, is that psychological debriefing as an early intervention "is likely ineffective and some evidence suggests that some forms of debriefing may be counterproductive by slowing down natural recovery."[20]

Treatment for Prolonged Grief

If early, global interventions are so ineffective and may even be harmful, how can treatment for grief be a good thing? The answer, once again, turns out to be basic common sense. We can and should treat grief reactions the same way we treat all other emotional disorders, like depression or phobia. We first establish that a person is, in fact, in need of help, that is, has a specific, identifiable psychological problem that will probably not improve on its own. Then we use a treatment with a proven track record specific to that problem.

Let us stick with the case of a more general psychological trauma. When someone has been exposed to a potentially devastating event—for example, a serious automobile accident, a physical or sexual assault, or a terrorist attack—it is reasonable to assume that that person may have suffered a psychological trauma. But as we saw in Chapter 4, most people recover from these kinds of events without lasting harm and without professional intervention. On the other hand, people with severe trauma reactions are more likely to benefit from intervention. We will need a reliable criterion, some sort of agreed-upon marker to help us to distinguish people with severe trauma reactions from people who will recover or already have recovered on their own. We already have such a criterion in the form of posttraumatic stress disorder, or PTSD. There are also empirically validated treatments for PTSD.[21]

If we apply this same simple logic to bereavement, we should also be able to help people who are suffering from prolonged grief. To be fair, one of the reasons that grief counseling has had such a poor track record is that until recently there was little appreciation of the difference between normal and severe grief reactions. Again, the emerging research on resilience has helped clear things up. As we began to see just how resilient most people are in the aftermath of loss or potentially traumatic events, we were also able to see more easily when someone might need help. And there is now a relatively well-established diagnostic category for extreme grief reactions, called prolonged grief disorder, or PGD.[22]

One of the key factors in determining whether someone has PDG is the severity of the person's reaction. The symptoms must be severe enough that the person is unable to function as he or she did before the loss. Another crucial component is time. Although there is still no clear consensus, six months is generally considered the minimal time passage for identifying a prolonged grief reaction.[23] That is, as much as we might want to encourage a person to seek treatment after a loss, we can't reliably determine whether there is a true psychological problem until at least six months have passed.

Once the critical time period has passed and a reliable diagnosis has been made, the question of treatment becomes much more straightforward. Although no single treatment approach yet stands out clearly as the gold standard for prolonged grief, several treatments have shown promising results,[24] and these treatments share a number of elements. One of those elements is a technique generally known as *exposure,* which is also a core element of the common treatment for PTSD. Exposure involves having patients confront those aspects of the event that they most dread. For trauma, the patient gradually relives the traumatic experience in the safety of the therapist's office and with the therapist's guidance. With time, the patient becomes able to tolerate the memories of the trauma and learns to control his or her fearful reactions to those memories.

Exposure treatments for extreme grief reactions are a little bit different. To begin with, the focus is usually less clearly on the specific event of the loss. Generally speaking, exposure for grief therapy focuses

broadly on those aspects of the loss or the lost relationship that most haunt the bereaved survivor.

To identify the trouble spots in bereavement, Dutch researcher Paul Boelen developed an approach in which the therapist asks patients to tell their story about the loss, what happened when their loved one died and how they experienced the death.[25] As the story unfolds, the areas that are most distressing usually stand out. These areas are then gradually covered in the treatment. The therapist may help patients organize the different aspects of their loss in a hierarchy of difficulty so they can gradually come to terms with the things that bother them, beginning with the least distressing and eventually working their way up to the most difficult aspects of the loss. For Rachel Tomasino, for example, such an exposure hierarchy might put Rachel's guilt over the couple's lack of children near the top of the list.

The therapist can also help prolonged grief patients to *understand* what might be behind the most difficult or disturbing aspects of the loss. This process often involves helping patients to see how irrational some of their beliefs are. The pain of severe grief is real—there is no mistake about that—but often it is fueled by an illogical chain of reasoning, as we saw in Rachel's case. When Frank died, and Rachel's grief took over, she began to worry and fret. She spun her regrets about not having children into an elaborate tale that she had ruined Frank's life. She came to believe that her inability to bear children had made Frank deeply unhappy, and that it had caused his poor health, ultimately killing him.

There may be a kernel of truth in Rachel's story but clearly many irrational and exaggerated aspects as well. The therapist's job is to help separate fact from fiction. In Rachel's case, the core facts were that she could not have children and that Frank may have harbored private regrets. But it also seemed true that Frank had genuine affection for Rachel and did his best to conceal from her any displeasure he felt. The rest of the story was pretty much Rachel's invention. Her inability to have children did not cause Frank deep unhappiness; it did not ruin his life or cause his poor health, and it certainly did not kill him.

Another useful treatment element for PGD is to work with the patient to develop concrete goals to begin moving back toward a normal life. People overwhelmed by grief simply give up. They stop participating in life and dwell increasingly in the past. They need help structuring more activity into their lives. They need help finding ways to be with other people, to revitalize old relationships and to begin developing new relationships. Of course, new, active approaches are difficult for people who struggle with dependency. They have not done much independently in their entire lives. And beginning this kind of new course while grieving is doubly difficult.

But dependency can actually help move therapy along. We tend to think of dependency in exclusively negative terms, but in fact, it has some plainly adaptive aspects.[26] For example, dependent people are inclined to be compliant and responsive to authority, so in a prolonged therapy the patient will trust the therapist and abide by her or his instructions. A dependent patient is also apt to be more open to the therapist's suggestions about the irrationality of some of the patient's painful thoughts.

Even more important, dependent people are usually sensitive to the nuances of interpersonal communication. They pick up cues in social interactions that others might miss. Therapists can work with this ability and help dependent people to use this sensitivity to their advantage.

CHAPTER 8

Terror and Curiosity

On the morning of the day John Lindquist died, he seemed happy, even chipper. "There was all this life in John," Heather Lindquist recalled, "that day, in particular. He got up in a good mood. I can still see him smiling. I forget what he said exactly. We were getting dressed and he made some sort of joke. We both laughed." John had put his arms around Heather's shoulders and squeezed her in a bear hug. "It was affectionate, you know, the way guys are affectionate," Heather said. "John was such a guy. Only he squeezed a little too hard. This funny sound came out of me. It made us both laugh."

Later that day John was a stiff mass on a hospital gurney, a body without a life in it. "I stood there, asking myself, 'Where did he go?'" Heather told me. "I saw him there in the hospital. I wanted him back. I wanted to do something, anything, to bring him back. But then I thought, 'Maybe he's not even there anymore.' He still looked like John—the body did—but John was gone. I could see that. It was eerie; John wasn't in that body anymore."

* * *

The death of a loved one is painful and sad. It is also confusing.

The death of a loved one is not a normal, everyday event, and the confusion that often surrounds the death is not a normal, everyday kind of confusion. It's bigger than that. It can be strange. It can be disturbing, and sometimes it can be mystifying. Death pulls at the veil of mundane life and, at least temporarily, exposes us to a universe of questions, many of which have no clear answer.

It would not be accurate to call bereavement a crisis of meaning. Most bereaved people do not find themselves searching for meaning in the traditional sense of questioning how or why the death came about.[1] This is not where the mystery lies. More often than not the why and the how of a death are all too clear: "His heart stopped"; "She fell and never recovered"; "The infection spread to his kidneys and overwhelmed his immune system"; "The impact was immediate, and she was killed instantly."

Sometimes, of course, the "why" is tricky—"It was just one of those things; she was in the wrong place at the wrong time, but why her?"—yet most people eventually find their way to accepting the death. They don't like it. They wish it weren't true, but they eventually stop thinking about it.

But even though most people cope remarkably well and are not troubled by nagging questions about the nature of a loved one's death, they often find themselves perplexed. They find themselves pondering weighty matters, questions about life and death, and the possibility of a soul.

Terror

Around the time I started college, I was living in a small New England town where I struck up a close friendship with an elderly woman. Alice was well into her nineties and lived by herself in the small red house next to mine. She was quite a character. This was obvious right from the start.

I met Alice on a warm summer day. I had been working in my small vegetable garden and had taken off my shirt. I heard what sounded like a wolf whistle, the kind of whistle men used to make when a beautiful woman walked by. I looked around but didn't see anybody. Assuming that I had imagined the sound, I went back to work. Then I heard it again. This time when I looked up I noticed an elderly woman standing behind the screen door of the adjacent house. It was Alice. I stared at her and she stared back; then she whistled again. I couldn't believe it. I walked over to her door and we began to talk. It was a long and intriguing conversation, the first of many we shared over the next few years.

I had never met anyone quite like Alice. She was old and frail and moved around slowly, but she always had something interesting to say, and there was usually a playful glimmer of a smile in the corner of her eyes.

Alice had worked most of her life in a small bookstore that served as the cultural center of the town. She was also an amateur historian of sorts and for years had written a column for the local newspaper about the town's past. She remained curious and thoughtful to the very last days of her life.

Alice knew her time was just about up, but she spoke frankly about death. "Soon," she told me, "I will know something no living person knows. Soon," she leaned forward and smiled, "I will know what happens when we die."

Was Alice genuinely unperturbed by death? Or were her playful remarks part of some ruse—maybe self-deception or outright denial? I trusted Alice, and I believed her curiosity to be genuine. Maybe this was self-deception on my part. Maybe I wanted to believe her as a way of dealing with my own anxieties about death.

These are big questions. Fear and anxiety about the end of life are not uncommon. Many social scientists believe, in fact, that such fears lie just below the surface and that much of what we do—indeed, much of human culture—is nothing more than an elaborate symbolic defense against the knowledge that we will all someday die. This basic thesis first gained prominence in 1973 with the publication of philosopher Ernest Becker's book *The Denial of Death.*[2] A year after its publication, the book was awarded the Pulitzer Prize. Several decades later, a group of social psychologists elaborated Becker's views into a more precise and testable theory they called terror management theory (TMT).

The theory goes something like this: During the course of human evolution, as we developed increasingly larger brains and more sophisticated cognitive abilities and intelligence, we also developed an awareness of our own vulnerability and mortality. That is, we became the first animals to manipulate and control nature, and also the first animals to worry about death. This awareness, combined with our extraordinary ability to imagine the countless ways in which we might be injured or killed, could produce an almost paralyzing terror about the end of life.

Dealing with this terror in the modern world has become increasingly difficult. For starters, we now have the sobering lens of science. Breathtakingly rapid advances in our understanding of the biological processes that sustain life, as well as those that bring life to an end, have laid bare many of the delicate secrets of nature. One unmistakable implication, many believe, is that consciousness is merely a by-product of the activity in our brains, and when we die not only do our biological processes cease, but quite likely so does all consciousness.

How do we live with this knowledge? The answer, according to TMT theorists, is that although our sophisticated brains create fears about death, our inherent intelligence also equips us with clever ways to keep harrowing thoughts at bay.[3] One way is plain old denial. TMT theorists see death-related denial as similar to other kinds of defenses we employ to fend off potential blows to our self-esteem. For example, if we fail a crucial test, we can simply deny the painful feelings by telling ourselves the test was not valid or fair. It might be more difficult to deny the reality of death, of course, especially during bereavement, but the suppression of unwanted thoughts is certainly within human capability.

If suppression doesn't work, we can always try to find comfort in the idea that we might pass on our genes through our progeny. This idea grants us a kind of quasi immortality. Our children and our children's children are, quite literally, a continuation of our genetic selves. They come from us. They look like us, and to some extent they act like us. Of course, this hand-me-down process contains elements that might make us cringe, as, for example, when our worst habits are replicated to perfection by our children. But this is a tolerable price to pay for the comfort we gain from the idea that we are passing on a bit of ourselves.

The bigger problem is that this kind of immortality has a built-in limit. Each child we produce will carry approximately half of our genetic makeup, and with each successive generation, the proportion is halved again: Our children's children will each have only about a quarter of our genes, and so on down the line. Even those of us who are not mathematically inclined can see without too much effort that within a few hundred years, the genetic similarity between ourselves and our eventual kin will have been stretched thin.

There are still other symbolic routes we can try, thanks to the brain's stunning capacity for imagination. We can, for example, strive to leave our mark on a culture in the form of lasting accomplishments or through leadership and fame. We can make other people remember us, even after we have perished. But this route, too, has its obvious limits. All we have to do is visit a city park to find a statue of someone who at one time was well known for some great accomplishment or civic achievement. Who remembers that person now? For the most part, these once-glorious commemorations are now nothing more than convenient perches for pigeons, not exactly what the civic leaders of the past had in mind.

According to TMT theorists, the simplest and most effective way to quell the fear of death is to buy into a shared cultural worldview. TMT theorists define worldviews as "humanly created and transmitted beliefs about the nature of reality shared by groups of individuals."[4] Examples include the belief that individual rights are more important than any other ethical concern, or that our country and political system are better than any other country and any other political system.[5] We invest in these shared beliefs, TMT theorists argue, because they "provide the universe with order, meaning, value, and the possibility of either literal or symbolic immortality."[6] Shared worldviews allow us to feel we are part of a larger whole, a group or culture that is bigger and more enduring then ourselves. This feeling, in turn, gives us a sense of being immortal.

A testimony to the strength with which we tend to cling to worldviews comes from the fact that usually we fail to see them as views at all. Rather, we see them as objective truth, as reality, and we assume that they are shared by everyone. Research has shown, in fact, that most people overestimate the extent to which other people share their beliefs.

This phenomenon is called the "false consensus" effect. In the original experiment that identified the effect, college students were asked whether they would be willing to walk around campus wearing a sandwich board inscribed in large letters with the word *repent*. The students who agreed to wear the sign believed that the majority of students on campus would also be willing to wear the sign, whereas the students who refused believed that the majority of students would also refuse. There are many other examples: During elections, voters typically assume their favorite candidates are more popular than they actually are, and sexually active college students overestimate the frequency of sexual activity in their peers.[7]

Mortality Salience

One of the strongest claims TMT researchers have made is that when people are reminded of their own mortality, they cling all the more tenaciously to shared worldviews, thereby fending off the threat of death. The procedure researchers have used to demonstrate this claim is deceptively simple; it begins with a "mortality salience" prompt that usually consists of nothing more than asking a few basic questions about death, for example, "Jot down as specifically as you can what you think will happen to you when you die and once you are physically dead," or "Write briefly about the emotions you feel when you think about your own death."[8] To ensure that the people who participate in this research don't catch on to what the researchers are up to, the mortality questions are usually embedded in a host of questions on other subjects.

These simple questions about death have produced some remarkable effects. For example, one of the more compelling experiments involved municipal court judges who were tested just before setting bail for accused prostitutes. Using the typical mortality salience prompt, the researchers asked half the judges the above two questions about death. The other half were asked two innocuous questions. The results were striking: The judges who answered the death questions set a higher bail bond for the prostitutes than the other judges. We assume that court judges are objective in their interpretation of the law and shouldn't be so easily influenced. Yet the only difference in the two conditions was that one group of judges answered those two simple questions about their own death. The explanation, according to TMT, is that because prostitution is generally considered a violation of American morals, the judges upheld this view and when reminded of their own mortality clung to it more strongly. This same result came through even more clearly in a follow-up study with college students. In this study the researchers first ascertained the students' attitudes toward prostitution and then presented the same bail bond task. The mortality salience questions again caused the students to set a higher bail bond for prostitutes, but this reaction was strongest in the students who had earlier said that they found prostitution immoral.

TMT also predicts that when our mortality is made salient we should react more favorably toward other people who we perceive as doing something consistent with our shared worldview. Most of us share the belief that standing up to crime is morally correct. When we are reminded of our own mortality, then, we should value this behavior even more. To test this idea, some researchers had subjects read a description of a woman who called a police hotline with crucial information about a dangerous mugger who had terrorized her neighborhood. The woman was described as acting courageously. She called the hotline even though she greatly feared the possible harm that might come to her if the mugger learned of her identity. After reading about the woman's behavior, the people in the experiment were told that the woman would receive a monetary reward for her heroic behavior and that their task was to set the amount of her reward. As predicted, those that had been given the mortality salience prompt assigned a higher reward to the woman.[9]

Yet another means by which we control our fear of death, the TMT theorists hold, is to deny our animal nature. When we acknowledge that we are animals, we have to face the fact that all animals die. To counter this threat, we convince ourselves that human existence means more in the grand scheme of things than does mere animal existence. If the TMT perspective is correct, this defense should be exaggerated whenever we are reminded of our own mortality. This is precisely the result that the TMT researchers have found. A group of subjects exposed to a mortality salience prompt tended to overstate the differences between themselves and other animals, to react with increased disgust toward human body products and toward animals, and to prefer essays that emphasized a greater distinction between humans and animals. In keeping with the symbolic immortality we may achieve through progeny, discussed earlier, mortality salience questions have also been shown to evoke in people a greater desire to have children.[10]

* * *

The great discovery of TMT research is that most of us have, somewhere, simmering just below the surface of conscious awareness, a vague and fleeting dread of our own vulnerability and mortality. Even the simplest reminder of our mortality may dramatically alter our attitudes and behavior in ways that appear to be consistent with some of the larger claims of the theory.

Yet many psychologists find it difficult to accept the sweeping nature of the TMT theorists' claims. For one thing, TMT assumes that the primary function of worldviews is to ward off death anxiety. Although the results of the TMT experiments are consistent with this hypothesis, there is nothing in these tests to show that lessening death anxiety is the sole or even the primary function of worldviews. More to the point, as critics of the TMT approach have been quick to point out, our brains probably evolved global belief systems in the service of far more pedestrian ends. Belief systems condense and catalog the world around us, for example, and thus help us to reliably predict what is likely to happen in a given situation. Shared beliefs also reinforce our membership in groups and cultures. When we feel that we belong to a larger whole, we are more likely to cooperate, to pool resources, and to work together to solve common problems.[11] These functions promote survival and suggest that worldviews more than likely evolved for more basic purposes than to help us deal with death anxiety.

There is an even more intriguing limitation to the TMT paradigm. The mortality salience prompt works only when it is presented "at the fringes of consciousness" and not to full conscious attention.[12] For example, in one study, American college students were given the standard mortality salience prompt ("briefly describe the emotions that the thought of your own death arouses in you") and showed the typical increase in worldview strength, in this case greater pro-American bias in their evaluations of a political essay. However, the effect of the death questions was dramatically reduced if the students were asked to contemplate their own death at a deeper, more explicit level or for a longer period of time.[13]

Why would deeper or longer contemplation of death reduce the usual mortality salience effects seen in these studies? The explanation that TMT theorists give is somewhat circular: This result is caused by the worldview's already having done its job in reducing death anxiety.[14] Possibly, but there is another explanation: When we confront the idea of death in a more measured, reflective context, we react with less distress because we have time to contemplate its meaning. Most of us lead busy, hectic lives. We have places to be, schedules to keep, children to comfort, deadlines to meet, bills to pay, food to cook, and so on. A fleeting reminder of our own mortality in the midst of that activity may trigger a cascade of worries and fears, but even the busiest of us slow down eventually, and when we do, we can and often do ponder the larger questions in life. When we confront death head-on, we have no choice but to embrace its meaning.

Meditating on Death

As part of their daily meditation, Buddhist monks believe it is healthy to reflect on the vulnerability of the human body. In Asia, Buddhists even go so far as to take their mediation practice to human burial grounds. The presence of decaying corpses, they believe, fosters a greater appreciation of the impermanence of life. Buddhists in the West espouse a similar belief, but finding corpses to meditate with is not quite so easy. Burial is strictly regulated in the West and hanging around with dead bodies is most definitely frowned upon. But then Rande Brown, an active Buddhist and executive director of a Buddhist foundation in New York City, had an idea.[15]

"Bodies: The Exhibition" was in New York at the time. The exhibit, which had become extremely popular all over the world, displayed a number of actual human corpses, preserved by a unique process that removes the water from the dead tissue and replaces it with a rubbery polymer. Each corpse was skinless and arranged in a unique pose to allow spectators an intimate glimpse into the wonders of anatomy. Admittedly, an exhibit of this nature is not for the fainthearted, but visitors were often surprised by how pleasant, and even calming, the show turned out to be.[16]

To Rande Brown, it seemed like a perfect place for Buddhist meditation. "It just quickly came to me," she told the *New York Times*. "I called the Bodies exhibit and told them, 'I'd really like to do a meditation in your space.'"[17] The exhibitors were willing, and not long after, arrangements were made for around 180 meditators to use the space. They filled the room, set up their meditation cushions among the displayed corpses, and got down to a half hour of contemplation.

How do Buddhists gain such comfort with the idea of death? This is an intriguing question, because, at least on the surface, Buddhist ideas about culture and the human tendency to cling to illusions would seem to be quite similar to TMT.[18] But although Buddhists have been musing on the human struggle with death and impermanence for more than two millennia, in many ways this belief system takes a more hopeful view of human nature and mourning.

The central tenets of Buddhist philosophy are captured in what have been called the Four Noble Truths. Probably the best way to explain these truths is to take a look at how they came about. Around 500 BCE, Siddhartha Gautama, the young man who would eventually become the Buddha, grew up in a small town in the Himalayan foothills of what is now India. His family was wealthy and provided him with the pampered and protected existence of a prince. His life was more or less insulated from the pains and troubles of daily existence—maybe a bit too insulated.

At the time of Buddha's youth, life in the region was rife with political and social unrest. Religious sects were springing up in the area and, as the Buddhist scriptures tell it, young Siddhartha's father greatly feared that his son would run off to join one of them. For that reason he kept the young prince sequestered within the walls of the family compound. As the prince grew to be a young man, of course, keeping the world from his eyes became impossible. Not surprisingly, his father's plan backfired. When the innocent and privileged Siddhartha finally set eyes on the world, he was immediately taken by the profound suffering of those around him. He soon realized that nobody was immune to such suffering; that all people, rich and poor alike, eventually grow old and weak; and that in due course everyone must come to terms with death. Siddhartha also realized that even though he led a comparatively comfortable and trouble-free life, he would face his own death one day.[19] This was the First Noble Truth: Life is suffering.

Like the TMT theorists, Buddha eventually came to believe that the human dread of death and vulnerability was the fundamental motivator for much of human behavior and culture. Just as the TMT theorists describe the anxiety-buffering function of worldviews, Buddha came to realize that humans try to mollify their dread of death and vulnerability by clinging to illusions of immortality. Here we have the Second Noble Truth, that suffering is caused by our clinging to and grasping at the illusion of permanence. It *seems* to us that our own existence must be permanent. Most of us simply cannot let go of the idea that whoever or whatever we are will live on, even as our bodies decay. We seek pleasure, but pleasures never last. We strive for wealth and power, but whatever wealth and power we acquire is never enough. We always want more. We carve our bodies and dye our hair so as to forestall the appearance of aging. As the TMT research so thoroughly demonstrates, we invest in cultural symbols and shared beliefs in the hope of belonging to something larger than ourselves.

When he saw the ubiquity of human suffering, the young Siddhartha left his cloistered sanctuary and spent years wandering the countryside in search of a solution. He explored and mastered a number of different spiritual methods but finally came to realize that the ability to transcend existential anxieties about the impermanence of life was deceptively simple. Rather than overcoming the human condition through sheer will or denial of bodily needs, as many ascetics of the day were preaching, the Buddha realized, one had only to *understand,* to become aware of, the link between impermanence and suffering. In other words, the Buddha came to believe, paradoxically, that by accepting the reality of our impermanence, we can eventually find our way to happiness.[20] This realization became the Third Noble Truth: Genuine acceptance of the impermanence of life is the only way to find true happiness.

Buddhist writers often compare this insight to waking from a dream. The experiences we have while dreaming feel absolutely real—until we awaken, when it becomes apparent that the experiences were only an illusion.[21] In a famous anecdote in the Buddhist literature, a stranger by chance encounters the Buddha not long after he has achieved enlightenment.[22] The stranger is immediately struck by the radiance and serenity that the Buddha exudes and stops him to ask, "My friend, what are you? Are you a celestial being or a God?" The Buddha simply says no. "Well, then, are you some kind of magician or wizard?" The Buddha again simply answers no. "Well, my friend, what, then, are you?" to which the Buddha replies, "I am awake."

To their credit, Buddhists accept that their philosophy is at odds with the way most of us view life. One of the classic Buddhist texts points out, for example, that although happiness can come about only through the "ceasing of identity," surely this realization "runs counter to the entire world."[23] For this reason Buddhist teachers commonly advise those new to the philosophy to remain critical or even to doubt the core doctrine. Rather than simply accept the teachings, they suggest, the neophyte should test the validity of Buddhist ideas directly through contemplation and meditation.

However, the kind of contemplative practice Buddhists aspire to requires years, if not a lifetime, of devotion, and the Fourth Noble Truth spells out how a practicing Buddhist can live his or her life so as to better ingrain these habits and insights.

* * *

Do Buddhists cope better with loss? It would certainly seem that a Buddhist should handle bereavement with greater equanimity. For one thing, Buddhists cope well with adversity generally. The Buddhist refugees who fled Tibet, for example, had been exposed to any number of trying circumstances, including imprisonment, rape, beatings, torture, and forced labor. Yet researchers who studied these groups reported that "despite a high prevalence of potentially traumatizing events, [their] levels of psychological distress were extremely low."[24]

As we saw earlier, Buddhists believe it is healthy to confront death head-on. As the Dalai Lama notes, "The reality of death has always been a major spur to virtuous and intelligent action in all Buddhist societies. It is not considered morbid to contemplate it, but rather liberating from fear, and even beneficial to the health of the living."[25] We've already seen an example in the practice of meditating among corpses. There are also guided meditation exercises, such as those developed by Vietnamese Buddhist teacher Thich Nhat Hahn, that instruct practitioners to imagine their own death: "Imagine you were on an airplane and the pilot announced that the plane was in trouble and might crash." That idea would launch a cascade of frightening thoughts and images in most of us. But Thich Nhat Hahn advises that the meditator focus on the Buddha, his teachings, and the community of other meditators as abiding sources of peace: "If you were indeed to die, you would be able to die beautifully, as you have lived beautifully in mindfulness. You would have enough calm and clarity in that moment and would know exactly what to do and what not to do."[26] In an even more explicit exercise, Thich Nhat Hahn instructs his followers to contemplate in vivid detail nine separate stages of decomposition of a corpse as if the corpse were their own decaying body. The exercise is explained as being a way to help its practitioners grow to accept the idea that everyone must die and to begin to let go of the normal worries and sufferings that plague them.

Beyond Terror

Many of us do not follow the basic tenets of Buddhism, but we may hold similarly benign attitudes toward death. The same can be said of other religious or spiritual belief systems. On the other hand, some people are especially prone to death anxiety. Even TMT research finds differences in whether or not people react defensively when reminded of their own mortality.

Differences in attitudes toward death can be explained, at least to some extent, by differences in personality. One type that seems to be especially susceptible to death anxiety is the authoritarian personality.[27] There was a great deal of interest in this personality type immediately following World War II. The passive compliance evidenced by ordinary German citizens in going along with Hitler's genocidal Nazi regime led to questions about how such a tragedy could happen. It was possible, of course, that the horrors of Nazi Germany came about because of a flaw in the German national character, but that explanation was just too simpleminded. A more plausible account was that the conditions in Germany in the 1930s were ripe for the exploitation of a global element of human nature: authoritarianism. We are all capable of mindless obedience to authority, a propensity that has been demonstrated by experimenters like Stanley Milgram.[28] But some people, those who have an "authoritarian personality," are more obedient to authority than others.

The connection between authoritarianism and death anxiety was discovered in a TMT experiment about in-groups and out-groups. The classic in-group/out-group effect occurs when we blindly favor people we perceive as more like ourselves, that is, the in-group. We are also sometimes blindly unfavorable or unfair to people we perceive as different from ourselves, the out-group. This effect is at the root of much of the prejudice and racism we see in modern life. It is also related to our need to adhere to shared worldviews. The more we define ourselves as part of a specific group or type, the more we can relish a shared reality. Given the results of the experiments on mortality salience discussed earlier, it should come as no surprise that having people think briefly about their own death seems to exacerbate the in-group/out-group effect. That is, when we are confronted with questions about death, we are more likely to derogate and reject people we perceive as different from or inferior to ourselves. However, people high in authoritarianism are especially likely to derogate the out-group, and not surprisingly, it is mostly authoritarian personalities that do so when reminded of their own mortality. The converse is also true: People who are less obedient to authority are also less susceptible to death anxiety and less likely to derogate the out-group, even when reminded of their own mortality.[29]

There are also simple sex differences in the effects of death anxiety. I mentioned earlier that making people aware of their own mortality tends to increase their desire to have children. It turns out, however, that this effect is clearest in men. The mortality salience prompt's influence on women's desire for children depended on the extent to which they were concerned about career success. Women who had more pronounced career goals were less likely to desire children regardless of whether they were reminded of their own mortality. However, in another study, women who were shown a fake newspaper article that touted the benefits of children for career success responded to the mortality salience prompt with a greater desire for children.[30] Another study found that making people aware of their own mortality resulted in a greater willingness to engage in risky activities, like bungee jumping, white-water rafting, skydiving, or drinking large quantities of alcohol. However, this kind of effect was found primarily in men.[31]

I know of no research that examined differences in the extent that being reminded of death influences our tendency to distance ourselves from our animal nature. However, it seems likely that such differences do exist. Frans de Waal, the noted primatologist, has written, for example, "I often get the impression of being surrounded by two distinct categories of people: those who do and those who do not mind being compared to animals."[32]

Another personality quality related to how a person reacts to death-related thoughts, and one of particular relevance to resilience and bereavement, has to do with attachment behavior. We touched on this subject briefly in the last chapter. The ability to feel close to and safe with another person is a crucial aspect of normal, healthy development. The extent that we can do this depends at least to some extent on our history of interactions in close relationships throughout our lives, especially our early bonding experiences. Normal, healthy attachment is assumed to provide an inner resource; when we feel threatened or stressed, we can evoke mental images of the people we are attached to—the internal hologram we discussed in the last chapter—as a way to comfort ourselves.

Some people find this process easier than others. Psychologists describe consistent differences in attachment behavior in terms of attachment styles.[33] Those who have difficulties experiencing intimacy in close relationships are said to have an *insecure attachment style*. These people tend to be less confident that others will be available when they are needed, and not surprisingly, these people are also more likely to suffer prolonged grief reactions. Insecure attachment is not uncommon, but it is also not the norm. Most people tend toward a more *secure attachment style* and are generally able to get close to others and feel confident about depending on other people. Securely attached people also tend to handle grief better and are less susceptible to death anxiety.[34]

The CLOC study I described in Chapter 5 provided a unique opportunity to examine whether views about death are truly related to resilience during bereavement. To recap, in that study people had been interviewed years before their spouse died. Included in the initial interviews were various questions related to death anxiety. For example, the people in the study were asked to rate how much they agreed with statements like "Death is simply part of the process of life" or "I don't see any point in worrying about death." This study found that the people who years earlier had said they didn't worry about death or who generally accepted that death happens were the same people who tended to cope best with the pain of grief when their spouse died. Also, when they were asked the same questions several years later, after their spouse had died and they had actually confronted death, most still gave more or less the same answer. In other words, they still didn't see any point in worrying about death even after having come close to it.

Curiosity

When my friend Alice hinted that she was actually curious about what happens when we die, I believed her. We are thinking creatures, and although at times we don't exactly act the part, we tend to seek explanations for the world around us. The impermanence of life may be anxiety-provoking or even terrifying, but it is also a mystery that has piqued our interest and wonder since *Homo sapiens* first walked the earth.

"Death excites an enormous curiosity," wrote the pathologist F. Gonzalez-Crussi. "How could it be otherwise? From the beginning of time human beings have left this life to emigrate to the unknown, dark realm, without any one of them ever coming back to hand us a report on the beyond. Any form of report. Not a word about what awaits us! We are curious by nature, but by nature we are doomed never to know."[35]

Yet we have always wanted to know. Ruins of the first human settlements include ancient stone structures aligned with the pathways of planets and stars. They suggest a precocious desire to understand the heavens. Early humans also appear to have shown a profound need to grasp life beyond the grave. Indeed, the capacity to conceptualize death and the possibility of an afterlife is widely considered an emergent property of mind that sets humans apart from other animals. Archaeological evidence of ritualized burial of the dead, found at prehistoric sites, for example, is often cited as a marker of the emergence of human self consciousness and the origins of society.[36]

The human inquiry into the mysteries of life and the nature of the soul is acute during bereavement. When a loved one dies, we have no choice but to face up to nearly imponderable questions, the kind of questions I mentioned at the beginning of the chapter. Most of us open ourselves up to the questions death demands of us. We don't necessarily do this by choice, mind you. Death does not ask permission. Although we may accept death's invitation with trepidation, many of us find that the experience is not as frightening as we anticipated. Many of us discover, in fact, that we have found something quite profound hidden in the experience.

CHAPTER 9

Between Was and Is and Will Be

After C. S. Lewis's wife died, he wondered what had become of her: "Can I honestly say that I believe she now is anything? That vast majority of people I meet, say, at work, would certainly think she is not. Though naturally they wouldn't press the point on me. Not just now anyway. What do I really think? I have always been able to pray for other dead, and I still do, with some confidence. But when I try to pray for H, I halt. Bewilderment and amazement come over me. I have a ghastly sense of unreality, of speaking into a vacuum about a nonentity."[1]

Like Karen Everly with her daughter, C. S. Lewis found it difficult to accept that his wife had vanished completely. He accepted that she had physically died; it took a while, but he came to terms with her physical death. It was much more difficult, however, to accept that everything about her was gone. Some part of H, he was sure, still existed, but where and in what form?

The logic of Lewis's internal questioning propelled him almost to absurdity as he tried to work the problem out:

> Where is she now? That is, in what place is she at the present time. But if H is not a body—and the body I loved is certainly no longer she—she

> is in no place at all. And "the present time" is a date or point in our time series. It is as if she were on a journey without me and I said, looking at my watch, "I wonder is she at Euston now." But unless she is proceeding at sixty seconds a minute along the same timeline that all we living people travel by, what does now mean? If the dead are not in time, or not in our sort of time, is there any clear difference, when we speak of them, between was and is and will be?[2]

The way questions like these take shape can be surprising. Most of us are ill equipped to handle them. Some of us hold strong religious beliefs with prepackaged stories about the afterlife. Some of us have intellectual arguments about existential dilemmas or the relationship of consciousness to the brain. Such views tend to refute the possibility of any kind of life after death. Some people have no beliefs at all. They simply haven't given the possibility of an afterlife much thought. When someone close or important to us dies, though, and we find ourselves puzzling over where that person has gone, and often whatever we previously believed simply falls apart.

* * *

Serge and Sondra Beaulieu were married for over twenty-five years. They had a passionate and loving relationship. Then Serge was diagnosed with lung cancer. His death came slowly, and it was hard on Sondra. But like so many bereaved people, she stood up to the pain and did what she had to do to get on with her life.

Sondra is a professional journalist and radio producer. Not long after Serge's death, she gave me a short essay she had written about her experience with loss. The essay, titled "The Final Good-Bye," highlights lucid accounts of Sondra's struggle, her loneliness, fear, and guilt. It also describes moments when Sondra seemed to fall into odd, almost mystical states and had the kind of experiences Joan Didion described as "magical thinking." Yet Sondra's essay is neither stark nor foreboding. Somewhere in the experience, soon after Serge's death, Sondra found peace.

Hallucinations again

"I had been doing my best," she wrote, "to put everything in order." Sondra and Serge had often worked together. She was "taking care of some of the projects Serge had developed in his lifetime." But Sondra was concerned that she might not be able to manage it all: "I felt I was letting Serge down. I worried that I wasn't carrying on his legacy, and it saddened me."

Then, one night, she woke up and saw Serge standing in the bedroom doorway. He wasn't actually present, but his blurred image was there momentarily. She was left with a lingering conviction that Serge had visited her to assess the situation.

A few days later, Sondra was awake but still in bed and she smiled. It was the same kind of smile, she realized, that she had seen on Serge's face in the ambulance on his way to his death. The attendant had said at the time that Serge looked as if he was "seeing angels." Sondra continued to smile broadly, and then she saw a white light in front of her bed. She described it as "cloud-shaped but not opaque," and it evoked in her a tranquillity she had never before experienced. Sondra's first thought was that perhaps *she* was dying. She reflected a moment and concluded that she was in fact awake and that there was no evidence she was being transported or altered in any way. Then she saw Serge: There he was again, this time larger than life. He seemed to be floating upright next to her. His image fanned out from one side of the white cloud shape to the other. Then, just as quickly, the light was gone and she was alone again.

The experience was not in the least disturbing to Sondra. On the contrary, she wrote, "I felt a lingering calmness, and I sensed that Serge was telling me that he was in this extraordinarily tranquil place and that he was all right. He had no worries about what was happening here, and no matter what I was able to do—or not do—it was all right. He was at peace, and I didn't need to worry about him."

Was Serge really there? Had some aspect of his spirit or soul actually visited Sondra? Perhaps what she experienced was only the vestige of a lingering dream?

Does it matter?

Like Karen Everly, C. S. Lewis, and countless others, Sondra had experiences after her husband's death that were as profound as they were unexpected. They gave her something to believe in. On the second anniversary of Serge's death, Sondra wrote a poem. The last line read, "I lost his body but not his soul. He's with me every day."

The Enduring Bond

In the terms we have used so far in this book, Sondra was unquestionably resilient. She mourned Serge's passing and at times suffered acute emptiness over all she had lost. But not only was she able to move on, she also continued to embrace life. She basked in old friendships and began new ones. She resumed her writing career and explored new forms. She began writing poetry and planned a memoir of her life with Serge. Once again she discovered passion in the things she did. She continued to live a rewarding and productive life.

Sondra's quasi-hallucinatory exchanges with Serge are more difficult to assess. From a traditional perspective, they could only mean trouble. Traditional theories about bereavement discussed in Chapter 2, inspired as they were by Freud's theorizing about grief work, assume that the only way to recover from a loss is to sever the emotional bond with the deceased. This dictum is unambiguous. When bereaved people fail to sever this bond or, as in Sondra's case, even revel in it, something is supposed to have gone wrong. According to the traditional theories, the behavior of bereaved people who maintain rather than break bonds with dead loved ones is pathological.[3] And from this point of view, Sondra was using the enduring bond as some sort of fantasy experience to mask a deeper pain.

The science of bereavement shows us that we need to take a broader view of these experiences. For starters, the bereaved people who find it most difficult to let go of a lost loved one are typically *not* those who have coped well. Rather, they tend to be people like Rachel Tomasino who are overwhelmed by grief. Rachel was stuck in an endless cycle of rumination and yearning for her dead husband. Sadly, she also found it almost impossible to gain any pleasure from holding on. In her case, the memories of her husband acted more like a purgatorial ball and chain than a comforting connection.

Most of us can locate comforting memories of dead loved ones and find reassurance, hope, and soothing calm in our recollections. Certainly, this experience is beneficial. Sometimes an emotional bond takes the form of a spiritual connection that is also beneficial. But sometimes, as for Sondra, the connection becomes more tangible. C. S. Lewis wrote that his recovery from grief felt "as if the lifting of the sorrow removed a barrier."[4] What if the barrier disappears? What if the loved one seems to exist again, even briefly, as if brought back from the dead or transformed in some altered state? How healthy can that be?

The first thing we need to find out is how common such experiences are. If we discover, for example, that a palpable sense of a deceased loved one's presence is rare, we have to accept the traditional idea that it represents a malfunction of the normal grieving mechanism, or at least something to be concerned about. If, on the other hand, the vast majority of bereaved people have these experiences, we must conclude that they are part of the normal grieving process, a bit strange but essentially benign, perhaps even healthy.

Remarkably, the question of how common such experiences are hasn't been answered until quite recently. The reason is simple: Nobody had ever asked.

When researchers finally investigated this phenomenon, the results were intriguing, if not a bit surprising. For one thing, some bereaved have sensed the presence of a deceased loved one to a profound extent, whereas others have never experienced anything of the sort. In fact, when asked about such experiences, many often find the question odd if not downright silly. I've seen this kind of polarity in my own studies. When I bring up the subject of a continued relationship with the deceased, many people immediately light up. They are delighted that I have finally broached the issue. Others, though, simply shake their heads or shrug: "Nope, never felt anything like that."

A large-scale survey study revealed the same pattern. A clear majority of those surveyed felt that their lost loved one was still in some way with them or "watching over" them. However, only about a third of the bereaved people in the survey reported that they talked regularly with deceased loved ones. Slightly more reported that they talked regularly to the deceased's photo. For these people, however, the conversations continued at about the same frequency even more than a year after the loved one's death.[5]

* * *

When Daniel Levy wanted to "have a little talk" with his deceased wife, Janet, he would walk to a marshy area near his home. "She liked the way the trees looked," he told me. "There isn't much there really, a smattering of trees, lots of empty space, salt water, but it's private. Nobody ever went there, I think, except us. It was always our spot, our own private little place."

Daniel had a set routine. He visited the marsh about an hour before sunset and walked directly to a large rock with a bowl-like depression on one side. The rock formed a natural seat that faced the water and the setting sun. Although the insects were plentiful at that time of day, Daniel said he didn't mind: "The scene is too beautiful. There are pine trees and eucalyptus there. Janet loved the way the colors of those trees contrasted."

One day, several months after Janet's death, Daniel decided to visit the marsh: "I had been thinking about her all day. I guess I was feeling lonely. I went to the marsh around the same time I normally did, only this time I had a very strong feeling. It seemed as if she was there. She was telling me she wanted to talk." Daniel called out Janet's name. He didn't hear anything or see anything. But it was crystal clear to him: He knew she was there.

Daniel went into "some kind of trance" and spoke to Janet at length. To an observer, it would have looked as though he was talking to himself, but for Daniel it was definitely a "conversation." When he asked Janet questions, she seemed to him to answer. I asked Daniel if he had actually heard Janet's voice. He said, "I don't know. I heard her say things, but I don't know if there was really a voice out there in the marsh saying things. I can't answer that. But it felt real. Man, it felt real."

Robert Ewing's experiences after his sister, Kate, died fell toward the opposite end of the spectrum. For Robert Ewing, recollecting his "good egg" sister was grounding. "She was part of me, you know, actually part of me, my blood. The memories come easily. At times, I still forget. It's as if she is going to walk through that door and sit down and talk to me. The images are so sharp, like a movie. I can see her talking, in that busy, taking-care-of-everybody way she had. She was loving. Even right now, as I am talking to you, I can see her." Despite the clarity of his memories, Robert never experienced Kate's presence in any tangible sense. When I asked him whether he'd ever had this kind of experience, he was defensive, as if I had implied there might be something wrong with him: "Not at all. I know Kate is dead. She is not actually here. She is not in this room. As much as I'd love that to be true, I know she is dead. I've accepted that. She is not coming back; she can't. I can't actually talk to her. It doesn't work that way."

Like Robert Ewing and his recollections of Kate, Julia Martinez found succor in recollections of her father. She said she knew that the love and safety he had given her would always be a part of her. And like Robert, Julia reported she had never felt that her father was physically present or was in some way guiding her. When I asked her about this possibility, her face grew serious: "Never." Did she ever talk with him? "No." She began to stare at me, as if to ask, "Why are you asking these weird questions?" Then she laughed and gave a shrug: "Is this some sort of test you guys do?" I reassured her. I told her I asked these questions of everyone in the study because not all bereaved people have the same experiences.

Heather Lindquist was a bit different. She told me that after her husband John died, she stopped thinking about where he might have gone and whether there was such a thing as a soul: "I'm not much of a theologian. The way I figure it, who knows what happens?" But Heather did occasionally talk with John, typically when she was uncertain about something and she wanted John's advice. She usually held these conversations in her garage: "John was always in the garage, tinkering with things, fixing something. Some of his tools are still there. The kids use them now. The tools remind me of John. It's a good place to talk with him. It's quiet there—private."

When I asked Heather if she felt John was actually present during the times when she spoke with him, she thought for a moment and then said, "I kind of assume he's probably *not* there, you know, hovering or anything like that. But like I said, what do I know? It feels as if I am with him when we talk. That's all that matters. When I talk, it makes me feel good, as if we can have a little chat."

* * *

This seems like a good place to put my own experiences on the table: I have, in fact, periodically engaged in something of a continued relationship with my deceased father. My perceptions of these experiences are probably most similar to the halfway state described by Heather Lindquist. I've already written about my reactions to my father's death in earlier chapters. I didn't grieve a lot at the time, and if anything, I felt relieved: His suffering had ended and my life could take a fresh course. But I never stopped thinking about my father. As I grew older, I found myself having conversations with him—much to my amazement.

The first time this happened was a good seven or eight years after his death. I was in graduate school at the time, earning my PhD from Yale. This choice had meant a major change in course for me, and I wished there was some way my father could see that. He died believing that I was a failure, that I was not going to make anything of myself, and also that he had failed me. If he had handled my rebelliousness differently, perhaps tried another approach, I might not have strayed so far. I longed to reassure him that everything had turned out OK. I wanted him to know that nothing was his fault, that I knew he had done the best he could. I wanted so much to speak with him, to tell him these things. Then one day, while walking down a quiet street at dusk, I did.

At first, I felt a bit odd speaking out loud. I looked around to double-check: Nobody was there; nobody was watching me. I spoke at a normal conversational level. "Hello Dad," I began, and then I paused. I didn't hear anything, but I felt my father's presence. It was warm and comforting.

I knew almost immediately that this experience was something I would not be able to describe later. The instant I tried to identify the experience and categorize it—after all, I was a psychologist in training—it was gone. So I pulled back and just let it come. It appeared to me not so much that my father was actually there as that the *possibility* was there. I felt a sense of expansion. If I opened myself to it, without thinking too much about what was happening, I could talk with him. And that's all I wanted to do. I didn't want him back. His life had been painful, so why would I want to bring him back? No, all I wanted was to talk. Actually, all I wanted was to tell him a few things. I told my father that I knew our battles had not been his fault. I told him that everything was turning out just fine. I told him that I still wanted him as a father. When I told him all this, I felt relieved.

There was a bit of apprehension, I must admit. I had just spoken aloud with my dead father. Was this a slippery slope? I wondered. Was I losing it, maybe just a little bit? Was graduate school too much for me?

The doubts didn't last. I soon realized that language gives ideas structure and clarity.

Saying I needed him, out loud, gave me back a bit of my father.

* * *

Although it was never something I did with any frequency, from time to time I felt an overwhelming desire to speak again with my father, and from time to time I did. These conversations had several elements that seem to match the experiences of many other bereaved people. For one thing, I had always had a strong need to have my father's council and support. Initially, after his death, I just wanted to talk with him. Later, the conversations seemed to occur at times when was I mulling over an important decision. I would describe the options to my father and often ask for his advice. Of course, I never heard an answer, but nonetheless I had a definite sense of what his response was.

Like most bereaved people who have had these experiences, I found I needed privacy. The fragile, almost hypnotic nature of the conversations seemed to require it. Initially, I spoke with my father while walking, almost always at twilight. If anybody approached, I immediately stopped. Later, I discovered to my own amusement that elevators worked well, especially old elevators in old buildings: The doors open slowly; the car moves slowly; and when it reaches the desired floor, the car usually requires a few extra seconds to bring itself to a slow stop. The elevator in the apartment building where I live in New York City is just such an elevator. If I am in a rush, which unfortunately is most of the time, the elevator's sluggishness can be annoying. But when I need to speak with my father, it provides a perfect layer of privacy.

Is It Healthy?

The fact that these behaviors are common means that in most cases they are *not* pathological. By the same token, however, just because behaviors are common does not necessarily mean that they are healthy either. We are still left with the question, then, of whether maintaining an ongoing emotional bond with a deceased loved one is a good thing to do.

Somewhat ironically, as the limits of the traditional grief work idea became apparent, a new generation of bereavement theorists began turning in the opposite direction. In other words, they began to argue that what was necessary for successful grieving was not the breaking of the emotional bond with the deceased but its continuation. This sea change was heralded more than a decade ago with the publication of a collection of scholarly papers bearing the title *Continuing Bonds: New Understandings of Grief.* The book gave "voice," its jacket claimed, "to an emerging consensus among bereavement scholars" and demonstrated that "the healthy resolution of grief enables one to maintain a continued bond with the deceased."[6] Other books express similar views. One pair of researchers argued, for example, that effective grieving involves a kind of "transformation . . . in which the actual ('living and breathing') relationship has been lost, but the other forms remain or may even develop in more elaborate forms."[7]

Along with these new ideas came a wave of new research. But contrary to the one-sided optimism for the continuing bond among bereavement theorists, the picture that emerged from the new research was a good deal more complex. Some studies suggested that an enduring bond between the living and the deceased was useful and adaptive, whereas others indicated that a continuing relationship with a deceased loved one was unhealthy. When this happens, when research findings on a particular question seem to go in opposite directions, it almost always indicates that other factors have not yet been taken into account. Researchers call these factors *moderating variables.*

In this case, one of the most robust moderating variables is the form that the bond takes. There is strong evidence, for example, that clinging to the deceased's possessions or using the deceased's possessions for comfort only makes grief worse.[8] To understand this, let us first consider a more benign form of holding onto a loved one's possessions. It is not uncommon for bereaved people to keep objects that were prized by the deceased, such as a favorite piece of clothing or jewelry, perhaps a book. Sometimes they are objects related to the deceased's hobbies, such as a golf club or knitting basket. Sometimes the objects people choose to hold onto had no particular meaning to the deceased but remind the survivor of a particular event or cherished memory connected with the deceased. Preserving these objects feels like a way to honor lost loved ones, a way to say, "I will not forget."

Clinging to the deceased's possessions is different. Some people, for example, attempt to maintain the deceased's personal belongings exactly as they were prior to the death. This behavior becomes obsessive: There is only one way a room can be arranged; there is only one place this or that object can go—where he had it, the way she would have wanted it. We can see intuitively that there is something wrong here; the need to maintain a certain order is too extreme. It is as if the bereaved is engaged in a desperate struggle to forestall the reality of the death, as if somehow a connection to the deceased's soul depends on the right arrangement of the furniture.

What about the more literal connections in the continued-bond idea, the kind of quasi-hallucinatory interactions Sondra Beaulieu and Daniel Levy had with their deceased spouses and, to some extent, the kind of conversational exchange both Heather Lindquist and I described? Bereaved people who have these kinds of interactions often say they are comforting. I cannot speak about the consequences of my own experiences with any objectivity, but when I interviewed Sondra and Daniel, I saw no signs of defensiveness or denial. Nor were they trying to convince me that there is an afterlife. They did not seem to want to push their experiences onto other people. If anything, they were reticent. Yet when I questioned them about the reality of the experiences, they explained that there was something tangible and compelling that made them feel that they had had contact with their deceased spouse. They were equally certain that these experiences had helped them, not only to get over their loss but to find meaning in it.

The research on this question is still coming into focus, but it is clear that several important factors determine whether these kinds of connections are healthy. One factor is time. The experience of an ongoing relationship with a deceased loved one tends to be salubrious later in bereavement. Early after a loss, we are still vulnerable to oscillating swings in and out of sadness. Indulging in an imagined conversation or dwelling on the sense of a lost loved one's presence while in such a vulnerable state can easily tip our mood in the direction of greater pain and distress. As we progress past grief and toward emotional equilibrium, it becomes easier to utilize these kinds of bonding experiences to sustain a sense of calm and connection.[9]

Another factor is the intensity of the bond. Almost any kind of continued relationship is potentially comforting as long as it occurs in moderation. When the bond becomes too strong, or too encompassing, we can lose ourselves in loneliness and yearning. There is also the quality of attachment, which we discussed in the previous chapter. When we feel helpless and insecure about a relationship, especially in the early months following a loss, a sense of the deceased's presence can be unnerving. It might even further exacerbate the pain of our grief. If, on the other hand, we are more secure and confident about the quality of the relationship, the bond is more likely to provide comfort.

I explored these ideas with Nigel Field, one of the leading researchers on continued bonds in bereavement. What Nigel and I did was ask a group of recent widows and widowers to engage in an imaginary conversation with their deceased spouses. We asked each to envision that the deceased was sitting in an empty chair that we had placed across from him or her. We then turned on a tape player with additional instructions and left the room so the participant could complete the task in private. The taped instructions suggested to our subjects that they think of the conversation as an opportunity to speak with the spouse "one last time" and that they should feel free to say whatever they had longed to say after their spouse had died. To render the conversation more realistic, we also encouraged the subjects to speak to the spouse directly, using his or her name. Once the conversation began, we videotaped it from another room using a one-way mirror—we got permission from our subjects beforehand—so that later we could code their attachment behaviors.

Some of the people in the study clearly evidenced attachment insecurity and helplessness during the imaginary conversation. They spoke about themselves as worthless without the deceased or described feelings of being lost, empty, weak, or overwhelmed by the loss. The bereaved people who did this were also more likely to experience an elaborate and extreme ongoing relationship with the spouse in their private life. And as we had anticipated, they also had more severe grief reactions.[10]

These studies led to important advances in our understanding of some of the factors that influenced whether continued bonds were healthy or not, but there was still more to the picture. Many of the theorists who have championed the value of the continued bond have agreed that an essential factor is culture. Indeed, to justify their claims, they have pointed to the prevalence of an ongoing relationship with the dead in non-Western cultures, and to the important role continued bonds have played in ancient cultural rituals. But *culture* is a term that's hard to define, and when we examine it in the context of life and death and bereavement, one way or another it boils down to differences in how people think about the afterlife.

CHAPTER 10

Imagining the Afterlife

In 1977, the National Aeronautics and Space Administration (NASA) launched *Voyager I,* the first of two space probes sent off on a one-way trip into deep space. *Voyager I* was scheduled to pass Jupiter and Saturn. If all went well, it was hoped, it might even get as far as the vast empty region at the periphery of our solar system. The number of new data the craft might potentially send back was staggering, as were the continuous technical difficulties and scientific challenges that kept cropping up. But despite the ambitious nature of the *Voyager* project, NASA scientists still found time to indulge their curiosity. They placed onboard *Voyager I* a number of cultural artifacts. The idea was that if the spacecraft should by some slim chance encounter extraterrestrial beings, it would be able to provide them with a glimpse of life on our planet. So what was included among the artifacts? One of the objects the scientists chose was a 1920s blues recording, *Soul of a Man,* by Blind Willie Johnson. The plaintive refrain to the song speaks for itself: "Won't somebody tell me, answer if you can! Won't somebody tell me, what is the soul of a man?"

Most of us, at some point in our lives, have wondered about the possibility of an enduring soul that might live on in the afterlife. How we think about the afterlife, if we think of it at all, almost certainly plays a role in determining whether we experience a continued sense of connection to deceased loved ones and, ultimately, how we cope with loss. In this chapter we will take a closer look at the different ways peoples across the globe have thought about the afterlife. Before we begin that journey, however, we will linger a bit longer close to home. We will begin with the Western concept of heaven.

A Heavenly Reunion—or a Hellish Separation?

Each of the three major monotheistic religions, Judaism, Christianity, and Islam, in their most elemental form, includes some basic idea about a final resting place in heaven. The concept also crops up in the popular culture, in books, movies, advertisements, even jokes. Not everyone takes the idea seriously. Some of us are uncertain. Christopher Buckley, the noted writer, and son of the famous conservative pundit William F. Buckley, Jr., was asked recently whether he believed in the afterlife. His reply: "Alas, no. But I find myself wondering at the oddest times; So, Pup [his father], are you in Heaven? Is it true after all?"[1]

The idea is simple enough. Most people envision heaven as a tranquil place, free of the trials and tribulations of life on earth, where departed souls find rest and comfort for all eternity. Under normal circumstances, such a benign concept potentially soothes the otherwise savage dread we typically associate with death. In fact, highly religious people with strong beliefs about the afterlife generally report good mental health.[2] They also report less worry and fewer anxieties about death.[3]

On the surface, the idea of heaven should be a comfort for bereaved people, at least during the initial period of mourning. For those who sincerely believe that heaven awaits the faithful, the death of a loved one is not a true good-bye. It is more like a prolonged absence, one that will end, eventually when the loved one and the survivor are reunited.

This was Robert Ewing's belief. About a year and a half after the death of his sister, Kate, Robert told me he had come to understand that death is a part of life: "We've all got to go through it, sooner or later. We all have our time. I don't want to push it because I'm happy with the life God has given me. I'm happy with the family that I have and the people I know and love. But when it's time to go, it's just another part of life. Death is part of life, and I think it possibly begins another existence of some kind. Something like heaven. I think of Kate in that kind of place. I feel comfortable with that thought: Kate safe in heaven. And God willing, when it's my time, I will join her. The entire family, Kate, my wife, the children, all of us, there someday, up in heaven."

Unfortunately, this kind of scenario is a bit more difficult for many of us to hold onto. Survey data show, in fact, that only about one-third of bereaved Americans can actually find comfort in the idea that a deceased loved one may be in heaven.[4] One of the reasons is that heaven comes with a built-in problem: It's not a sure thing. As our understanding of heaven evolved over the millennia, so did our conceptualizations of its polar opposite: the hateful fires of hell. As has been true of nearly every human attempt to give order and structure to the cosmos, these concepts gradually took on a dialectical quality: The more peaceful and distant heaven became, the more horrific and painful were the opposing hellfires below.[5] Surveys have shown that the majority of Americans believe in the existence of hell.[6] For bereaved people, the uncertainty about the fate of their loved one's soul and whether it has made its way to heaven or hell can lead to serious distress.[7]

The torment we might experience about a loved one's ultimate destination in the afterlife was poignantly illustrated in the 1998 film *What Dreams May Come*. The movie begins with the chance meeting of two American tourists, Chris and Annie, at an idyllic Swiss mountain lake. They fall in love, marry, raise two beautiful children, and go on to successful individual careers. Everything is perfect, but then tragedy strikes: Their life is torn apart when their children die in an auto accident. Although Chris and Annie's grief is severe, after several years the couple begin to show clear signs of mending. Then tragedy strikes again when Chris is killed.

The scenes that follow create a stunning visual fantasy as Chris ascends to heaven and is eventually reunited with his two children. But their blissful reunion is short-lived. As he pieces the events together, Chris discovers that not long after his own death, his wife Annie sank into depression. Then, in a fit of despair, she took her own life. Because Christianity strongly prohibits suicide, Chris knows that Annie has to have been banished to hell. He is deeply anguished. Heaven or no heaven, he realizes he cannot live without Annie and spends the rest of the movie on a distress-filled quest to rejoin her.

Even if we bypass our concern about hell and assume our loved ones have made it to heaven, another problem is that heaven severely restricts the kinds of interactions a bereaved person can envisage with the deceased. No matter how fancifully the eventual reunion may be imagined, a separation still intervenes, a painful, irreversible, and seemingly indefinite separation. Many bereaved people have a sense that they are watched over by loved ones in heaven, or that those in heaven can hear or see them "from above." This belief can be reassuring, but loved ones in heaven cannot influence or interact with the living. They cannot visit or hold conversations with living relations. A bereaved person who accepts the heaven idea but longs for this kind of connection is likely to struggle.

Probably the biggest stumbling block, whether we are actively religious or not, is that heaven just doesn't hold up as a believable concept. A large-scale survey of religious and spiritual beliefs across the globe found that belief in heaven was widespread only in the poorer and less-well-educated agrarian nations. Industrial and postindustrial countries like the United States have seen belief in the idea plummet. More than half of the people surveyed in postindustrial countries said they did *not* believe heaven existed, and over two-thirds said they did not believe in the existence of anything like a soul.[8]

In 1997, a cover story in *Time* magazine boldly asked its readers, "Does Heaven Exist?"[9] The tone of the article revealed a deep discord about the viability of the concept. There were, of course, quotes from steadfast Christians endorsing the traditionally idyllic portrait of heaven as a blissful and effortless paradise. But the story also contained quotes about nagging doubts, even among believers, about the improbability of such a wish. In addition, priests and theologians admonished their communities not to take the metaphor of heaven too literally. There is a growing movement among religious scholars to downplay the concept in the service of modernizing and legitimizing their faith. Some religious leaders have taken an even harder line, arguing that the modern idea of heaven results from too literal a reading of the old religious texts and includes plainly "infantile" and "materialistic" and in many ways "unbiblical Elements."[10]

The dissonance surrounding our wish for a heavenly reunion is given colorful voice in Don DeLillo's poignant novel *White Noise.*[11] In the passage that follows, DeLillo's protagonist has just suffered a gun wound. He finds himself in a hospital run by the Catholic church. The nurse that dresses his wound is a nun. As she attends him, he studies a painting hanging just above him depicting an idealized meeting in heaven between assassinated President John Kennedy and the pope. He asks the nun if, for the church, it is "still the old Heaven, like that, in the sky?" Her response stuns him:

> "Do you think we are stupid?" she said.
>
> I was surprised by the force of her reply.
>
> "Then what is heaven, according to the Church, if it isn't the abode of God and the angels and the souls of those who are saved?"
>
> "Saved? What is saved? This is a dumb head, who would come in here to talk about angels. Show me an angel. Please. I want to see."
>
> "But you're a nun. Nuns believe these things. . . ."
>
> "You would have a head so dumb to believe this?"
>
> "It's not what I believe that counts. It's what you believe."
>
> "This is true," she said. "The nonbelievers need the believers. They are desperate to have someone believe. . . ."
>
> "Why are you a nun anyway? Why do you have that picture on the wall?"
>
> She drew back, her eyes filled with contemptuous pleasure.
>
> "It is for others. Not for us."
>
> "But that's ridiculous. What others?"
>
> "All the others. The others who spend their lives believing that we still believe. . . . If we did not pretend to believe these things, the world would collapse."

"Pretend?"

"Of course pretend. Do you think we are stupid? Get out from here."

"You don't believe in heaven? A nun?"

"If you don't, why should I?"

"If you did, maybe I would."

"If I did, you would not have to."

Coming Back

Science is often granted the final word in debates about the afterlife, but an empirical approach cannot answer every question. Buddhist scholars like Robert Thurman have been quick to address this point. The Western scientific worldview, Thurman observed, equates the cessation of heartbeat and brain activity with the cessation of consciousness, "yet the picture of death as a nothing in consciousness is not a scientific finding. It is a conceptual notion. . . . Science should not neglect to question this picture."[12] Buddhists, like Hindus and followers of numerous religions, do in fact question the idea that death brings an end to consciousness. In fact, they share the belief that the end of corporeal life is not the end of being, that a vague remnant or essence of consciousness persists and eventually enters life anew through the process of reincarnation.

Westerners often dismiss the idea of reincarnation, using the same axe that was applied to heaven: It is simplistic and almost impossible to reconcile with the broader knowledge base of the modern world. Most of our ideas about the afterlife, including those about heaven and reincarnation, are rooted in concepts developed at a much earlier point in human history, a time when humans lived in small groups or tribes, often with vast swathes of uninhabited landscape in between them. Our ancient ancestors experienced the world locally rather than globally. They knew nothing of the size and shape of the planet or, for that matter, of the evolution of life. From this perspective came relatively simple ideas about life after death.

These concepts are quite awkward in a modern context.[13] If souls are continually recycled through reincarnation, we might ask, for example, why does the global population continue to expand? Where do the new souls come from?

It is important to keep in mind, though, that at least part of the Western aversion to reincarnation is cultural. Just as images of heaven have insinuated themselves into Westerners' minds, the notion of reincarnation has taken on an archetypal quality within Eastern cultures. The cultural divide leaves us much room for misunderstanding.

I learned about this kind of misunderstanding firsthand once while speaking with a friend and colleague from India. The subject of reincarnation had come up and I assumed my friend would be quite skeptical about the topic. He is a well-seasoned global traveler and divides his time between residences in Mumbai, London, and New York. He is a well-regarded scholar, highly intellectual, knowledgeable on an impressive array of subjects, and, if the truth be told, also a bit of a cynic.

I asked him if, since he had grown up in a Hindu country, he had ever believed in reincarnation. Surely, I reasoned, he must have struggled at some point in his life with the realization that a concept so prevalent in his native culture was at the same time deeply at odds with the Western intellectual tradition in which he seemed equally at home. To my surprise, he said that he had never doubted the reality of reincarnation. Seeing the look of bafflement I couldn't conceal, he explained that he had been raised with the idea of reincarnation. Even though he might find it hard to justify the concept from a logical or evidentiary point of view, it had always been a core element of his personal and cultural background, and he simply accepted it.

In this same context, we might consider this rather amusing anecdote. The noted astronomer Carl Sagan purportedly once asked the Dalai Lama, "What would you do if we could show you conclusively that reincarnation is not possible?" Buddhists emphasize the importance of direct knowledge, including scientific findings. The Dalai Lama responded straightaway. He would immediately put the word out, he told Sagan, notifying everyone of this fact and telling them that reincarnation was no longer a viable concept. However, after a pause, the Dalai Lama wryly asked, "But how would you show that?" a question to which, of course, Sagan had no reply.[14]

Evidentiary debates aside, does reincarnation offer anything useful to alleviate the suffering of bereavement? Although reincarnation is a key spiritual construct in Eastern religions, it does not actually deny the reality of death and, more important, does not necessarily lessen the pain of grief. In this regard, although there are similarities between heaven and reincarnation, there are also key differences. One crucial difference is that whereas heaven promises an eventual reunion with deceased loved ones, reincarnation is decidedly more opaque on the subject. It is entirely possible that two people who knew each other in past lives could meet again in future incarnations but, except in the rarest of cases, would have no knowledge of their past relationship. Westerners who have latched onto the reincarnation idea have tried to get around this somewhat thorny problem by inventing mystical, if not mystifying, techniques such as past lives regressions that purport to help people identify their past selves. Ultimately, however, the cultlike nature of these techniques seems to marginalize the idea of incarnation even further in the West.

Tibetan Buddhists have their own approach to reincarnation. Using a system that has its roots in the ancient, pre-Buddhist Bön religion, Tibetans have developed elaborate ideas about the suspended state that exists between incarnations. They call it the Bardo, or in-between,[15] and it is described in remarkably specific detail in *The Great Book of Natural Liberation Through Understanding in the Between,* or as it is more commonly known, *The Tibetan Book of the Dead*.

The origins of *The Tibetan Book of the Dead* are mystical. The manuscript is attributed to the semimythical spiritual adept Padma Sambhava, who is believed to have dictated the work in the sixth century and then hid it along with other writings in the caves and mountains of Tibet. The lost manuscript is said to have been discovered in the fourteenth century by a monk purported to be an incarnation of Padma Sambhava.[16] The text claims knowledge of the spirit world and the states between incarnations, knowledge that followers argue could come only from advanced spiritual beings with sacred access to unseen realms. Although one could just as easily suggest that Padma Sambhava simply made it all up, for centuries Tibetans have turned to this text for spiritual guidance.

Tibetans also use *The Book of the Dead* as an aid in preparing loved ones for death. Commentaries that accompany modern translations encourage the reading aloud of the text to dying loved ones as a way of helping them prepare for and exert some control over their voyage into the Bardo realm. One can see how this practice might provide comfort to the dying and also help surviving friends and relatives with their own anxieties about the loved one's death.

Although the directness of this approach to death is appealing, for many Westerners the idea of leading a dying person toward the state between death and her or his next incarnation is a bit of a cultural leap. Westerners are interested in the idea (workshops and self-help books claiming to guide a bereaved person toward the reincarnation of a lost loved one are readily available), but in practice reincarnation falls prey to the same fears and fantasies that plague the heaven concept.

The crowning problem with almost all conceptions of the afterlife, including heaven and reincarnation, is that we tend to take these ideas too literally. The human condition is such that we can never know for sure what happens after we are dead. This is what we are stuck with. Yet our desire to be reunited with those we have lost propels us to bend our beliefs. We stretch and simplify them until we get what we want; or at least what we think we want. Ultimately this process fails to satisfy.

* * *

Julia Martinez has never had a conversation with her deceased father. Initially, when I interviewed her, she emphatically denied that she had ever sensed his presence or felt that he was watching over her. But later on, somewhat sheepishly, she admitted that she did in fact harbor a secret belief about her dad: She thought that her father had been reborn as a cat. She believed that he had come back so that he could care for her while she was away at college: "The first time it happened, I was outside of my dorm. I was coming home and there was this black cat.

He came right up to me, purring and all that, you know, the things cats do when they want milk or something. He looked right at me; right into my eyes. He looked at me, and without even thinking, I said, 'Dad?' It just came out of me. He purred and rubbed against my leg."

Julia was never 100 percent certain about these beliefs: "Who can say? He is a cat, you know. But he did act just like my father, really just like him. . . . He didn't want much from me. I fed him and all. But then I didn't see him, you know, for days. But when I was feeling down or upset or something, it never failed. He was always there. Just like my dad. I would come home and there he would be, and that cat, you know, he always came right up to me and looked at me. It was just like Dad saying, 'It will be OK, Jay.' That's what my dad called me, Jay."

Julia had kept these thoughts to herself: "I never told anyone. I figured my friends probably wouldn't get it, except maybe Tara. She probably knows about reincarnation and would have been OK with it. But I didn't want to tell her. What if she thought I was some kind of weirdo?"

In part, Julia told me, she was also reluctant to discuss her experience because she didn't want to be talked out of it. I have heard many stories like Julia's. Bereaved people, driven by the pain and yearning of grief, imagine signs of communication from a lost loved one. Often, they believe a loved one is reaching out to them, sending a signal, in the form of another being, typically an animal.

Whatever comfort the perception of these signals might bring, it never seems to last. Initially, perhaps, there is a kind of anticipation, almost excitement, about the possibility of renewed contact, but then comes the sobering up: The new relationship is limited. It could be no other way. A cat is not a father, no matter how much Julia might have wished it. As she said, "Cats don't talk." As most cat owners know, they don't listen very well either.

Thoroughly Akin to It All

There is a great irony in the way Westerners and even some Easterners have embellished the idea of reincarnation. In the Eastern religious traditions, where belief in reincarnation first developed, the idea has always held a more complex and elusive meaning. It was readily understood, for example, that the people we know and love could not actually return after death. The barest essence of that person might survive in another life, but even so, there is nothing that can be recognized.

The idea of rebirth, or the transmigration of souls as it is sometimes called, originated around the ninth century BCE in India. The Eastern religious texts from this period, such as the Upanishads, are complex and often deliberately ambiguous. Compared to the philosophical arguments of the Greeks that emerged later in the West, these early Eastern writings are downright recondite,[17] which may be one reason why the idea of reincarnation has been so easily subjugated. Modern "new age" philosophers on the subject of reincarnation are not likely to have bothered to work their way through the ancient texts, and those who had would have found sufficient ambiguity to allow for almost any kind of self-serving interpretation.

Scholars of classic Hindu philosophy are generally in agreement, however, that reincarnation does *not* mean that an individual person with a memory of a specific life can return. The self in Hindu philosophy is broader than the individual, somewhat akin to the self in Buddhism. Buddhism developed out of the same context as the Upanishads, which tell us that the self of everyday life is illusory. We mistakenly assign our material desires and needs to the self, when actually, according to the Upanishads, our true self, the atman, is not at all personal. Actually, the English word *self* is not even a relevant term because, Hindus believe, the atman can be understood only through a negation of the personal. It is grounded in something larger that we all share at the core of our being, like a universal world soul that is ageless. There is no reason to fear death, the Upanishads tell us, because when we die, all personal attributes and memories are shed; only the atman remains.[18]

The same idea runs through Buddhist writings. In attempting to explain the Buddhist concept of reincarnation to a Western audience, the French-born Buddhist monk Matthieu Ricard argued that "reincarnation has nothing to do with the transmigration of some 'entity' or other. It is not a process of metapsychosis because there is no 'soul.'"[19]

The Buddha himself actively discouraged his followers from contemplating questions like "What was I in the past?" or "What shall I be in the future?" because, he cautioned, such questions lead only to self-doubt, fear, and distraction.[20]

But what exactly do Buddhists believe persists when we die? The answer would go well beyond the scope of this book, and unfortunately the explanations offered in Buddhist writings, much as in the Hindu texts, are vague at best. We find terms like *luminosity*[21] and the *ultimate dimension*.[22] American Buddhist Robert Thurman writes of a state of "extremely subtle body-mind," which is "very hard to describe or understand" and should not be misconstrued "as a rigid, fixed identity." Rather, "this most essential state of an individual being is beyond body-mind duality; it consists of the finest, most sensitive, alive and intelligent energy in the universe."[23] Although Thurman described this state as an "indestructible drop" and the "living soul of every being," he again hastened to emphasize that it is still not an eternal self.[24] The inconclusiveness can be exasperating, but that may be part of the point.

Take, for example, a famous Buddhist sutra in which the poor wanderer Vacchagotta asks the Buddha, "Is the world eternal?" The Buddha replies, "Vacchagotta, I have not declared this." Vacchagotta asks, "Then . . . is the world not eternal?" The Buddha replies, "Vacchagotta, I have not declared this either."[25] Undaunted, the hapless Vacchagotta persists with his questioning: "Why then do you remain silent on these issues when leaders of other religious sects do not? Why are they willing to take a stand one way or another?" To which the Buddha responds, "Leaders of other sects provide answers to such questions only because they mistakenly accept the illusion of the self as real and permanent."

As intractable as all of this seems, we might wonder whether it will ever be possible to reconcile such ideas with the science-oriented Western worldview, or at least to do so without succumbing to oversimplifications. Many have tried, including a surprising number of intellectual luminaries like the great American psychologist William James. James is widely acknowledged as the father of modern psychology. He possessed a sweeping intellect, and in the late nineteenth and early twentieth centuries he published an influential series of books and articles on the workings of the human mind, many of which continue to be heavily cited in psychology journals.

Throughout his career James nurtured an ardent interest in spiritual concerns. In 1893, he delivered a now famous lecture in which he described the desire for human immortality as "one of the great spiritual needs of man."[26] Prophetically, James pointed to the growing conflict—one that now dominates Western philosophical discourse—between this most elementary of desires and the evidence coming from the biological and physiological sciences. Scientists and the lay public alike, James noted, had come to share the seemingly unavoidable conclusion that, beyond all doubt, our inner life, our experience of consciousness, comes solely from the functioning of our brain, and that when the brain is physically dead, so, too, must consciousness die.

Surprisingly, though, James offered a counterargument. He proposed that the evidence available at the time he was writing—and we can easily extend his argument to the present—does not necessarily preclude the possibility that "life may still continue when the brain itself is dead."[27] The problem, James thought, lay not in the evidence about brain function but rather in the narrow view that the brain's *exclusive* function is to produce consciousness: "When the physiologist who thinks that his science cuts off all hope of immortality pronounces the phrase, 'thought is a function of the brain,' he thinks of the matter just as he thinks when he says, 'Steam is a function of the tea-kettle,' 'Light is a function of the electric circuit.'"[28] James's contrarian position was that this view emphasized only the "productive function" of the brain. Natural entities, he noted, serve functions beyond mere production: A prism refracts light and thus serves a "transmissive" function; the valves of a pipe organ release air and thus serve a "permissive" function. These same functions also characterize various part of the human body. For example, the retina of the eye detects and "transmits" color information to the brain via the optic nerve; a heart valve "permits" blood to flow in and out. Could not the brain also serve transmissive or permissive functions for the normally unseen forces of the universe?

Having made these somewhat startling points, James then asked his audience to entertain a series of suppositions that came surprisingly close to Eastern religious epistemology. Echoing the Hindu concept of an atman, he conjectured that "consciousness in this process does not have to be generated. . . . It exists already, behind the scenes, coeval with the world."[29] Mirroring the Buddhist axiom of the impermanence and illusory nature of the self, he supposed "that the whole universe of material things—the furniture of earth and choir of Heaven—should turn out to be a mere surface-veil of phenomena, hiding, and keeping back the world of genuine realities."[30] James also attempted to address the common criticism that ideas about an afterlife are naive and illogical. In response to the question about reincarnation and global population growth, for example, he observed, "It is not as if there were a bounded room where the minds in possession had to move up or make place and crowd together to accommodate each new occupant."[31] On the contrary, "each new mind brings its own edition of the universe of space along with it, its own room to inhabit. . . . When one man wakes up, or one is born, another does not have to go to sleep, or die in order to keep the consciousness of the universe a constant quality."[32]

James concluded, "I speak, you see, from the point of view of all the other individual beings, realizing and enjoying inwardly their own existence. . . . Through them as through so many diversified channels of expression, the external Spirit of the Universe affirms and realizes its own infinite life."[33]

* * *

Of course, when we are coping with loss, we usually have little time for or interest in grand metaphysical theories. Most of the time, we want to know where our loved ones have gone. We want to know what it means to sense another presence. And even if we know that such questions are probably unanswerable, the bottom line is that we still need something to hold onto.

A clue to where we might turn for that "something" is beautifully explored in William Steig's delightful children's book *Amos and Boris*.[34] The story begins with Amos, a tiny mouse who builds himself a boat and sets off on a grand adventure, a metaphorical journey in search of himself.[35] "One night, in a phosphorescent sea, he marveled at the sight of some whales spouting luminous water, and later, lying on the deck of his boat gazing at the immense, starry sky, the tiny mouse Amos, a little speck of a living thing in the vast living universe, felt thoroughly akin to it all." But in the middle of this universal bliss, tragedy strikes. Amos is so "overwhelmed by the beauty and mystery of everything," he accidentally rolls right off the deck and plunges into the sea. He nearly drowns, but fortunately is saved by a huge whale named Boris. The two creatures strike up an improbable friendship. Boris is curious about the tiny mouse, the likes of which he has never seen before. Amos is just as curious about Boris, and each marvels at the fact that although they are both animals, they are of dramatically different size and live in different worlds. "They told each other about their lives, their ambitions. They shared their deepest secrets with each other. The whale was very curious about life on land and was sorry that he could never experience it. Amos was fascinated by the whale's account of what went on deep under the sea."

Steig's delightful story illustrates something crucial: the unexpected and often unimaginable insights that can be had when we experience life through someone else's eyes. And so we return to the topic of bereavement. We've so far considered how we tend to *think* about the afterlife. We've looked at concepts like heavenly reunions, reincarnated souls, and the transmission of a universal spirit. But the world is vast and there is more to cultural variation than these few concepts. Indeed, in some cultures, people think about the afterlife hardly at all; they simply live with it. And when they do, they find humor, comfort, and sometimes transcendence.

"Are You Pleased with Your Living Relatives?"

F. Gonzalez-Crussi tells the story of a rural Mexican woman who, each year on November 2, set up an altar, diligently tidied up the house, and then went out to the street to hold pleasant conversations, speaking aloud and listening in turn, with the invisible souls of her ancestors:

> Come in, blessed souls of my father, my mother, and my sisters. Please, come in. How did you do this year? Are you pleased with your living relatives? In the kitchen we have tamales, tostadas, pumpkin with honey, apples, oranges, sugarcane, chicken broth, a great deal of salt, and even a little tequila so you may drink. Are you happy with what we have? My sons worked very hard this year so we could offer you this feast, as usual. Tell me, how is Saint Joseph? Did you receive the Masses we ordered for him?[36]

We can only guess what went through the woman's mind that day. One thing is certain: she was probably *not* thinking about the ineluctable nature of the universe. Rather, she was simply having a good time. The reason is that on the day that she was visited by her deceased loved ones, people all over Mexico were engaged in similar conversations with their own deceased friends and relatives. That day was the day of the annual celebration of El Día de los Muertos, the Day of the Dead.

Much like festivals in China and other countries around the globe, the Mexican Day of the Dead is based on the popular belief that the souls of deceased loved ones are given special "license" to visit the living once a year. The custom is ancient, dating back to pagan ancestral rituals from the precolonial Aztec civilization and probably much earlier. When the Spanish conquered the region in the sixteenth century, they imposed their Catholic rites and beliefs on the inhabitants, but the pagan rituals connected to dead loved ones did not vanish. Instead, they morphed with an existing Catholic holiday, All Souls Day, and eventually took the form of the Day of the Dead celebration.

The Day of the Dead keeps the participants from taking it too seriously. At a superficial level, the Day of the Dead bears some resemblance to the American holiday of Halloween. Both evolved out of pagan ceremonies and once included a veneer of religion, although Halloween has long since shed that connection, and both make great use of costume and humor. But unlike Halloween, which is now seen primarily as an entertainment for children, the Mexican Day of the Dead has retained much of its original spiritual aura. Although the sincerity of the celebration may have been diluted in recent years, in part because of its popularity with tourists, the Mexican rite nonetheless continues to thrive, especially in villages and rural areas.

The air of lightheartedness and humor that pervades the Day of the Dead is in many ways typical of Mexican culture and its generally blithe attitude toward many otherwise serious subjects, including death. As the great Mexican poet Octavio Paz has observed, "The Mexican is familiar with death, jokes about it, caresses it, sleeps with it, celebrates it; it is one of his favorite toys and his most steadfast love."[37]

We still see signs of the Mexican familiarity with death among expatriate Mexicans living in the United States. During funerals, Mexican Americans spend more time than other Americans viewing, even touching and kissing, the bodies of their deceased loved ones. They also spend more time at burials and grave sites. Not surprisingly, when these habits are carried outside their original cultural context, there can be problems. Mexican Americans have, for example, reported frequent conflicts with professionals in the American funeral and cemetery industries, who bristle at such "odd" practices.[38] An especially poignant illustration of Mexican comfort with death imagery is found in the festive use of the *calavera,* or skeleton. During the Day of the Dead festival, skulls and skeletons are everywhere, in shop windows or dancing among the ubiquitous traditional *ofrendas,* makeshift altars that bear "sugar skulls painted with gaudy floral motifs among piles of candies, foodstuff, and images of saints."[39] As compelling as they may be, the explicit purpose of these offerings is to appease the souls of dead relatives and to entice them to come for a visit. The tiny ceramic and papier-mâché skeleton theaters often play out tiny scenes, arranged with equally small furniture and accoutrements, depicted in frozen moments from the ancestor's life or enacting the ancestor's favorite activities and pleasures. It is not uncommon, for example, to find groups of small skeletons playing musical instruments, eating, dancing, preparing food, or enjoying a game of baseball.

Although the skeleton theaters are designed to amuse and appease deceased ancestors, they are also unmistakably comforting and heartwarming for the living. To be sure, the skeleton can also be found in Western art, as, for example, in Albert Dürer's engravings or Hans Holbein the Younger's famous woodcuts in the *Danse Macabre.* But these Western skeletons are calculated to frighten, to compel us to repent our sins. The Mexican *calavera,* though a skeleton, poses no threat.[40] Rather, the *calavera* most typically appears as a benign, and smiling, dear old friend.[41]

Jovial skeletons and benign images of death are not limited to Mexican culture. Wherever Tibetans reside, for example, we are likely to find *thangkas,* richly colored scroll paintings depicting the core Buddhist narratives and symbols. *Thangkas* are commonly used for educational and meditational purposes, but they are also extraordinarily beautiful. Like the Mexican *calavera,* the *thangka* imagery is often intermingled with skeletons. Sometimes there are even more grotesquely corporeal images, like decaying corpses.

A particularly compelling *thangka,* with striking similarities to Mexican imagery, is the Chitipati, a pair of dancing skeletons, possibly a brother and sister, who rein as guardians of the cemetery or charnel ground.[42] There are various legends regarding the origins of the Chitipati, the most colorful being that they were originally monks and so lost in meditation that they failed to notice the approach of a band of thieves. The thieves promptly robbed the monks and then killed them. But owing to their deep spiritual state at the time of death, the pair were instantly transformed into eternal deities and given the charge of protecting the spirits of the recently deceased.

The Chitipati's portrayal in *thangkas* usually includes a number of rather gruesome death images. For example, each of the dancing skeletons holds a human skull, or *kapala,* filled with human brain tissue. Decaying body parts are strewn about the painting; scavenging animals prowl the corners looking for a meal or sometimes actually feasting on body parts. Often depicted in the background is a temple of some sort that is constructed entirely from human bones.

Despite the morbid details, the Chitipati themselves are not the least bit morbid. In fact, they are always portrayed in the midst of an ebullient dance, like a deranged couple, or perhaps a vaudeville duo. They wear playful, almost silly grins and look deeply and fondly into each other's eyes. Even if they intended any harm, they look as if they would be too busy smiling and dancing to bother.

Did You Hear the One About . . .

The Dahomey people of Western Africa enjoy a different kind of death-related humor: They tell dirty jokes. The Dahomey once formed a great African kingdom, which thrived for centuries until succumbing to French colonization in the mid nineteenth century. Today the region is an independent state, the Republic of Benin. Despite the political changes, the people have retained many of the ancient ways, including the traditional mourning rites. Dahomey funerals celebrate the life of the deceased, but the Dahomey don't let the funerals get too serious. They usually conclude in bouts of drinking, dancing, and singing that often go on well into the night. In the midst of it all, it is not at all unusual for friends and loved ones to recount lascivious tales about the deceased. The colorful stories and the humor undoubtedly help relieve the pain of grief, but that is not their sole purpose. The primary purpose of the tales, in fact, is to "amuse the dead," for according to the Dahomey view of life, "to moralize to a dead person is both indelicate and senseless."[43] Similarly to Mexicans, Africans in general take a casual if not a conversational approach to the spirits of the dead. Like the Mexican Day of the Dead, African ancestral ceremonies often include carnival-like elements, such as a parade of costumed villagers known as the ancestral masquerade.[44]

Humor and laughter connect us to one another, and in this context it is not surprising that African funeral rites also place strong emphasis on the broader community. Africans have a proverb: *"Owu antweri obaako mforo."* A rough translation is "The ladder of death is not climbed by only one person." For Africans, death traditionally is "not an individual affair" but "binds up relationships in society, revitalizing the living and underscoring their sense of community."[45] The death of a villager becomes an opportunity to "give concrete expression to community solidarity."[46] The emphasis on the communal is often observed in African American communities as well,[47] and not surprisingly African Americans are more likely than most other Americans to describe a continued relationship with a deceased loved one.[48]

Elaborate community bereavement rituals are seen in many non-Western cultures. The Hmong people of Laos and Southeast Asia believe, for example, that the successful mourning of the dead requires a richly detailed set of funerary rites that necessarily involve huge numbers of friends, relatives, and neighbors.[49] For the Hopi Indians, the "maintenance of proper relations with the dead" is seen as the responsibility of the entire "clan" to which the deceased belonged.[50] When a villager dies among the Saramaka of Surinam, ritual specialists are brought in to manage the funeral, but the "rites of separation" are shared by the entire community. The Saramaka believe that a collective ceremony is necessary so that the deceased can make a "final separation from the village itself." The community ceremony always takes precedence over the personal grief any one individual may feel. In fact, if a surviving family member should become so distressed as to interrupt the proceedings, he or she is likely to be strongly reprimanded and if necessary forcibly restrained.

The Saramakan rites conclude with a transcendent group experience, one that sometimes goes on for days. All those involved, usually thirty to forty relatives and neighbors, engage in a *kóntu-kôndè,* a mutual exchange of fantasy stories through which they, in effect, transport themselves into a separate reality. The term *kóntu-kôndè* literally refers to folktale land. When night falls, the villagers gather around and begin sharing wild stories of transcendent struggles with age-old existential problems. They are "by turns frightened by the antics of a villainous monster, doubled over with laughter at a lascivious song, or touched by a character's sentimental farewell, they experience an intellectually and emotionally rich evening of multimedia entertainment." The stories bear little resemblance to the actual realities of a funeral. Rather, "everyone present steps over the invisible barrier into folktale-land."[51]

Transcendent group rituals are often used for the express purpose of communicating directly with spirits of the dead. Anthropologist Emily Ahern witnessed one such ritual, a group trip to the underworld, while researching ancestral rites in northern Taiwan. She described in vivid detail what she saw: It was dusk, as a shaman's assistant, Ong Bieng-tiek, made his way through his village to announce that "a trip to the underworld would be starting soon."[52] On his way back, he stopped at a local store to buy packs of ritual paper money and incense for the ceremony. Meanwhile, at the house where the ritual was slated to take place, the shaman, or *tang-ki,* arranged bowls of fruit and candy as offerings to the god they would summon to lead them on their journey. The *tang-ki* began filling out small cards with the names of the four people who wished to make contact with deceased relatives that evening.

A short while later, a crowd gathered at the home. The *tang-ki* announced that only those who intended to voyage to the underworld should have their feet on the floor. Most of the participants clambered up onto one of the two platform beds in the house. The four remaining "would-be travelers" were blindfolded and sat on stools with their hands resting on their knees.

Although the villagers were respectful of the ceremony, "the atmosphere was excited, very like the feeling at the start of an excursion: children giggled and shrieked at each other, adults chattered loudly." Ong Bieng-tiek, playing the role of the *tang-ki*'s assistant, beat incessantly on a wooden clapper. The *tang-ki* warned the audience to keep clear of the doorway so that the gods could enter freely. Then he chanted the gods' names and burned the paper money, known as joss paper, as offerings. Three of the four would-be travelers convulsed periodically. Only one, a young woman, remained still. After about an hour, she gave up and left, complaining that sitting for so long on a stool was uncomfortable.

Eventually, one of the participants, a middle-aged man named Kim-Ci, appeared to enter a trance state. The *tang-ki* concentrated all his attentions on Kim-Ci, "filling the air around his head with smoke, shouting at him to 'Go!' and feeling his hands to see if they were cold." Cold hands were considered a sure sign that someone was "beginning the trip."[53]

The voyage that followed lasted several hours. The *tang-ki* questioned Kim-Ci about what he was seeing. He offered advice about how to enter and move around the underworld. The trip was not easy. At times Kim-Ci became visibly frustrated and confused. He had difficulty finding the right road. He had to climb steep mountains and became weary. The *tang-ki* continued burning paper money as offerings to the denizens of the underworld so that they would ease Kim-Ci's journey. At one point, Kim-Ci encountered a bridge and claimed that the people of the underworld would not let him pass. The *tang-ki* burned more joss paper money but seemed to be growing impatient. He exhorted Kim-Ci to "find another one, but hurry up." A bit later Kim-Ci encountered "terrible animals" and pleaded, "I'm frightened; I don't want to go on."

The *tang-ki* tried to reassure Kim-Ci, but although his authority was respected, it seemed obvious the villagers recognized these trips as personal journeys. Eventually Kim-Ci relented and continued the trip, but he never stopped complaining. After some time, he encountered a cluster of houses and saw various relations inside. He tried to speak with them but got no response. They had either failed to notice him or were simply ignoring him.

The most difficult moment came when Kim-Ci encountered his deceased elder brother. He made several attempts to speak with his brother. The *tang-ki* burned even more joss paper money. But Kim-Ci received no reply. He buried his face in his hands and cried, "My brother won't talk to me. My own brother won't talk to me." A few minutes later, he announced, "What's the use of coming here if no one will talk to me? I'm going home."

The *tang-ki* tried to persuade him to explore further, but Kim-Ci was adamant. He wanted to return. After several minutes of incantations, during which time the audience called out his name to help him back, Kim-Ci removed the blindfold and wiped his teary eyes. He was exhausted. The journey was still fresh in his memory, though. He repeated his disappointment over his brother's refusal to speak to him, then stretched out on a bed in another room and promptly fell into a deep sleep.

At different points in the ceremony, the other would-be travelers also fell into trance states. Even Bieng-tiek, the *tang-ki*'s assistant, had a go. Bieng-tiek enjoyed these trips. He had visited the underworld on several previous occasions and had usually found the voyage fascinating, in part, no doubt, because he gravitated toward those sides of the underworld that were likely to capture a young man's attention. He found movie theaters, for example, and once even a house of prostitution. On this trip, Bieng-tiek encountered a group of young girls, but the *tang-ki* was taking no chances. Knowing Bieng-tiek's propensities, he immediately began to read the incantation to bring him back. He feared, as he explained later, that Bieng-tiek might fall in love with one of the girls and refuse to leave. If that happened, he would have to remain in the underworld forever.

Most people do not make the voyage to the underworld to have a good time. The most common reason they go is to check on deceased loved ones. They want to find out how they are doing, whether they are happy and have the things they need for a good existence in the afterlife. If they need anything, such as money, clothing, or a proper house, their living relatives can arrange for it. They do this the same way the *tang-ki* did: They burn joss paper money or paper replicas of other objects like houses, cars, furniture, clothing, food, anything their loves ones might need. The act of burning the paper offerings, they believe, transports these objects to the land of the dead.

* * *

Although the ritual in the Taiwanese journey to the underworld is primarily symbolic, the reverence that goes along with these practices makes it hard to believe that there isn't more to it. The villagers who attempted to travel to the underworld certainly seemed to behave as if they thought the ceremony was real, at least in part. And the burning of paper offerings is widespread. Why would so many people engage in such a practice if it were nothing more than a symbolic gesture?

The answer may be difficult for Westerners to understand. Grief and curiosity propel us Westerners to think about the afterlife, but we also have a deep-seated need to justify our beliefs. We try on concepts like heaven or reincarnation. We simplify them and bend them until they fit our needs. Yet ultimately we find them lacking because they are so difficult to reconcile with the imposing machinery of science and reason. So we explain them away, and we are left empty-handed.

Other cultures do things differently, though not all other cultures, of course. Globalization has made the world a smaller, more homogeneous place. But many people still embrace the old rituals. They suspend disbelief. They let the humor unfold and the ceremony take over. It is hard to know how much they truly believe in what they are doing, but that's not the point. The ritual is the point. The ritual is what matters.

Might it be possible for a Westerner to have this same kind of experience? What would happen if we let go, just for a little while, and lost ourselves inside a transcendent mourning ritual? Would that be beneficial, or even possible? Or maybe just a waste of time?

Several years ago I decided to find out. At the time I had an abiding interest in ancient Chinese culture and in particular in the bereavement and ancestral ceremonies from the early stages of the empire. These rituals are still alive in China. They have changed only slightly from the time of their ancient origins, and they still play a role in contemporary Chinese society. I thought they might still be vibrant and meaningful, perhaps even to a Westerner. I hoped to have the chance to experience the rituals firsthand, and then as China gradually relaxed its borders, the opportunity presented itself.

CHAPTER 11

Chinese Bereavement Ritual

I visited China for the first time in 1997. My wife, Paulette, who speaks fluent Mandarin, made the trip with me. Over a decade earlier, when China was first opening up to the West and well before she met me, Paulette had spent a year in Beijing as an exchange student. She later traveled widely across both eastern and western China, and she also worked for a survey company on the island of Taiwan.

Knowing that Paulette would serve as my guide gave me enough confidence to arrange visits to several different universities in the most heavily populated regions of the eastern mainland. The goal was to set up a collaborative research project to study bereavement. But it gave me a perfect excuse to nose around the ancestral temples.

We arrived in Hong Kong, a city I would eventually come to know quite well, and then made our way to the mainland. Travel in those days was not easy. The stunning rise in prosperity that has so characterized modern China was just beginning. Poverty was a pernicious problem, and China's cities were just waking from the slumber of their narrow *hutong* alleyways and dilapidated buildings.

Eventually, we found our way to Nankai University in Tianjin and then to several universities in Beijing. Although I met with several researchers, I was unable to get a project off the ground. Exchange between Chinese and Western scholars at that time was still new. Few

Chinese spoke English, even at the universities. I spoke no Chinese. Paulette did her best to communicate for me, but although it's a cliché to say so, something was definitely lost in the translation. In addition, for years the communist government had outlawed psychology as a self-indulgent, bourgeois discipline. By the time I visited, the ban on psychology had been relaxed, but everyone I met was still obviously cautious.

I was ready to give up when we decided to make one more visit, this time to the Nanjing Medical University in Jiangsu Province. I had arranged a meeting with Professor Wang Chunfang, a psychiatrist at the Nanjing Brain Hospital. Nanjing is a beautiful city. It was once the capital of China and still retains its ancient city walls. Modernization was coming and the now ubiquitous glass and stone buildings were on the rise, but at the time I visited, Nanjing was still dominated by the elegant old *siheyuan* courtyard homes, street peddlers, and what seemed like millions of bicycles.

On our way to the hospital, we turned a corner and noticed a sign made of enormous letters fastened to a curved brick wall. It didn't look promising. The sign was obviously new, but several letters had already fallen off. It read: NANJING BRA N HOS. Below the sign a vendor stood beside a sprawling pile of watermelons.

We passed through a gate and entered a small, ramshackle building. Paulette informed a guard of the nature of our visit. The guard pointed to an open courtyard and told us to wait there. We sat on a bench and watched people milling about. It was hot and sticky. As the heat slowly overtook me, my spirits sagged, and I thought to myself, "What on earth made me think I could pull this off?"

* * *

China is the one of the world's oldest continuous civilizations, and for most of its long history Chinese culture has embraced the possibility of ritualized contact with deceased ancestors. One reason the rituals have endured for so long has to do with the political solutions the Chinese used to keep the empire intact. The geographic reach of the Chinese world has extended at one time or another from Siberia to the Equator and from Asia's Pacific coast into the heart of the Eurasian continent. In its earliest recorded history, Chinese culture consisted of clusters of disparate city-states, often preoccupied in wars with one another. Then, in the year 221 BCE, Qin Shi Huangdi, ruler of the kingdom of Qin, conquered his neighbors and created the first unified "Chinese" empire.

The formation of empire is by no means unique to China, but where other great civilizations have come and gone, the Chinese have endured. Somehow they have managed to capture an extraordinarily heterogeneous mix of cultures and languages within the boundaries of a single, enduring, centralized state.[1] And they have been able to hold it together for well over two thousand years. The key has been cultural standardization, and here is where we get back to mourning rites.

The independent states that originally formed the Chinese empire were culturally distinct and for the most part hostile to each other. Assimilation came only after long and very bloody conquests. But once it happened, it was essential that the city-states function as a single entity. One of the ways empire builders have tried to achieve unification throughout history is to make their constituents feel like part of the whole. The Greek and Roman Empires did this by creating uniform cultural, political, and religious practices across the empire. So did Napoleon. And for two millennia, so have the Chinese.

The process wasn't completely random. The kingdoms that would eventually compose the Chinese Empire already shared some cultural norms. One was that they were polytheistic. There were, for example, gods of the sea, gods of agriculture, gods of thunder, gods of war and commerce and fire. There were even gods for manmade structures like moats and walls. And there were gods that regulated the boundary between the living and the dead.

The spirits of the dead were also thought to have supernatural or godlike power. The contrast here with the concept of heaven that was developing in the monotheistic religions of the Western world could not be more pronounced. Whereas heaven requires a tangible boundary, the afterlife as it developed in polytheistic cultures was permeable.

The dead held power over the living and needed to be placated by properly performed ancestral rites. In the earliest periods of Chinese history, this usually consisted of animal and human sacrifices, regular offerings of food or livestock, and, later, maintenance of ancestral halls or shrines. If the rites were performed properly, the spirits of the dead would be better off in the afterlife. As repayment for that veneration, the spirits could be evoked by the living in times of need, to bless their crops or help defeat an enemy, for example. If the rites were not performed properly, if they were neglected or ignored, the ancestral spirits would suffer in the afterlife—and suffering spirits can easily become vengeful spirits.[2]

As always, the rules were different for kings. Royalty were assumed to have acquired godlike status at birth. When they died it was assumed they would continue to serve their regal functions in the afterlife. Therefore they would need extra special offerings, the kind of supplies fit for a king. Chinese royalty were buried with a remarkable array of goods, literally thousands of bronze and ceramic vessels and containers filled with food and drink, cooking equipment, oil lamps, sumptuous textiles, magnificent jewelry, and abundant weaponry.[3]

Of course, it was assumed that the spirits of dead kings, being royalty, would not actually bother with mundane chores in the afterlife. These would be left to their servants, who unfortunately would need to be sacrificed to accompany their masters into the afterlife. In fact, the death of a king was extremely bad news for anyone in the king's retinue; family members, soldiers, servants and attendants, and even horses were often sacrificed and buried along with the king.

When Qin Shi Huangdi unified the empire, he immediately set to work remaking both its government and its society. Although he is remembered as a ruthless tyrant, he was also a great reformer and saw unification and standardization of the Chinese Empire as his great legacy. Qin Shi Huangdi did little to dispel the idea that royalty should be viewed as demigods, but to the great relief, no doubt, of his family and army, he changed the royal burial practices. Rather than sacrifice his entire retinue, Qin Shi Huangdi arranged for the manufacture of life-size ceramic replicas that could accompany him to the afterlife in their stead. These ultimately became, of course, the now famous ceramic army that was discovered and began to be excavated in the 1970s near present-day Xian.

The introduction of ceramic figures initiated a cascade of changes across the empire. Ceramic figures were relatively cheap to manufacture, and before long their use in burial rites was quite common. Over time, the ceramic replicas were reduced in size and detail, and they became readily available in marketplaces. Eventually, most people could afford these figures as a means of honoring their own dead. In addition to the use of symbolic ceramic objects to replace actual sacrifice, Qin Shi Huangdi also enforced unified rules about the appropriate method for dressing and handling the corpse as well the proper timing and sequence of funeral behaviors.[4] But even with these changes, it is remarkable that an empire as vast and heterogeneous as China could manage to enforce a uniform procedure for burial and worship.

This was done through the use of a stunning bit of psychology. The emperor did not legislate his people's beliefs about death or the afterlife; he merely enforced a uniform code of mourning behavior practices.[5] Simply put, people were free to believe whatever they liked about the afterlife, as long as they performed the burial and ancestral rites in the dictated way. Although generic, these changes made it possible to incorporate tribes with divergent backgrounds into a growing Chinese state without stepping too heavily on their personal cultural values. In addition, regulating behavior through ritual contains within it a deceptively powerful force: With enough repetition, collective ritual encourages a uniformity of belief.

The Chinese emphasis on behavior, on the proper way to carry out the mourning rituals, rather than on the *experience* of the ritual, is illuminating, and it foreshadows the way these rituals are understood in contemporary China. As anthropologist James Watson, one of the foremost experts on Chinese burial practices, notes:

> To be Chinese is to understand, and accept the view, that there is a correct way to perform rites associated with the life-cycle, the most important being weddings and funerals. By following accepted ritual routines ordinary

> citizens participated in the process of cultural unification. . . . Performance, in other words, took precedence over belief—it mattered little what one believed about death or the afterlife as long as the rituals were performed properly. . . . However . . . ritual is about transformation. . . . Rituals are repeated because they are expected to have transformative powers. Rituals change people and things.[6]

* * *

Around 100 CE, an important development in the spread of Chinese mourning rites occurred: Paper was invented. Although accounts vary, the most popular version of the story holds that a eunuch and minor official named Cai Lun first came upon the methods for making paper,[7] and that by the sixth century the burning of joss paper as a way of symbolically providing for deceased ancestors was well established.[8]

In contrast to ceramic or bronze objects, paper offerings were considerably more practical and affordable. With the widespread availability of inexpensive paper, literally any object that a deceased ancestor might desire could be represented by a paper replica, burned, and thus symbolically transported for the ancestor's use to the land of the dead. An impressive joss paper manufacture sprang up across the Chinese Empire, making available paper models of food, cooking pots and utensils, even animals. For wealthier patrons, there were paper boats and houses and even custom-made paper surrogates of servants or sexual companions.

Joss paper offerings can be burned at any time, but they are most often used as part of the funeral ceremony to provide for the deceased's journey to the land of the dead. These offerings include paper money, passports to the underworld, and paper gifts for the guards at the gates of the underworld. Then of course there are paper replicas of the household items the deceased will need: kitchen appliances, clothing, televisions, and the like. Joss paper is also commonly burned long after the funeral during times of need. For example, a troubled relative might seek to appease an ancestral spirit to obtain his or her help with a personal problem, or on specified ancestral worship holidays. In a sense, sending a paper replica of a gift greases the wheels of ancestral benevolence.

During the Qingming Festival, which takes place in the second or third lunar month of each year, families come together to clean their ancestral graves and to leave offerings so that the ancestors may continue to prosper in the other world. Joss paper offerings are also burned during Yulan, the Feast of the Hungry Ghosts, which takes place in the middle of the seventh month. Although the Yulan holiday typically includes offerings to deceased ancestors, the primary purpose of this holiday is to placate potentially dangerous wandering spirits of the dead and to keep them from interfering with the living. Part of this belief centers on the idea that the spirits of recently deceased ancestors are still somewhat unstable and unpredictable, whereas long-dead and well-venerated ancestors have more stable and reliable ghosts.[9]

There is a Buddhist element in the Yulan Festival. It is based on the idea that people who were particularly avaricious while alive tend to carry this quality into the afterlife and will thus take the form of an insatiable and potentially troublesome "hungry ghost."[10] To placate these restless spirits, the Yulan Festival gradually evolved to include offerings at Buddhist temples and monasteries as a way of recruiting the monks' help and spiritual resources.[11]

Although it retains the quality of folk religion, the growth and development of the Yulan ghost festival nonetheless bears the unmistakable imprint of the Chinese state. In the seventh century CE, for example, during the Tang Dynasty, the ritual offerings to Buddhist and Taoist temples were supplied directly from the state's coffers. Honorific offerings to previous emperors were carried out by none other than the emperor himself.[12]

Westerners often dismiss the Chinese rites as mere denial, a defense against the finality of death and the terror of human vulnerability. But there is an aspect of these rites that flies in the face of that kind of objection: Chinese bereaved handle the decaying body. A core element of all ancestor worship rites is the separation of the spirit from the earthly body. It is not uncommon for surviving ancestors to disinter a corpse after several years to clean the deceased's bones. To do this, they literally clean and remove any remaining tissue from the bones and then relocate the bones in a more formal ancestral vessel.[13]

It is hard to imagine someone doing this in a Western culture, where it would be seen as shockingly ghoulish. But in China, the cleaning of a dead loved one's bones is treated not as repulsive but as a duty and a responsibility. The reason is that the Chinese believe the spirit of the deceased has already long vacated the body.[14] Old human bones, in this case, are not very different from old chicken bones.

* * *

Paulette and I passed several dreary hours outside the entrance to the Nanjing Brain Hospital before we were finally taken to see Dr. Wang. His cheery company immediately lifted our spirits. He was cordial and solicitous, and after many rounds of tea and pleasantries, he instructed us to return to the hospital the next day so that we could meet the staff of the newly constructed Social Psychiatry Unit. The mere existence of such a unit was a clear sign of a sea change in China's attitudes toward mental health. When we returned the following morning, we were led immediately to a sparkling and apparently empty hospital wing. After a short tour of the facilities, we gathered in a small conference room. There we sat in a large circle and smiled at each other.

I had by this time become familiar with this routine.

Eventually, after various starts and stops, I got it across that I was hoping to study bereavement in China. Often the Chinese researchers had trouble understanding what I meant. There isn't really a direct Chinese translation that matches the English word *grief*. The closest alternatives are *bei shang* and *ju sang,* which indicate feeling depressed or dejected. Neither specifically refers to the emotional reaction following the death of a loved one, as *grief* does. In and of itself, this was a fascinating cultural discovery for me.

Then we had a breakthrough. Somehow I managed to convey my intentions to one of the researchers, Zhang Nanping. He knew about bereavement in Western cultures and understood that I hoped to compare practices and reactions in China and the United States.

It required two full days of meetings, but at the end of the second day, we had finalized the plans for the first cross-cultural research study of bereavement. Zhang Nanping and his colleagues would recruit recently bereaved people in Nanjing through the university hospital. In turn, I would gather a comparable group of bereaved people in the United States. We would ask people in both countries the same questions at several points during their bereavement, and then we would compare the answers. Excited about this new endeavor, I bid farewell to my new collaborators, and Paulette and I made our way back to the States so I could begin my research.

* * *

One of the biggest questions I had at the time was whether the ancient practices and attitudes about the veneration of deceased loved ones were still honored in China. I knew for certain that these practices had thrived well into the twentieth century, but in 1949, the Communist Party rose to power and forcibly changed many of the ancient customs. Communists frown on the belief in dead spirits as a superstitious relic of the past, and until recently the government in Beijing strongly prohibited virtually all of the ancient mourning rites. Ancestral temples were retooled as public buildings for "the people's use" or were simply destroyed, and the burning of joss paper all but disappeared.

But old rituals die hard and in the broader sweep of history, the communist ban was only temporary. As the party began to loosen its hold in the 1980s to allow for greater economic development, the old rites returned with a flourish. Temples were rebuilt, and once again vendors specializing in the sale of ritual joss paper became common throughout China. In fact, joss paper vendors can now be found almost anywhere across the globe where Chinese populations thrive.[15] The paper is the same, but the objects have changed to satisfy the tastes of modern ancestors. There are now paper replicas of cell phones and televisions, fast food, and health care products, and of course it is still possible to custom-order the manufacture of paper surrogates for servants or sexual companions.

This very same pattern replicated itself in Vietnam, another communist country and China's neighbor.[16] As in China, the Vietnamese Communist Party tried in vain to outlaw the ancient spirit rites. It even substituted an official state ceremony, the commemoration of war heroes, for the older cults. That didn't work either. The Vietnamese populace held onto their cultural beliefs and whenever possible found ways to continue to make offerings to the spirits of the dead.[17] Like the Chinese communists, the government in Hanoi gradually came to see the wisdom in relaxing its policies. As it loosened its economy to allow for the influences of the free market, it also gradually freed its people to openly engage in the customs of the past. The two have developed in tandem. Renovating and rebuilding the ancestral temples and ghost shrines have in fact become a central feature of Vietnam's local economic development. The Hanoi government has even hired a traditional "spirit master" to help locate the ghosts of the war dead.[18]

The research I did with Zhang Nanping and his enthusiastic colleagues in Nanjing captured these sweeping cultural changes. Our research revealed clear-cut differences in the bereavement experiences of Americans and Chinese.[19] For one thing, bereaved people in China were, on the whole, more successful in dealing with grief than were their American counterparts. The difference had at least something to do with the way the Chinese engage in what we in the West have called grief work.

Many of the questions we asked in our Chinese/American study had to do with grief work. For example, we asked how much the bereaved people had thought about their loss, how much they had talked about it or let their feelings show, and how often they had memories of the deceased and searched for meaning or tried to make sense of the loss. As we had seen in other studies, the more Americans reported this kind of grief work in the early months after the loss, the more likely they were to experience chronically difficult grief symptoms. This was not the case for the Chinese. The Chinese reported *more* grief work than Americans, but for the Chinese, it was almost completely unre-

chinese crying

lated to suffering. Whether someone in China was thinking about or talking about a deceased loved one or trying to make sense of the death had very little relation to the actual level of distress.

At first, this finding seemed to make little sense, but then we remembered that for the Chinese, mourning and ancestral worship rites are not about the pain and suffering of the bereaved. The Chinese rites are focused almost exclusively on the imagined experience of the deceased person, their express purpose being to help the deceased loved one successfully make her or his way to the land of the dead and, once there, to ensure that she or he finds a good life.

Crying is a perfect example of how grief takes on dramatically different meanings in diverse cultures. In the West we cry at funerals when we cannot hold back our pain. A Western bereaved person's tears mean only one thing: an outpouring of emotion; as if the pain is literally leaking out of the eyes.

Crying at Chinese funerals is much more deliberate. In fact, it is tightly orchestrated so that it occurs at just the right moments in the ritual. Professional mourners and musicians are often hired to help. The musicians play a specific kind of mournful music, called *suona,* to enhance the somber mood, while the hired mourners cry at the designated points in the ceremony to cue the others to unleash their own tears.

The primary function of crying at Chinese funerals is not at all about the release of pain. Rather, crying sends a signal to the deceased loved one. In villages of northern Taiwan, near Taipei, for example, on the seventh day of mourning the deceased's family members rise early, make their offerings, and then set forth with unbridled wailing.[20] Custom dictates they should do this as early as possible on the seventh day because on that day their deceased love one will finally come to realize he is actually dead. They anticipate he will experience great sorrow at this realization. The crying is intended to help assuage his pain. As one mourner put it, "If we get up early enough to wail before the ancestor finds out he is really dead, then his own sorrow will be lessened. The more we weep, the less he must."[21]

The Chinese focus on the imagined reactions of the dead loved one, rather than on their own grief, harkens back to the continued bond discussed in Chapter 9. The evidence concerning the usefulness of the bond to bereaved people in the West, as we have already seen, was inconclusive. Some feel a continued bond with a deceased loved one, and others do not. For some people this bond is healthy, and for some it is not.

But what about the Chinese? The traditional mourning rites are clearly focused on an ongoing relationship. Then, shouldn't the continued bond be more ubiquitous in China? And shouldn't it also be more consistently healthy as well?

The answer to both questions is a resounding yes. In our study, the overall sense of a continued bond was more common among the Chinese than among the Americans, and it was also healthier for the Chinese.[22] For Americans, as in the earlier studies, a continuing relationship with a lost loved one was not always adaptive. Some American bereaved people who reported a continued bond had less distress over the next year of bereavement, whereas some experienced greater distress. For the Chinese, however, continued bonds were much more universally positive. In general, the more our Chinese subjects experienced a connection to the deceased early in bereavement, the less distress they felt over the long run.

I was delighted with these results. They pointed toward an important piece of the continued-bond puzzle. Western psychologists had come to believe strongly in the salubrious nature of the continuing connection with deceased loved ones. They had couched their arguments in anecdotal and historical accounts from other cultures. Because the ongoing connection to the dead has for so long played a key role in China and Japan, for example, they argued it had to be useful in all cultures.[23]

Yet, as we saw when we discussed the idea of reincarnation, a little bit of cultural knowledge can be a dangerous thing. Common sense tells us that just because an ongoing relationship with deceased loved ones is healthy in one culture, it will not necessarily be healthy in another.[24] The research findings in our Chinese/American study plainly supported this idea. I would not conclude from these findings that the continuing bond is unhealthy in Western culture. A better way to put it would be that continuing bonds are more adaptive in a context where they are understood and culturally supported.

I am reminded again of those conversations I had with my deceased father in the cranky old elevator of my New York apartment building. I chose the elevator because it gave me privacy. Because the doors opened slowly, I didn't have to worry about being caught by other people in the building, or about what they might think if they found their psychologist neighbor talking with a dead person. But the very fact that Westerners fret about engaging in such rituals may itself be enough to strip those rituals of their vitality.

In China and many other Asian countries the rituals are sewn into the very fabric of the culture. The Chinese need not fear they will be thought strange if they appeal to a dead ancestor. Indeed, many Chinese towns and villages are dotted with ancestral temples where families honor their dead and also commune with them. These temples are often the most prominent and elaborate buildings in the neighborhood. It is also quite common, especially in cities, to find small ancestral altars openly displayed in homes and businesses.

Modernization

As intriguing as the differences were between Chinese and Americans in grief and continuing bonds, one question kept nagging at me: Would the differences still hold in twenty-first-century China? I conducted the continued-bond research in Nanjing in the mid-1990s. Although the opening up of China was well under way at that time, it had not yet fully permeated the well-populated eastern region of the country. For reasons more complex than I can go into here, Nanjing seemed to have been on a slower pace of modernization than the other Chinese cities. There were, for example, still few cars at that time.

In 2003, Zhang Nanping wrote me to say that he had purchased a "motor car" and suggested that I visit Nanjing again so he could take me on a tour of the countryside. He had also tasted what it was like to travel, to visit, and to learn about other cultures. The entire Zhang family had even come to see me in New York. I wondered how this kind of exposure would affect the traditional mourning ceremony.

Might it do what the Communist Party had only hoped to do? Would modernization finally kill off the old rites?

I had a chance to find out in 2004 when my friend and collaborator, Samuel Ho of the University of Hong Kong, suggested that Paulette and I return to China, this time with our two children. Sam and I had been planning several different collaborative research projects, and to make our work together easier, he invited me to spend time with him in Hong Kong as a visiting professor at the university. I had an academic sabbatical coming up, so the timing was perfect. In the back of my mind, I knew the trip would also allow me to revisit the ancient ancestral temples. This time I wanted to see firsthand whether the Chinese people still took the old rites seriously, and maybe, just maybe, I might even try out the rituals for myself.

Hong Kong provided the perfect laboratory for this kind of exploration. When social change and economic prosperity spread on the mainland, the old rituals were revived, but prosperity brought modernization, and the older customs eventually gave way to an innovative hybrid. In the words of a former professional mourner, "My village has easy access to modern transportation. When a person passes away, a family just has to make a phone call. A company specializing in funeral preparations will show up right away, offering a wide range of services, from wreath rentals to the organization of wakes and funeral processions. They call it one-stop service."[25]

Hong Kong, by contrast, had gone through that phase many years earlier. Hong Kong was a modern, highly cosmopolitan city when the mainland was still largely agrarian and closed off to the rest of the world. If the rites and ancient customs could thrive in Hong Kong, they should be able to thrive anywhere. And I had been told that there were still plenty of ancestral temples on the island.

I was reluctant at first to tell Sam about my desire to participate in the ancestral rites. Most Chinese psychologists, I found, were more than happy to answer questions from a scholarly angle. They took pride in the fact that Chinese culture had been around so long, and that a Westerner might be interested in its history. But the idea that Chinese people might still practice the ancestral rites was, I think, something of an embarrassment for them; they felt it made China seem provincial.

When I inquired about the locations of active temples, the response was often dismissive: "Nobody cares about those old rituals anymore. Only old people continue to practice the old ways, like my grandmother."

There was an obvious defensiveness in these responses, and I suspected there was probably more to the story. One colleague, for example, was surprisingly angry: "Why would you want to do that? This is not your culture." Perhaps this kind of reaction had to do with the nature of the ritual itself. Remember, the old customs dictate that if a surviving relative fails to adequately honor his ancestors, the ancestor will suffer, and a suffering ancestor is vindictive.

For example, in Ha Jin's novel *A Free Life,* two Chinese immigrants to the United States find themselves in a quandary when they buy a restaurant from an older Chinese couple. Upon moving into the restaurant, they discover that the old couple had worshipped the god of wealth. "In a tiny alcove in the restaurant's dining room, this deity was represented by a porcelain statuette. . . . At his bare feet sat bowls of tangerines, apples, peaches, cookies, two miniature cups of rice wine, and four smoking joss sticks stuck in a brass censer." The restaurant's new owners had "mixed feelings about this superstitious practice, but should they evict the god? What if there indeed existed such a supernatural power that could decide the vicissitudes of their fortunes? In any event, they mustn't offend this deity, so they decided to leave him undisturbed and make similar offerings to him."[26]

Modern Chinese who refuse to engage in their filial obligation to send money or luxury goods by burning paper offerings are essentially saying they don't care, they no longer believe. But given the indelible mark these rituals have left on the collective Chinese psyche, this refusal becomes a bit of a dare. It's as if they said to the ghosts, "Go ahead, make my day. Do your worst; I don't believe you exist." But even the slightest apprehension that on some level there may be something to the old beliefs could lead to a cascade of second-guessing.

* * *

I decided to first visit one of the oldest and most distinguished temples in Hong Kong: the Man Mo Temple. The day before the trip to the temple, my family and I walked to the top of Victoria Peak at the island's center. The vista from the peak is magnificent. The sprawling density of the city spreads out across steep green mountains and gives way only to the busy harbor below. Up high, one is reminded that Hong Kong is tropical. A verdant junglelike mass of brush and small trees hangs and twists from every available angle. Moisture gathers in drips and small rivulets and trickles past, unseen in the brush. The rain forest cascades down the mountain but then comes to an abrupt halt as glass and steel take over; offices and vertiginous apartment buildings crowd what seems like every possible remaining inch. I once mentioned to Sam Ho that because the buildings are so tall and narrow in Hong Kong, it looked to me as if a bunch of pencils had fallen from the sky and stuck in the ground. "Not pencils," Sam corrected me, then smiled, "Chopsticks."

Taking in the view and thinking about the various reactions my plans had evoked, I was beginning to find it hard to imagine that anyone would bother to practice the ancient rituals in this bustling city.

The next day as we walked to the temple, the light rain that had been falling all morning began to pick up. We followed our map and walked along Tai Ping Shan Street to Kui in Fong, then to Square Street and down the steps of Ladder Street. And there it was, nestled in among the high-rise apartment towers, a cluster of small white buildings with a green tile roofs: the Man Mo Temple.

I stood for a moment, craning my neck up toward the lofty high-rises, pink and yellow and mint green, and their thousands and thousands of uniform windows, and then looking back down to the inviting little white buildings.

The temple was built in the 1880s to honor Man and Mo, the gods of civil bureaucracy (or literature) and war. Over the years, more gods had been included in the worship, and plaques were added to honor deceased relatives; as a Chinese colleague put it, "It's all the same here. There is very little distinction. Ancestors are worshipped the same as if they were gods."

The temple was still in good shape; obviously somebody was taking care of it. The eaves were carved in elaborate figures and symbols. Below red wooden spears, a tall doorway opened to the dark interior. The view of the interior was concealed by an elaborately carved wooden screen.

I noticed a large metallic boxlike structure in front of the temple. The placement seemed odd. The structure had an industrial ugliness that contrasted sharply with the poetry of the temple and partially blocked the otherwise welcoming facade. Then I noticed a small door in the metal box. I walked closer and saw that inside was a blazing flame. It was a furnace. A sign in Chinese characters was taped next to the door. Scrawled in English, underneath it, were the words "joss paper." This was obviously the place to burn paper offerings.

The interior was dark and smoke-filled. Red pillars and stone steps defined a central chamber and several side rooms. There were richly colored statues of Buddhist and Taoist deities crowded together behind marble altars, partially hidden by piles of soup, buns, bowls of fruit, and exotic brass animal statues. Large golden censer pots speared with incense sticks stood nearby.

The walls at the sides of the temple were completely covered in orderly rows of small tiles bearing the names and faces of countless deceased ancestors. Perched on shelves below the tiles were votive candles, flowers, and more food offerings: soft drinks, oranges, steamed buns, and sticky rice wrapped in lotus leaves.

A number of patrons were milling about. Several knelt or stood before altars with their heads bowed in silent prayer. Some clasped smoldering incense sticks, which they waved up and down in a Buddhist salutation. There was a pleasing solemnity to the scene.

I stood for a moment, taking this all in. Then my attention was drawn upward. The temple's rafters, I realized, were completely filled with multiple tiers of low-hanging spiral objects. Each spiral was tan-colored, and they were all identical in shape, with a red and gold paper strip dangling from the center. The spirals were arrayed tightly together in orderly rows, one row layered atop the next. The dense smoke, which was now beginning to overwhelm me, filtered streaks of light from openings in the ceiling to lend the spirals an otherworldly beauty.

I learned that the spirals were incense coils, purchased by the temple's patrons. On the dangling paper strips were written prayers to the gods. The incense was lit at the bottom, and the flame slowly worked its way up the spiral; the rising smoke lifted the prayer to the heavens. Years of smoky prayers had tarred the wooden ceiling to a deep black.

Temples and ancestral halls are surprisingly easy to find, even in the densest parts of modern Hong Kong. Not far from the Man Mo temple we came across a number of smaller temples, and further up Tai Ping Shan Street, a large ancestral hall. The entrance to the ancestral hall consisted of a simple wooden structure with a modest, corrugated fiberglass roof. We climbed a rickety staircase and entered a room absolutely brimming with the spiral coil incense. As we ventured further inside the hall, we found ourselves in a labyrinth of small worship rooms.

In one of the larger backrooms, we found a group of four or five young women, a mix of teenagers and young adults, busy preparing and folding joss paper in readiness for making offerings. Skylights allowed in plenty of light. The brightness of the room contrasted markedly with the cavelike interior of the Man Mo Temple. In part this effect was produced by the ancestral tiles on the wall, which were a bright yellow.

I watched the scene from the corner, my four-year-old daughter, Angelica, at my side. Older relatives stood nearby or sat in chairs, casually talking and eating, as the young women worked. There was a feeling of shared respect among all present, but the occasion wasn't the least bit melodramatic. If anything, the atmosphere was relaxed and pleasant.

I wondered if perhaps our presence was invasive. Yet nobody seemed to mind. In fact, nobody seemed to be paying us the least bit of attention. Then Angelica walked up and stood next to the young women. My thoughts turned to panic; surely this would violate the privacy of the ritual. But the women only smiled at her, as they talked among themselves in Chinese.

Then Angelica pulled from her pocket a small plastic figurine of Snow White. She had been carrying the figurine with her during the entire trip. Now she held it up in what seemed like an offering to the women. They understood the gesture instantly and laughed warmly. They patted Angelica on the head and continued to talk and banter with her in Chinese. I had no idea what they said, of course, but it was obvious they were more than happy to have her join them.

In the process of researching a book about Chinese paper offerings, another Westerner, Roderick Cave, admitted to experiencing a similar hesitation about intruding on the ancient rites. Just as I had, Cave feared that the "worshippers might feel that conspicuous foreigners would be defiling their shrines." He also came to realize that his apprehension was nothing more than "a mistaken cultural sensitivity," for in actuality "the degree of acceptance" he found among the worshippers in the temples "was remarkable."[27]

Several days later, my family and I visited a flourishing street market in Shau Kei Wan, an area on the eastern end of the island. The coast at Shau Kei Wan forms a natural harbor that once supported numerous fishing villages. Modern high-rises have since crowded out the old villages, but there are still temples to honor Tin Hau, a female god of the sea, and Tam Kung, god of weather and health.

Outside the market area, I noticed in the distance at the top of a steep hill what seemed to be another collection of ancestral temples set back in a wooded area. Although at first we could not discern a way to ascend the hill, eventually we discovered a crumbling stone stairway and made our way up.

To our delight, at the top we found a surprisingly opulent complex of buildings, almost like a small medieval city. There was an iron fence and an elaborate entry gate that led to a brightly painted red walkway. On either side of the walkway were several elevated temples, each with a small red stairway leading up to it. The entryways were framed by statuary: large bronze horses, ceramic tigers, and large iron or brass censer cauldrons for incense. The buildings themselves were decorated with standing flowerpots and red lanterns, and in the corners of the complex stood furnaces for burning offerings.

As we explored in and around the buildings, my son, Raphael, excitedly called out to me. He had discovered a stairway and was waving to us from the top. We hurried after him and to our astonishment found yet another enclave of buildings; this was a second tier of the complex, and with the exception of a few slight stylistic differences, it was laid out very much like the first. We hardly had the chance to take it in when Raphael found another stairway to still a third tier of temples.

We had stumbled upon something truly extraordinary. This was the center of ancestral worship for the old Shau Kei Wan village. For centuries clusters of temples much like these would have been a common sight in small villages and towns throughout China. The temples became the primary means of ancestral veneration, and in this way they functioned in much the same way as the paper offerings. Inside each temple were ancestral tablets or plaques and other honorifics to represent dead clan members. Once the tablet or plaque was placed in the temple, it was believed that the ancestor's sprit now dwelled there.

Each family or clan in the town kept its own ancestral temple. The living members of the clan were responsible for the temple's upkeep. Failing to keep an ancestral hall in good working order reflected poorly on the ancestor and of course evoked his or her wrath. By the same token, the best way to please or curry favor with deceased ancestors was to build and maintain as lavish a structure as possible. Not surprisingly, the result was great competition among villagers, a kind of one-upsmanship. Erecting a more elaborate ancestral hall than the neighboring clan was a sure way to please an ancestor, and it was also a great source of status among the living.

Ancestral complexes like this are no longer easy to find on the Chinese mainland. Most were destroyed or converted to public buildings during the Cultural Revolution of the 1950s. But Hong Kong was a British territory at that time, and the Cultural Revolution stopped at its doorstep; the old ways were free to continue. It was obvious that the Shau Kei Wan village ancestral complex was still very much in use. The temple buildings were clean and well maintained, and there were signs of recent visits; as in other temples around the city, we found food offerings and freshly lit votive candles on the altars. Later we came across still more temples in isolated locations further into the jungle. These, too, were clean and well maintained, with recent offerings still in evidence.

What struck me most of all about these temples was that they were completely open and unguarded. Such is the reverence for the old rites, it seemed, that nobody would dare to vandalize the buildings or use them as temporary shelter. In and of itself, this attitude is not so amazing, but it does contrast markedly with the attitude toward churches and other religious buildings throughout most of the Western world, which are now almost always locked.

"Ni Hao, Dad"

I am not sure why I deliberated so long. For days I had been thinking about trying out a ritual myself. I wanted to send a paper offering to my father.

I was hesitant and I didn't quite understand why. Maybe it was my academic colleagues' remonstrances. Maybe it was the fact that I was a scientist, and participating in this ancient rite was like acknowledging the limits of science. Or maybe I was a bit unsure, perhaps even a bit frightened, about what I might experience. It is easy to dismiss old customs as silly superstitions, but the very fact that the rites had endured so long, and I had seen evidence of their vitality all over Hong Kong, told me that they were probably powerful. After all, this was a ritual, and as James Watson wrote, rituals "have transformative powers. Rituals change people."[28] I decided to burn my offerings in the Man Mo Temple.

The first thing I was going to have to do was select the right paper object. That task I discovered was not insignificant. With my family in tow, I wandered over to Tai Ping Shan Street, near the temple. There we knew we would find several long city blocks of joss paper vendors. Store after store sold almost nothing else; there were mountains of paper objects, neatly stacked in rows, spilling out onto the sidewalk, and hanging in chaotic bunches from the awnings. There were paper houses, cars, radios and televisions; food, cooking pots and pans, even fast food; there were paper shoes and paper clothing, and of course there was an abundance of paper money and paper credit cards.

But what to burn for my father?

We entered one of the shops, and as I mulled this question over, I noticed that my daughter had wandered to the back of the store. What had drawn her there was the sight of a woman packaging paper shoes into clear plastic wrappers for display. By this point, Angelica had grown enamored of the paper objects, especially the paper houses. She walked over to the woman packaging the paper shoes and, entranced, intently watched her every move. Obviously paper shoes were for her as delightful as paper houses. But I grew concerned. I had read that joss paper manufacture is often seen as a spiritual function.[29] Would Angelica's curiosity violate some taboo of the ancient custom? Again I was wrong. The woman couldn't have been more delighted by Angelica's interest, and soon, despite the language barrier, she had engaged my daughter in an amusing game.

Angelica's unabashed curiosity and the welcome response it evoked showed me something important: I had been taking it all too seriously. Up to that point, I had assumed that I would do the paper burning ritual by myself, so as to lend it a proper solemnity. Now I realized that this would be a mistake. The burning of paper offerings is not about individual grief. Nothing in the Chinese bereavement ceremony is about individual grief. The ancestral rites are about honoring lost loved ones, and above all, they are about family and connection. As Roderick Cave noted, the preparation of the paper for offering "is in itself one of the rituals which helps to strengthen family bonds."[30]

Emboldened by this realization, I no longer found the task of selecting the appropriate paper offering daunting. My father had worked hard all his life. He had worked hard so that his family could have a better life, and he had denied himself material pleasures. Sure, he liked simple things like baseball games and cigars. But he was frugal; that was part of his game plan. Without an advanced education, he didn't have much economic mobility, and he knew he was going to have to save in order to support his family. He accomplished that.

So what would I send him if I could send him anything? Not televisions or clothing; those were small things that I knew would interest him little. Not a car, or even a house. That would be too much and might make him feel uncomfortable because it was careless and pretentious.

Then I saw the perfect thing: paper gold bullion. Gold bullion bars were like money in the bank. Gold was rock-solid. This was something my father could rely on; this would make him feel safe, allow him to breathe a little easier. The more I thought about it and thought about his life, the more I became convinced that gold bullion would make the perfect offering.

And then I realized that *thinking* about my father this way was the whole point.

The insight was exhilarating.

* * *

An old woman stood before the large metal furnace in front of the Man Mo Temple. She was bent over a basket full of gold and red joss paper, and she slowly tossed handfuls through the small furnace doorway into the flames. We waited for our turn, several feet behind her.

Earlier we had walked back to the temple to offer a prayer to my father. The elation I had experienced picking out the gold bullion had given way to an enduring calm. But now that we were at the temple, I was not exactly sure how this next part of the ceremony worked or, for that matter, what I was supposed to do.

Intuition suggested that the best approach was probably to pray in a way that made the most sense to me.

Rituals change people.

I walked over to one of the altars at the side of the temple, where it was darker and I had a bit of privacy. I had seen others in the temple give the Buddhist salutation—three waves of the clasped hands to signify the Buddha, the teachings of Buddhism, and the *sangha,* or supportive community.

By following accepted ritual routines ordinary citizens participate in the process of cultural unification.

I wasn't a Buddhist but I was interested in Buddhism. It seemed like a reasonable way to begin. I knelt before the altar and gave the three salutations.

Then I thought about my father.

"Hello Dad," I whispered.

Scenes of my father's life flipped rapidly through my consciousness.

It mattered little what one believed about death or the afterlife as long as the rituals were performed properly.

A warm sensation enveloped me. I felt calm again, almost serene. But something new was happening. The words I had spoken were surprisingly forceful, as if I had summoned some great power. The act of reaching out to my father in this public temple, this place where such behavior was fully accepted, seemed to have magnified the effect. Immediately I began to feel my father's presence, much as I had when I had occasionally spoken with him in the past, but this was like opening a door to another world.

When I had spoken with my father previously, I had always imagined him alone. In the Man Mo Temple, I saw him in a world full of other people. They were amorphous, not fully realized, but I sensed them; there was a crowd. I was connected, automatically, to all of them.

Whatever my father was—a spirit, a memory, a cluster of neurons activated in my brain, a vague opening in the cosmos—it just didn't matter. All that I cared about at that moment was that I felt deeply and immutably bonded with him.

Rituals are repeated because they are expected to have transformative powers.

Then it struck me, right then and there, like a thunderbolt. I don't know why I hadn't realized it earlier. I was reaching out to my father from a temple *in China*. In and of itself, this was not especially unusual—travel to China had by this time become fairly common—but in the context of my relationship with my father, it was enormous. My father had given up his desire to travel so that he could support his family. I had defiantly left home at a young age with the irrepressible intent to do just the opposite. This issue had torn us asunder; now it was the ground on which we were coming together. The disparate strands of our relationship seemed to knit together for the first time. It seemed to wrap itself around me. I felt indelibly linked with my father. He was me and I was him.

This was the best offering I could have hoped for.

Before I knew it, the words came out of my mouth: "Ni hao, Dad." I couldn't speak Chinese, but I knew how to say hello.

* * *

The old woman had finished and it was now our turn at the furnace. Before moving forward I paused a moment to explain to Raphael and Angelica what we were about to do. Paulette busied herself trying to decipher the Chinese characters next to the furnace door.

Then finally I approached the open door and looked for the flame—but saw none.

This was odd. We had just seen the old woman tossing in joss paper a few minutes earlier. The flame had seemed to be roaring then.

There was a small candle for lighting incense nearby, but I was not sure if it would be appropriate to use this for igniting the paper offering. The old Chinese woman, still in the vicinity, glanced my way, smiled, and rushed back over. She gestured and spoke in Chinese. I didn't understand a word, but I got the idea that she was telling me I should light the corner of the paper bars with the candle and then toss them into the furnace. I did so, and immediately the paper burst into glorious flames. She nodded and smiled broadly. "This is a modern furnace," she seemed to say. "The flame is self-regulating."

And there it was. Paper gold sent, with the help of an elderly Chinese woman, to the spirit of my deceased father.

The act had been mechanical, almost an afterthought. I had noticed this same thing during the previous days when I had hung around the temples. There seemed to be nothing particularly sacred about the way people burned the paper offerings. They simply threw them into the flames as if they were, well, burning paper.

Now I understood why. The actual burning of the offerings *was* an afterthought, literally; the most vital part of the ceremony had already happened.

CHAPTER 12

Thriving in the Face of Adversity

I've emphasized our natural resilience throughout this book. We see it when we cope with the death of a loved one and also when we are confronted with horrific events like war, disaster, biological epidemic, terrorist attack, and countless others. We dread these events, but when they happen we have no choice but to deal with them as best we can. Fortunately, most of us deal with them remarkably well. In this sense our capacity to endure the pain of loss is not particularly special. Rather, it is one instance of our more general human capacity to thrive in the face of adversity.

But when we speak of thriving, we are usually thinking about a long period of time. Until recently, most of the research on extreme stress, especially bereavement, pertained to very short periods of time. Most of the early studies on the grieving process typically covered one or two years at the most. The reason is simple. It is difficult and expensive to follow people over longer periods of time. But gradually, we have begun to find ways to get around these problems, and now some of the first snapshots of the longer course of bereavement have emerged. What we've found remains wholly consistent with the earlier studies: Resilience in the face of loss is real, prevalent, and enduring.

In one study, for example, my colleagues and I took a longer look at the data from the CLOC project that I described in Chapter 5. We examined data from the full seven years of the project, beginning three years before the spouses' deaths and ending four years after. Some of those who had suffered chronically over the first two years had, by the fourth year, begun to recover. Unfortunately, this wasn't true of everyone; even four years after the loss there were still some bereaved people who were continually plagued by debilitating grief symptoms. By contrast, most of the people who had exhibited resilience earlier in the study—close to half—remained healthy throughout those seven years.[1]

In another study my colleagues and I used a much larger sample: 16,000 people. The data were from a preexisting study in which the participants had been tracked over an unusually long period of time: about twenty years.[2] The study was unique in another way; it included some novel questions that allowed us to take a slightly different perspective on adjustment. One of the questions, repeated each year, was "How *satisfied* are you with your life as a whole?" When we analyzed the resulting data, we found the same patterns as we had seen in our previous studies, only over much longer periods of time. Of particular importance, a substantial majority of bereaved people—approximately 60 percent—had consistently experienced high levels of life satisfaction over the years. In other words, although they had suffered the pain of grief, for the most part they were satisfied with their lives before, during, and in the many years after their loss.

* * *

Karen Everly never did start that kennel that she and her daughter had dreamed of. The first year after Claire's death, Karen felt compelled to see the idea through, largely because it was something she and Claire had thought about together. But gradually the demands of her life pulled at her. Her career continued to thrive, and she remained a devoted mother and wife. "Without Claire's constant input," she told me, "I came to see that the kennel project no longer made sense."

That did not mean that Karen had forgotten Claire. Far from it; she and her husband dedicated themselves to keeping Claire's memory alive. They maintained a steady relationship with the breeding association that Claire had been involved with. They set up a fund in Claire's name to help support humane care for unwanted dogs. They kept in touch with Claire's friends, even years after her death, and they made it a point to invite them to family activities when they were in town.

Above all, Karen remained strong and healthy: "Claire would have wanted it that way." On this point, she spoke with absolute certainty: "I couldn't just crumble. Other people needed me. I had—I have—a career. It is who I am. It would have made no sense to push that aside. The best way I can think of to honor Claire is to live my life. I need to do the things I am supposed to be doing, the things I am good at. That's what I would have expected of her, of Claire. That's what I wanted of her. It's my own way of saying I will never forget her."

Indeed, after the initial shock of grief wears off, many bereaved people realize that the best way to pay tribute to their loved ones is not through their own pain and suffering, not through their own metaphorical death, but by living on as fully as possible. Former Beatle Paul McCartney echoed this conclusion when he thought about the losses in his life. McCartney's mother died tragically when he was fourteen years old. Over the years, he had lost two of his closest friends, his "mates" from the Beatles, and more recently his much beloved wife of twenty-nine years. McCartney keeps his grief for each of these losses at a distance because "the idea that their deaths would plunge me into some sort of morose depression would bother them. I know that for a fact. So that helps me not go there."[3]

Daniel Levy did not forget Janet, but five years after her death, he was living with another woman. What about those conversations with Janet by the water?

"I still do it now and then. Janet was such a huge force in my life. I want to hold onto her. I like to think I can still find her."

Do memories of Janet interfere with his new relationship? "The connection I have with Lorrie is not the same as the one I had with

FINAL

Janet. Janet and I had this spiritual thing, which I think is rare; it doesn't happen every day. But Lorrie is fun; she makes me happy, and she is happy with me. I've told her about Janet. I talk about Janet a lot, actually. And Lorrie is OK with that."

Equipped for Grieving

The early theories of bereavement emphasized the importance of working through the pain of loss and viewed this process as unfolding in a series of predictable and necessary stages. There was never much research support for these ideas, largely because there was never much research on bereavement at all. When we finally got around to studying the details of the grieving process, however, a very different picture emerged.

We cope well with loss because we are equipped—wired, if you will—with a set of in-born psychological processes that help us do the job. The most obvious of these is our ability to feel and express sadness. When we feel sad, we are more likely to turn our attention inward, to reflect, take stock, and recalibrate to the reality of the loss. When we express sadness, we tell others that we are in pain, that our minds are elsewhere, and that we are likely to need their care and sympathy, especially during the early days and weeks of bereavement.

All emotions, including sadness, are designed to be short-term solutions. If we remain in a constant state of sadness or feel sad for too long a time, we run the risk of ruminating and withdrawing from the world around us. If we express too much sadness, we begin to alienate the very people whose help and support we most need.

Fortunately, nature has provided a built-in solution. Rather than staying sad for long periods of time, our experience of the emotion comes and goes. It oscillates. Over time the cycle widens, and gradually we return to a state of equilibrium.

One of the ways we achieve the kind of adaptive oscillation in and out of sadness is by switching to more positive states of mind. Most of us are surprised to learn that we can make this switch. We don't expect to find joy and even laughter within our pain, but when we do, it makes sense, and we feel better, even if temporarily. We can also find moments of comfort in positive reminiscences of the lost loved one. These positive states do more than propel us out of sadness; they also reconnect us to those around us. Laughter in particular has a contagious effect on other people, and in our research we've shown this to be true even during bereavement. Laughter makes other people feel better and pulls them toward us, in a way rewarding them for having bothered to stay with us through the painful moments.

Regrettably, not everyone copes so well with loss. It is important that we understand why so that we can foster healthy coping in a greater number of people and, hopefully, help those whose suffering has become disproportionate.

We know that there is almost certainly a genetic component in resilience. However, the science on this issue is not yet fully worked out. We also know that psychological factors are involved. One such factor is optimism. Another, revealed in my research, is coping flexibility. Earlier, I described resilient people as having more tools in their toolbox than people who are not resilient. One of those tools is being able to switch back and forth from sadness to positive emotions. Another is being more flexible in the way they use emotions.

There are still other routes to the same end. In relation to behavioral flexibility, my research has shown that people sometimes cope well by using behaviors or strategies that under normal circumstances are less than perfectly healthy. The use of self-serving biases is one such strategy. We tell ourselves we are stronger or more durable than we really are, or we blame external factors for our loss, for example, the care a loved one received in the hospital or the actions of his or her employer. We may also focus on a positive outcome as a way of looking on the bright side. In other circumstances, behavior like this can be problematic, but when the chips are down, it most definitely helps us get by.

The Enduring Bond

"I cannot believe so much time has passed," Sondra Beaulieu wrote to me in an e-mail on the fourth anniversary of Serge's death. She seemed to be doing well. I told her that I thought she was a resilient person and asked if she agreed. She did, although she was quick to add that not everything had been easy. Her mother had died recently. That had been taxing, and it had felt different from Serge's death. The effects of her mother's death had had more to do with the shifting complexities of her family life and with the changing responsibilities that come with aging.

On the anniversary of Serge's death, Sondra was planning to spend much of the day with a close friend. Sondra had told me about that friend. She had written a poem about the town where Sondra grew up. Sondra had read the poem to her dying mother, she said, because she "thought it would bring back good memories as she passed from this world into the next." On the anniversary of Serge's death, that same friendship was now making "a rough day for me better and happier, too."

But Sondra also reminded me that it is difficult being alone: "There is no one to keep you in line. Serge used to do that, and now I have had to do without it. When something upsets me I don't have Serge to come home to anymore. I can't come home and rant the way I used to. When I have doubts, he can't put his arm around me."

Still, she was optimistic: "Serge always encouraged me to manage my own activities; he encouraged independence. He encouraged me to write—when he died I felt I could carry on, develop my own writing."

When Serge came into her life, Sondra had found a way to open up, and after her mother died, "there was no one left to tell me what to do." Only Serge's influence remained. "I value Serge now more than ever," Sondra said. "I always appreciated how wonderful he was, but now I see that he was more amazing that I even realized."

There was another development. Sondra had begun to forge a relationship with a daughter Serge had from a previous marriage. Serge was not close to his daughter when he was alive. After his death, however, Sondra began to spend time with her. Sondra told me, "She never knew Serge that well, but she is learning more about Serge and about me."

After we talked a while, I reminded Sondra of her comments in earlier interviews. I reminded her of the visions she had described soon after Serge's death, when he appeared to her as if he were checking in with her. I asked Sondra if she remembered those experiences, and if anything of that nature still happened. She brightened immediately. "Oh yes, I still see him from time to time," she told me, "but not as strongly as that first time." Then she added, "I know Serge is still with me, watching over me. He is definitely still around."

Death evokes in us a powerful dissonance. It terrifies us but still we remain curious. When we grieve, we live with the dissonance. We are pulled toward the unknown. We want to know what has become of our loved ones. And sometimes we continue to sense their presence long after they are gone.

Traditional bereavement theories have always looked askance at any form of continued relationship with a deceased person. The ultimate goal of grieving, these theories held, was to completely sever the attachment, to break all unconscious connection. Failure to do so would only delay the final resolution of the grieving process. Over time it became apparent, however, that many healthy bereaved people did not relinquish the emotional bond. In fact, many continued to feel deeply connected and even held conversations with deceased loved ones years after the loss. To make sense of these observations, bereavement theorists reversed gears. They touted the importance of maintaining rather than breaking the emotional bond.

The research shows us that the picture is more complex. Whether or not a continued bond is healthy during bereavement depends on a number of factors. One is the type of bond. For example, maintaining the deceased's possessions is almost always maladaptive. Another factor is the timing. Experiencing the ongoing presence of a deceased loved one soon after the death often makes people feel worse, while later on in bereavement these experiences are more comforting and clearly more adaptive. Regardless of the form that continued bonds take, however, extreme or excessively frequent experiences of connection to a deceased loved one usually lead to a more protracted grief course.

Another crucial factor is culture. In the West, where scientific objectivity rules, we tend to recoil at the thought of communing with the dead. Yet, in many regions around the globe, this idea has long been sewn into the very fabric of people's lives. It is difficult to know for sure how seriously these cultures take the idea; ritual communication with the dead when we can observe it seems casual and is often accompanied by playfulness and levity. But rituals are powerful, and whether we fully believe in them or not, they can still move us. My research in China demonstrates this fact. It also shows us that we still have a lot to learn about culture and bereavement.

* * *

After my last trip to China, I was certain that I would continue to burn paper offerings for my father. It was a simple ritual, and it brought my relationship with my father back to life. To my delight, I discovered that joss paper was readily available in the Chinese neighborhoods of New York City. Even in the old "Chinatown" of lower Manhattan, which had of late become a major tourist destination, there were ancestral temples and paper shops remarkably similar to those I had seen in Hong Kong. I had walked in these areas many times in the past but never noticed the shops or the temples before.

There was another surprise, although a far less pleasant one. When I described the experience of burning paper offerings to friends and colleagues, they looked at me askance, as if they were not sure whether they should take me seriously. It quickly became apparent that this kind of thing was not something I could easily talk about. In fact, just about any topic pertaining to a dead person, I had to remind myself, still made people in the West uncomfortable.

In addition, the Chinese merchants in New York were suspicious when I visited. They questioned my intentions. "Why do you want those things?" they asked. "Do you know they are not real, only paper? What do you intend to do with them?" This kind of suspicion was also apparent when I visited ancestral temples in New York.

My desire to reenact the paper-burning ritual faded with time. I never repeated it, and actually in the end I had to admit that my academic colleagues in Hong Kong were right: As much as I was drawn to the joss paper ritual while in Hong Kong, it was not and could not be part of my experience in my home country.

But cultural differences were not the only factor. I realized over time that I no longer needed the ritual. My father had been dead for over twenty-five years. I had been young when he died. We fought then, and there was so much to our relationship that was still unresolved. Reaching out to him as I had, talking with him in imaginary conversations, was a way of continuing the relationship, a way of resurrecting it so that we could pick up where we had left off and maybe, if I was lucky, repair some of the rift between us. The ritual in Hong Kong was especially powerful in that regard. It worked. It served its purpose, and it gave me something to keep, something to take back home with me. There was no reason now to repeat it.

* * *

The longest bereavement study that I know of spanned a remarkable thirty-five years.[4] Some things stay constant, the study showed, but many aspects of bereavement fade only gradually, after many years have passed. In the first few years after a loss, for example, most bereaved people frequently reminisce about the lost loved one. We find ourselves indulging in reflection, replaying old memories. We do this at least several times a week. Fifteen years later, these kinds of reflective thoughts and memories happen less frequently, but they are not completely absent.

Anniversary reactions, like the kind Sondra Beaulieu felt, reveal the same gently sloping pattern. An "anniversary reaction" occurs anytime a bereaved person experiences a dramatic increase in sadness or loneliness on the anniversary of an important date related to the loss: the lost loved one's birthday, the first holiday after the death, and, of course, the date of the loved one's death. For most people, anniversary reactions last a few hours and not much longer. The duration does not seem to change much over time. What does change, though, is the frequency of these reactions.

Despite the durability of grief, bereaved people often worry that they will forget, that they will lose track of their memories, even years after a loved one's death. This is an especially thorny issue for bereaved parents.[5] Once a parent, always a parent; there is no switch to turn that off. When a child dies, parents never allow the memory to drift too far away.

I asked Karen Everly about this. I asked her if she could sum up what bereavement felt like years after the death of her daughter. She looked thoughtful. Her words apply, I think, to anyone who has ever mourned a loved one:

> It's a bit like a fading light. It grows dim but it never goes out, never, not completely anyway. I find that enormously reassuring. I used to worry that someday the light would disappear—that I would forget, and then I would really have lost Claire. I know, now, that doesn't happen. It can't. There is always a little flicker there. It is a bit like the small glowing embers you see after a fire dies down. I carry that around with me, that little ember, and if I need to, if I want to have Claire next to me, I blow on it, ever so gently, and it glows bright again.

Acknowledgments

I am humbled by the courage and generosity of each and every person who participated in my research. This book would not have been possible without their efforts. Despite their painful losses, despite the difficult events they endured, they unflinchingly answered my endless questions and willingly carried out whatever tedious task I set for them. Their openness started me on the road to understanding human resilience. I am especially grateful to Sondra Singer Beaulieu for our repeated conversations and exchanges over the years, and for allowing me to excerpt from her thoughtful essays and moving poetry.

I would not have had the luxury of time to write this book were it not for the patience and support of my wife, Paulette Roberts, and my two children, Raphael and Angelica. They have waited for me to return from the office, waited at the dinner table, and waited on weekends for me to turn off the computer. I am forever grateful.

I have been in a position to develop the ideas in this book thanks to Ira Sharkey, who first opened the door for me, and to the expert and generous guidance of my mentors Neil Stillings at Hamphire College, Jerome L. Singer at Yale University, and Mardi Horowtiz at the University of California, San Francisco, as well as myriad colleagues who have guided me along the path of my career: Robert Crowder, Penelope Davis, Paul Ekman, Barry Farber, Susan Folkman, Arè Holen, Steve Lepore, Randolph Ness, Bruce Wexler, Camille Wortman, and James Youniss. I am indebted to many friends and collaborators who have stimulated and inspired: John Archer, Diane Arnkoff, Jo-Anne Bachorowski, Lisa Feldman Barrett, Toni Bisconti, Paul Boelen, Kathrin Boerner, Richard Bryant, Lisa Capps, Louis Castonguay, Cecelia Chan, Andrew Clark, Nathan Consedine, Nigel Field, Chris Fraley, Barbara Fredrickson, Peter Freed, Sandro Galea, James Gross, Stevan Hobfoll, Susan Nolen-Hoeksema, Samuel Ho, John Jost, Dacher Keltner, Ann Kring, Darrin Lehman, Scott Lilienfeld, Tyler Lorig, Andreas Maercker, Anthony Mancini, Tracy Mayne, Richard McNally, Batja Mesquita, Mario Mikulincer, Constance Milbrath, Judith Moskowitz, Zhang Nanping, Robert Neimeyer, Yuval Neria, Jennie Noll, Kathleen O'Connell, Collin Murray Parks, Frank Putnam, Eshkol Rafaeli, Edward Rynearson, Marty Safer, Henk Schut, Gary Schwartz, Katherine Shear, Bryna Siegel, Roxanne Silver, Charles Stinson, Margaret and Wolfgang Stroebe, Robert Weiss, and Hansjorg Znoj.

Many thanks as well to my good friends Larry and Mary Hewes for urging me to write this book; to my literary agent, Linda Lowenthal, for helping me figure out how to translate my ideas into this book and for convincing me that I could do it; and to Amanda Moon at Basic Books for her patience, calm insight, and steady editorial eye. My thanks go as well to my fine copy editor, Margaret Ritchie.

Psychological research is not a solitary activity. It requires countless hands and multiple minds. I am grateful to the students who labored tirelessly with me in the lab and in particular to those with whom I wrote many of the papers mentioned in the book: Anthony Papa, Jack Bauer, Kathleen Lalande, David Pressmen, Karin Coifman, Maren Westphal, Azeminia Kovacevic, Stacey Kaltman, Joy Kassett, Rebecca Sherman, Courtney Rennicke, Sharon Dekel, Claudio Negrao, David Fazzari, Michael Mihalecz, Jenna Lejune, Deniz Colak, Lisa Wu, Kelly Cervellione, David Keuler, Laura Goorin, who also created the index for this book, Sumati Gupta, Isaac Galatzer-Levy, Donald Robinaugh, Michelle O'Neill, Lisa Horowitz, and Nicolas Seivert.

The research described in this book was generously funded by the National Institutes of Health, the National Science Foundation, the Research Grants Council of Hong Kong, and the Office of the Vice President of Administration, Columbia University.

Notes

Chapter 1

1. T. Holmes and R. Rahe, "The Social Readjustment Scale," *Journal of Psychosomatic Research* 11 (1967): 213–218.

2. J. E. Miller, *Winter Grief, Summer Grace: Returning to Life After a Loved One Dies* (Minneapolis, MN: Augsburg Fortress, 1995), and J. E. Welshons and W. Dyer, *Awakening from Grief: Finding the Way Back to Joy* (Novato, CA: New World Library, 2003).

3. C. Wortman and R. Silver, "The Myths of Coping with Loss," *Journal of Consulting and Clinical Psychology* 57 (1989): 349–357.

Chapter 2

1. E. Erikson, *Childhood and Society* (New York: Norton, 1950): 264.

2. S. Freud, "Mourning and Melancholia," originally published in *Zeitschrift*, vol. 4, 1917. Later appeared in *The Standard Edition of the Complete Psychological Works of Sigmund Freud,* vol. 14, ed. J. Strachey (London: Hogarth Press, 1917–1957): 152–170.

3. M. Bonaparte, A. Freud, and E. Ernst, eds., *The Origins of Psychoanalysis: Sigmund Freud's Letters* (New York: Basic Books, 1954): 103.

4. Ibid., 166.

5. Ibid., 154.

6. J. Didion, *The Year of Magical Thinking* (New York: Knopf, 2005): 35.

7. Freud, "Mourning and Melancholia," 54.

8. R. Kurzban and M. R. Leary, "Evolutionary Origins of Stigmatization: The Functions of Social Exclusion," *Psychological Bulletin* 127 (2001): 187–208,

and J. Tooby and L. Cosmides, "Friendship and the Banker's Paradox: Other Pathways to the Evolution of Adaptive Altruism," *Proceedings of the British Academy* 88 (1996): 119–143.

9. At the beginning of the paper, Freud warned that "our material here is limited to a small number of cases" and that "any claim to the general validity of our conclusions shall be forgone at the onset." Later in the paper, Freud also acknowledged that he would find it "impossible" to answer any objections to his idea about mourning, and that "we do not even know by what economic measures the work of mourning is carried through" (166).

10. L. R. Squire and E. R. Kandel, *Memory: From Mind to Molecules* (New York: Scientific American Library, 2000).

11. The paradoxical effects of thought suppression have been well documented in the research of Daniel Wegner and his colleagues. For a summary of that work, see R. M. Wenzlaff and D. M. Wegner, "Thought Suppression," *Annual Review of Psychology* 51 (2000): 59–91.

12. J. Archer, *The Nature of Grief: The Evolution and Psychology of Reactions to Loss* (London and New York: Routledge, 1999).

13. Helene Deutsch, "The Absence of Grief," *Psychoanalytic Quarterly* 6 (1937): 16.

14. E. Lindemann, "Symptomatology and Management of Acute Grief, *American Journal of Psychiatry* 101 (1944): 1141–1148.

15. W. Middleton et al., "The Bereavement Response: A Cluster Analysis," *British Journal of Psychiatry* 169 (1996): 167–171; G. A. Bonanno and N. P. Field, "Examining the Delayed Grief Hypothesis Across Five Years of Bereavement," *American Behavioral Scientist* 44 (2001): 798–806; and G. A. Bonanno et al., "Resilience to Loss and Chronic Grief: A Prospective Study from Pre-Loss to 18 Months Post-Loss," *Journal of Personality and Social Psychology* 83 (2002): 1150–1164.

16. E. Kübler-Ross, *On Death and Dying* (New York: Routledge, 1973), and E. Kübler-Ross and D. Kessler, *On Grief and Grieving: Finding the Meaning of Grief Through the Five Stages of Loss* (New York: Simon & Schuster, 2007).

17. J. Bowlby, *Attachment and Loss,* vol. 3, *Loss: Sadness and Depression* (New York: Basic Books, 1980).

Chapter 3

1. James Innell Packer, *A Grief Sanctified* (New York: Crossway Books, 2002): 9.

2. Readers interested in learning more about Paul Ekman's groundbreaking research will find his books highly readable, the most recent being *Emotions Revealed: Recognizing Faces and Feelings to Improve Communication and*

Emotional Life (New York: Macmillan, 2003). Although Dacher Keltner would later expand Ekman's work on emotion into uncharted territory, at the time we met he had not yet done so. Readers interested in learning more about Dacher's research and inspiring ideas might read his book *Born to Be Good: The Science of a Meaningful Life* (New York: W. W. Norton, 2008).

3. C. Darwin, *The Expression of Emotions in Man and Animals* (London: John Murray, 1872), and L. Parr, B. Waller, and S. Vick, "New Developments in Understanding Emotional Facial Signals in Chimpanzees," *Current Directions in Psychological Science* 16, no. 3 (2007): 117–122.

4. P. Ekman, "Are There Basic Emotions?" *Psychological Review* 99, no. 3 (1992): 550–553, and J. Tooby and L. Cosmides, "The Past Explains the Present: Emotional Adaptations and the Structure of Ancestral Environments," *Ethology and Sociobiology* 11 (1990): 375–424.

5. R. S. Lazarus, *Emotion and Adaptation* (New York: Oxford University Press, 1991).

6. F. de Waal, *Peacekeeping Among Primates* (Cambridge, MA: Harvard University Press, 1989).

7. M. Westphal and G. A. Bonanno, "Attachment and Attentional Biases for Facial Expressions of Disgust," unpublished manuscript, 2009.

8. Lazarus, *Emotion and Adaptation.*

9. C. E. Izard, "Innate and Universal Facial Expressions: Evidence from Developmental and Cross-cultural Research," *Psychological Bulletin* 115, no. 2 (1994): 288–299; C. Z. Stearns, "Sadness," in *Handbook of Emotions*, ed. M. Lewis and J. M. Haviland, 547–561 (New York: Guilford Press, 1993); and Lazarus, *Emotion and Adaptation.*

10. N. Schwarz, "Warmer and More Social: Recent Developments in Cognitive Social Psychology," *Annual Review of Sociology* 24 (1998): 239–264.

11. J. Storbeck and G. Clore, "With Sadness Comes Accuracy; With Happiness, False Memory: Mood and the False Memory Effect," *Psychological Science* 16, no. 10 (2005): 785–789.

12. G. V. Bodenhausen, L. A. Sheppard, and G. P. Kramer, "Negative Affect and Social Judgement: The Differential Impact of Anger and Sadness," *European Journal of Social Psychology* 24 (1994): 45–62.

13. H. Welling, "An Evolutionary Function of the Depressive Reaction: The Cognitive Map Hypothesis," *New Ideas in Psychology* 21, no. 2 (2003): 1.

14. G. A. Bonanno, L. Goorin, and K. G. Coifman, "Sadness and Grief," in *Handbook of Emotions,* 3rd ed., ed. M. Lewis, J. M. Haviland-Jones, and L. F. Barrett, 797–810 (New York: Guilford Press, 2008).

15. G. A. Bonanno and D. Keltner, "Facial Expressions of Emotion and the Course of Conjugal Bereavement," *Journal of Abnormal Psychology* 106 (1997): 126–137.

16. N. Eisenberg et al., "Relation of Sympathy and Distress to Prosocial Behavior: A Multimethod Study," *Journal of Personality and Social Psychology* 57 (1989): 55–66.

17. J. J. Gross and R. W. Levenson, "Emotion Elicitation Using Films," *Cognition and Emotion* 9, no. 1 (1995): 87–108.

18. L. Wang et al. "Amygdala Activation to Sad Pictures During High-Field (4 Tesla) Functional Magnetic Resonance Imaging," *Emotion* 5 (2005): 12–22.

19. M. Dondi, F. Simion, and G. Caltran, "Can Newborns Discriminate Between Their Own Cry and the Cry of Another Newborn Infant?" *Developmental Psychology* 35, no. 2 (1999): 418–426.

20. N. Eisenberg et al., "Differentiation of Vicariously Induced Emotional Reactions in Children," *Developmental Psychology* 24 (1988): 237–246.

21. Keltner and Kring, "Emotion, Social Function."

22. Murray Bowen, *Family Therapy in Clinical Practice* (Northvale, NJ: Jason Aronson, 1978).

23. Bonanno and Keltner, "Facial Expressions."

24. J. Lerner et al., "Facial Expressions of Emotion Reveal Neuroendocrine and Cardiovascular Stress Responses," *Biological Psychiatry* 61, no. 2 (2005): 253–260.

25. J. Bowlby, *Attachment and Loss* (New York: Basic Books, 1980). In this book on bereavement Bowlby described a form of "disordered mourning" in which there is a prolonged absence of grieving despite "tell-tale signs that the bereaved person has in fact been affected and that his mental equilibrium is disturbed" (153). Among the "tell-tale signs" indexed are the positive emotions of pride and cheerfulness, as well as optimism and the appearance of being "in good spirits" (156).

26. Bonanno and Keltner, "Facial Expressions"; D. Keltner and G. A. Bonanno, "A Study of Laughter and Dissociation: Distinct Correlates of Laughter and Smiling During Bereavement," *Journal of Personality and Social Psychology* 73 (1997): 687–702; B. L. Fredrickson, "The Role of Positive Emotions in Positive Psychology: The Broaden-and-Build Theory of Positive Emotions," *American Psychologist* 56 (2001): 218–226; and B. L. Fredrickson et al., "What Good Are Positive Emotions in Crisis? A Prospective Study of Resilience and Emotions Following the Terrorist Attacks on the United States on September 11th, 2001," *Journal of Personality and Social Psychology* 84 (2003): 365–376.

27. R. R. Provine, "Laughter Punctuates Speech: Linguistic Social and Gender Contexts of Laughter," *Ethology* 95 (1993): 291–298, and R. R. Provine, "Illusions of Intentionality, Shared and Unshared," *Behavioral and Brain Sciences* 28, no. 5 (2005): 713–714.

28. M. Iwase et al., "Neural Substrates of Human Facial Expression of Pleasant Emotion Induced by Comic Films: A PET Study," *Neuroimaging* 17 (2002): 758–768, and B. Wild et al., "Neural Correlates of Laughter and Humor," *Brain* 126 (2003): 2121–2138.

29. For an excellent review of the research literature, see M. Gervais, and D. S. Wilson, "The Evolution and Functions of Laughter and Humor: A Synthetic Approach," *Quarterly Review of Biology* 80 (2005): 395–430.

30. E. Hatfield, J. T. Cacioppo, and R. Rapson, "Primitive Emotional Contagion," *Review of Personality and Social Psychology* 14 (1992): 151–177, and R. R. Provine, "Contagious Laughter: Laughter Is a Sufficient Stimulus for Laughs and Smiles," *Bulletin of the Psychonomic Society* 30 (1992): 1–4.

31. G. E. Weisfield, "The Adaptive Value of Humor and Laughter," *Ethology and Sociobiology* 14 (1993): 141–169, and K. L. Vinton, "Humor in the Work Place: Is It More Than Telling Jokes?" *Small Group Behavior* 20 (1989): 151–166.

32. J. P. Scharlemann et al., "The Value of a Smile: Game Theory with a Human Face," *Journal of Economic Psychology* 22 (2001): 617–640.

33. L. A. Harker and D. Keltner, "Expression of Positive Emotion in Women's College Yearbook Pictures and Their Relationship to Personality and Life Outcomes Across Adulthood," *Journal of Personality and Social Psychology* 80 (2001): 112–124.

34. A. Papa and G. A. Bonanno, "Smiling in the Face of Adversity: Interpersonal and Intrapersonal Functions of Smiling," *Emotion* 8 (2008): 1–12.

35. Bonanno and Keltner, "Facial Expressions."

36. Ibid.

37. R. S. Lazarus, A. D. Kanner, and S. Folkman, "Emotions: A Cognitive-Phenomenological Analysis," in: *Emotions, Theory, Research, and Experience*, vol. 1, *Theories of Emotion,* ed. R. Plutchik and H. Kellerman, 189–217 (New York: Academic Press, 1980).

38. D. Keltner and G. A. Bonanno, "A Study of Laughter and Dissociation: Distinct Correlates of Laughter and Smiling During Bereavement," *Journal of Personality and Social Psychology* 73 (1997): 687–702.

39. R. J. Kastenbaum, *Death, Society, and Human Experience* (New York: Mosby, 1977): 138.

40. M. S. Stroebe and H. Schut, "The Dual Process Model of Coping with Bereavement: Rationale and Description," *Death Studies* 23, no. 3 (1999): 197–224.

41. Ibid., 212.

42. Two research studies have documented this oscillatory quality among bereaved people: T. L. Bisconti, C. S. Bergeman, and S. M. Boker, "Emotional Well-Being in Recently Bereaved Widows: A Dynamic Systems Approach," *Journals of Gerontology: Series B: Psychological Sciences and Social Sciences* 59B

(2004): 158–168, and T. L. Bisconti, C. S. Bergeman, and S. M. Boker, "Social Support as a Predictor of Variability: An Examination of the Adjustment Trajectories of Recent Widows," *Psychology and Aging* 21, no. 3 (2006): 590–599.

43. C. S. Lewis, *A Grief Observed* (San Francisco: HarperSan Francisco, 1961): 52, 53.

Chapter 4

1. G. A. Bonanno, "Loss, Trauma, and Human Resilience: Have We Underestimated the Human Capacity to Thrive After Extremely Adverse Events?" *American Psychologist* 59 (2004): 20–28.

2. Work on this issue by evolutionary psychologists Geoffrey Miller and Lars Penke is summarized in a brief report by Constance Holden, "An Evolutionary Squeeze on Brain Size," *Science* 312 (2006): 1867.

3. H. G. Birch and J. D. Gussow, *Disadvantaged Children: Health, Nutrition, and School Failure* (New York: Harcourt, Brace, & World, 1970); Children's Defense Fund, *Maternal and Child Health Date Book: The Health of American's Children* (Washington, DC: U.S. Government Printing Office, 1986); and N. Garmezy, "Resiliency and Vulnerability to Adverse Developmental Outcomes Associated with Poverty," *American Behavioral Scientist* 34 (1991): 416–430.

4. J. G. Noll et al., "Revictimization and Self-Harm in Females Who Experienced Childhood Sexual Abuse: Results from a Prospective Study," *Journal of Interpersonal Violence* 18, no. 12 (2003): 1452–1471, and J. L. Herman, *Trauma and Recovery* (New York: Basic Books, 1992).

5. S. Thompson, *The Folktale* (Berkeley: University of California Press, 1977); A. Dundes, "Projection in Folklore: A Plea for Psychoanalytic Semiotics," *MLN* 91 (1976): 1500–1533; and V. Propp, *The Morphology of the Folktale*, 2nd ed. (Austin: University of Texas Press, 1968).

6. Tatiana Serafin, "Tales of Success: Rags to Riches Billionaires," *Forbes,* June 26, 2007, http://www.forbes.com/2007/06/22/billionaires-gates-winfrey-biz-cz_ts_0626rags2riches.html.

7. A. M. Masten, "Ordinary Magic: Resilience Processes in Development," *American Psychologist* 56 (2001): 227–238. The term *superkids* was used in the title of a book review on resilience: S. E. Buggie "Superkids of the Ghetto," *Contemporary Psychology* 40 (1995): 1164–1165.

8. N. Garmezy, "Resilience and Vulnerability to Adverse Developmental Outcomes Associated with Poverty," *American Behavioral Scientist* 34 (1991): 416–430; L. B. Murphy, and A. E. Moriarty, *Vulnerability, Coping, and Growth* (New Haven, CT: Yale University Press, 1976); M. Rutter, "Protective Factors in Children's Responses to Stress and Disadvantage," in *Primary Prevention of Psychopathology: Social Competence in Children,* vol. 3, ed. M. W. Kent and J. E.

Rolf, 49–74 (Hanover, NH: University Press of New England, 1979); and E. E. Werner, "Resilience in Development," *Current Directions in Psychological Science* 4, no. 3 (June 1995): 81–85.

9. S. S. Luthar, C. H. Doernberger, and E. Zigler, "Resilience Is Not a Unidimensional Construct: Insights from a Prospective Study of Inner-City Adolescents," *Development and Psychopathology* 5, no. 4 (1993): 703–717.

10. A. J. Reynolds, "Resilience Among Black Urban Youth: Prevalence, Intervention Effects, and Mechanisms of Influence," *American Journal of Orthopsychiatry* 68, no. 1 (1998): 84–100.

11. G. H. Christ, *Healing Children's Grief* (New York: Oxford University Press, 2000).

12. F. H. Norris, "Epidemiology of Trauma: Frequency and Impact of Different Potentially Traumatic Events on Different Demographic Groups," *Journal of Consulting and Clinical Psychology* 60 (1992): 409–418.

13. W. E. Copeland et al., "Traumatic Events and Posttraumatic Stress in Childhood," *Archives of General Psychiatry* 62 (2007): 577–584.

14. This passage relies heavily on John Hersey's excellent essay "Hiroshima," first published as an entire issue of *New Yorker,* August 31, 1946, and later published in book form: J. Hersey, *Hiroshima* (New York: Knopf, 1946).

15. R. S. Lazarus, *Emotion and Adaptation* (New York: Oxford University Press, 1991).

16. Hersey, *Hiroshima.*

17. J. I. Janis, *Air War and Emotional Stress* (New York: McGraw-Hill, 1951).

18. Ibid.

19. Ibid., 86.

20. S. J. Rachman, *Fear and Courage* (New York: W. H. Freeman, 1978).

21. Janis, *Air War.*

22. Hideko Tamura Snider, *One Sunny Day: A Child's Memories of Hiroshima* (Chicago: Open Court, 1996).

23. Hersey, *Hiroshima,* 114.

24. Ibid., 64.

25. Ibid., 118.

26. Ibid., 69.

27. Takashi Nagai, *The Bells of Nagasaki*, trans. William Johnson (New York: Kodansha International, 1984): 37, 76.

28. George Weller, *First into Nagasaki* (New York: Crown, 2006).

29. Janis, *Air War.*

30. Ibid. The United States Strategic Bombing Survey: Summary Report (Pacific War). Washington, DC: U.S. Government Printing Office, 1946.

31. S. Galea et al., "Psychological Sequelae of the September 11 Terrorist Attacks in New York City," *New England Journal of Medicine* 346 (2002): 982–987.

32. S. Galea et al., "Trends of Probable Post-Traumatic Stress Disorder in New York City After the September 11 Terrorist Attacks," *American Journal of Epidemiology* 158, no. 6 (2003): 514–524.

33. G. A. Bonanno et al., "Psychological Resilience After Disaster: New York City in the Aftermath of the September 11th Terrorist Attack," *Psychological Science 17*, 181–186; G. A. Bonanno et al., "What Predicts Resilience After Disaster? The Role of Demographics, Resources, and Life Stress," *Journal of Consulting and Clinical Psychology, 75*, 671–682.

34. G. A. Bonanno, C. Rennicke, and S. Dekel, "Self-enhancement Among High-Exposure Survivors of the September 11th Terrorist Attack: Resilience or Social Maladjustment?" *Journal of Personality and Social Psychology* 88, no. 6 (2005): 984–998.

35. S. Zisook, Y. Chentsova-Dutton, and S. R. Shuchter, "PTSD Following Bereavement," *Annals of Clinical Psychiatry* 10 (1998): 157–163; G. A. Bonanno and S. Kaltman, "Toward an Integrative Perspective on Bereavement," *Psychological Bulletin* 125 (1999): 760–776; and S. Kaltman and G. A. Bonanno, "Trauma and Bereavement: Examining the Impact of Sudden and Violent Deaths," *Journal of Anxiety Disorders* 17 (2003): 131–147.

36. World Health Organization, *Update 49–SARS Case Fatality Ratio, Incubation Period,* May 7, 2003, http://www.who.int/csr/sarsarchive/2003_05_07a/en.

37. G. A. Bonanno et al., "Psychological Resilience and Dysfunction Among Hospitalized Survivors of the SARS Epidemic in Hong Kong: A Latent Class Approach," *Health Psychology* 27 (2008): 659–667.

Chapter 5

1. B. Raphael, *The Anatomy of Bereavement* (New York: Basic Books, 1983).

2. For more information about the CLOC study, visit the study's Web site: http://www.cloc.isr.umich.edu.

3. The papers in which we reported these results are as follows: G. A. Bonanno et al., "Resilience to Loss and Chronic Grief: A Prospective Study from Pre-loss to 18 Months Post-loss," *Journal of Personality and Social Psychology* 83 (2002): 1150–1164; G. A. Bonanno, C. B. Wortman, and R. M. Nesse, "Prospective Patterns of Resilience and Maladjustment During Widowhood," *Psychology and Aging* 19 (2004): 260–271; and K. Boerner, C. B. Wortman, and G. A. Bonanno, "Resilient or At Risk? A Four-Year Study of Older Adults Who Initially Showed High or Low Distress Following Conjugal Loss," *Journal of Gerontology: Psychological Science* 60B (2005): P67–P73.

4. Bonanno et al., "Resilience to Loss."

5. J. Fantuzzo et al., "Community-Based Resilient Peer Treatment of Withdrawn Maltreated Preschool Children," *Journal of Consulting and Clinical Psychology* 64 (December 1996): 1377–1386.

6. J. Kaufman et al., "Social Supports and Serotonin Transporter Gene Moderate Depression in Maltreated Children," *Proceedings of the National Academy of Sciences* 10 (December 2004): 17316–17321.

7. G. A. Bonanno et al., "Psychological Resilience After Disaster: New York City in the Aftermath of the September 11th Terrorist Attack," *Psychological Science* 17 (2006): 181–186, and C. Brewin, B. Andrews, and J. D. Valentine, "Analysis of Risk Factors for Posttraumatic Stress Disorder in Trauma," *Journal of Consulting and Clinical Psychology* 68, no. 5 (October 2000): 748–766.

8. C. S. Lewis, *A Grief Observed* (San Francisco: Harper San Francisco, 1961): 57.

9. Bonanno et al., "Resilience to Loss."

10. M. S. Stroebe and H. Schut, "The Dual Process Model of Coping with Bereavement: Rationale and Description," *Death Studies* 23, no. 3 (1999): 197–224.

11. For reviews of these factors, see G. A. Bonanno and S. Kaltman, "Toward an Integrative Perspective on Bereavement," *Psychological Bulletin* 125 (1999): 760–776; G. A. Bonanno and A. D. Mancini, "The Human Capacity to Thrive in the Face of Potential Trauma," *Pediatrics* 121 (2008): 369–375; and G. A. Bonanno et al., "What Predicts Psychological Resilience After Disaster: The Role of Demographics, Resources, and Life Stress," *Journal of Consulting and Clinical Psychology* 75 (2007): 671–682. For an interesting discussion and research on social support during bereavement, see W. Stroebe et al., "The Role of Loneliness and Social Support in Adjustment to Loss: A Test of Attachment Versus Stress Theory," *Journal of Personality and Social Psychology* 70 (1996): 1241–1249.

12. For a fascinating review of the history of this idea, see Gilbert Gottlieb, *Individual Development and Evolution* (Oxford: Oxford University Press, 1992). Highly readable summaries of this view are also available: Matt Ridley, *Nature via Nurture* (New York: HarperCollins, 2003), and David S. Moore, *The Dependent Gene* (New York: Times Books, 2003).

13. A. Caspi et al., "Influence of Life Stress on Depression: Moderation by a Polymorphism in the 5-HTT Gene," *Science* 301 (2003): 386–389; D. G. Kilpatrick et al., "The Serotonin Transporter Genotype and Social Support and Moderation of Posttraumatic Stress Disorder and Depression in Hurricane-Exposed Adults," *American Journal of Psychiatry* 164 (2007): 1693–1699; T. E. Moffitt, A. Caspi, and M. Rutter, "Measured Gene-Environment Interactions in Psychopathology: Concepts, Research Strategies, and Implications for Research, Intervention, and Public Understanding of Genetics," *Perspectives on Psychological Science* 1 (2006): 5–27; and J. Kaufman et al., "Social Supports."

14. Although there is no direct evidence linking genes to grief outcome, a key factor in the development of more severe grief and depression is rumination, the tendency to dwell repetitively and passively on distress and its possible causes. People with the same gene combination that has been associated with a

resistance to stress also tend to ruminate less; see T. Canli et al., "Neural Correlates of Epigenesist," *Proceedings of the National Academy of Sciences* 103, no. 43 (2005): 16033–16038. In one study, reduced rumination was found to mediate the relationship of the genetic disposition and depression; see L. M. Hilt et al., "The BDNF Val66Met Polymorphism Predicts Rumination and Depression Differently in Young Adolescent Girls and Their Mothers," *Neuroscience Letters* 429 (2007): 12–16.

15. For a review of some of the studies about personality characteristics in resilience, see M. Westphal, G. A. Bonanno, and P. Bartone, "Resilience and Personality," in *Biobehavioral Resilience to Stress,* ed. B. Lukey and V. Tepe, 219–258 (New York: Francis & Taylor, 2008). See also papers on the personality dimension of hardiness, a characteristic associated with resilience: S. C. Kobasa, "Stressful Life Events, Personality, and Health: An Inquiry into Hardiness," *Journal of Personality and Social Psychology* 37 (1979): 1–11; S. C. Kobasa, S. R. Maddi, and S. Kahn, "Hardiness and Health: A Prospective Study," *Journal of Personality and Social Psychology* 42 (1982): 168–177; S. R. Maddi, "Hardiness in Health and Effectiveness," in *Encyclopedia of Mental Health,* ed. H. S. Friedman, 323–335 (San Diego: Academic Press, 1998); and S. R. Maddi and D. M. Khoshaba, "Hardiness and Mental Health," *Journal of Personality Assessment* 63 (1994): 265–274.

16. G. A. Bonanno et al., "The Importance of Being Flexible: The Ability to Enhance and Suppress Emotional Expression Predicts Long-Term Adjustment," *Psychological Science* 157 (2004): 482–487.

17. K. G. Coifman and G. A. Bonanno, "Emotion Context Sensitivity, Depression, and Recovery from Bereavement," unpublished manuscript, 2009.

18. There were numerous media reports of gang violence and several incidents of rape during the emergency occupation of the New Orleans Superdome during and in the immediate aftermath of Hurricane Katrina (e.g., BBC News, September 6, 2005, http://news.bbc.co.uk/go/pr/fr/-/2/hi/uk_news/4214746.stm). However, owing to the chaos, few of the actual instances of violent behavior were ever verified.

19. G. A. Bonanno, "Grief, Trauma, and Resilience," in *Violent Death: Resilience and Intervention Beyond the Crisis,* ed. E. K. Rynearson, 31–46 (New York: Routledge, 2006), and Bonanno and Mancini, "Human Capacity to Thrive."

20. B. Gilbert and S. Jamison, *Winning Ugly: Mental Warfare in Tennis—Lessons from a Master* (New York: Fireside, 1994), and M. Madden, "Obama's Winning Ugly, but He's Winning," *Salon,* March 24, 2009, http://www.salon.com/news/feature/2009/02/12/stimulus_battle; and F. Barnes, "Winning Ugly," *Weekly Standard,* June 20, 2005.

21. John Lennon, composer and lyricist, "Whatever Gets You Through the Night," *Walls and Bridges,* John Lennon, Capitol Records, 1974.

22. For a classic review of this literature, see S. E. Taylor and J. D. Brown, "Illusion and Well-Being: A Social Psychological Perspective on Mental Health," *Psychological Bulletin* 103 (1988): 193–210.

23. M. E. Alicke et al., "Personal Contact, Individuation, and the Better-Than-Average Effect," *Journal of Personality and Social Psychology* 68 (1995): 804–825.

24. G. Keillor, *Home on the Prairie: Stories from Lake Wobegon,* audio recording (Minneapolis, MN: HighBridge, 2003).

25. G. A. Bonanno, C. Rennicke, and S. Dekel, "Self-enhancement Among High-Exposure Survivors of the September 11th Terrorist Attack: Resilience or Social Maladjustment?" *Journal of Personality and Social Psychology* 88, no. 6 (2005): 984–998, and G. A. Bonanno et al., "Self-enhancement as a Buffer Against Extreme Adversity," *Personality and Social Psychology Bulletin* 28 (2002): 184–196.

26. P. L. Tomich and V. S. Helgeson, "Is Finding Something Good in the Bad Always Good? Benefit Finding Among Women with Breast Cancer," *Health Psychology* 23 (2004): 16–23.

Chapter 6

1. The first time we were able to identify this pattern with any accuracy—that is, when we could actually follow people in our studies from before to after a major loss—we found that about 10 percent showed this kind of improvement; see G. Bonanno et al., "Resilience to Loss and Chronic Grief: A Prospective Study from Pre-loss to 18 Months Post-loss," *Journal of Personality and Social Psychology* 83 (2002): 1150–1164. We have since observed the same pattern—years of struggle before the loss and then improvement during bereavement—in several other studies, usually in around that same 10 percent proportion; see G. A. Bonanno et al., "Resilience to Loss in Bereaved Spouses, Bereaved Parents, and Bereaved Gay Men," *Journal of Personality and Social Psychology* 88 (2005): 827–843. Improvement during bereavement has also been observed in other studies: R. Schulz et al., "End of Life Care and the Effects of Bereavement Among Family Caregivers of Persons with Dementia," *New England Journal of Medicine* 349, no. 20 (2003): 1891–1892.

2. G. A. Bonanno et al., "Resilience to Loss and Chronic Grief: A Prospective Study from Pre-Loss to 18 Months Post-Loss," *Journal of Personality and Social Psychology* 83 (2002): 1150–1164.

3. B. Wheaton, "Life Transitions, Role Histories, and Mental Health," *American Sociological Review* 55 (1990): 209–223.

4. J. C. Bodnar and J. K. Kiecolt-Glaser, "Caregiver Depression After Bereavement: Chronic Stress Isn't Over When It's Over," *Psychology and Aging* 9 (1994): 372–380, and D. Cohen and E. Eisdorfer, "Depression in Family Members

Caring for a Relative with Alzheimer's Disease," *Journal of the American Geriatrics Society* 36 (1988): 885–889.

5. E. O. Wilson, *Naturalist* (Washington, DC: Island Press, 1994): 125.

6. Laurence J. Peter and Raymond Hull, *The Peter Principle: Why Things Always Go Wrong* (New York: William Morrow, 1969).

7. B. S. McEwen, "Protective and Damaging Effects of Stress Mediators," *New England Journal of Medicine* 38, no. 3 (1998): 171–179.

8. J. K. Kilecolt-Glaser et al., "Chronic Stress Alters the Immune Response to Influenza Virus Vaccine in Older Adults," *Proceedings of the National Academy of Sciences* 93 (1996): 3043–3047; A. M. Magariños et al., "Chronic Stress Alters Synaptic Terminal Structure in Hippocampus," *Proceedings of the National Academy of Sciences* 94 (1997): 14002–14008; and B. S. McEwen, "Protection and Damage from Acute and Chronic Stress: Allostasis and Allostatic Overload and Relevance to the Pathophysiology of Psychiatric Disorders," *Annals of the New York Academy of Sciences* 1032 (2004): 1–7.

Chapter 7

1. G. A. Bonanno and S. Kaltman, "The Varieties of Grief Experience," *Clinical Psychology Review* 21 (2001): 705–734.

2. J. Bauer and G. A. Bonanno, "Continuity and Discontinuity: Bridging One's Past and Present in Stories of Conjugal Bereavement," *Narrative Inquiry* 11 (2001): 1–36.

3. M. J. Horowitz et al., "Diagnostic Criteria for Complicated Grief Disorder," *American Journal of Psychiatry* 154 (1997): 904–910, and H. G. Prigerson et al., "Consensus Criteria for Complicated Grief: A Preliminary Empirical Test," *British Journal of Psychiatry* 174 (1999): 67–73.

4. For an excellent review of the contemporary research literature on adult attachment behavior, see M. Milulincer and P. Shaver, *Attachment in Adulthood: Structure, Dynamics, and Change* (New York: Guilford Press, 2007).

5. Kerstin Uvnäs-Moberg, "Neuroendocrinology of the Mother-Child Interaction," *Trends in Endocrinology and Metabolism* 7 (1996): 126–131.

6. G. A. Bonanno et al., "Interpersonal Ambivalence, Perceived Dyadic Adjustment, and Conjugal Loss," *Journal of Consulting and Clinical Psychology* 66 (1998): 1012–1022.

7. S. Strack and J. C. Coyne, "Social Confirmation of Dysphoria: Shared and Private Reactions to Depression," *Journal of Personality and Social Psychology* 44 (1983): 798–806.

8. R. F. Bornstein, "The Complex Relationship Between Dependency and Domestic Violence," *American Psychologist* 61 (2006): 595–606.

9. D. S. Kalmus and M. A. Strauss, "Wife's Marital Dependency and Wife Abuse," *Journal of Marriage and the Family* 44 (1982): 277–286.

10. R. G. Bornstein, "The Dependent Personality: Developmental, Social, and Clinical Perspectives," *Psychological Bulletin* 112 (1992): 3–23.

11. G. Bonanno et al., "Resilience to Loss and Chronic Grief: A Prospective Study from Pre-loss to 18 Months Post-loss," *Journal of Personality and Social Psychology* 83 (2002): 1150–1164.

12. M. W. Lipsey and D. B. Wilson, "The Efficacy of Psychological, Educational, and Behavioral Treatment: Confirmation and Meta-Analysis," *American Psychologist* 48 (1993): 1181–1209.

13. D. L. Chambless et al., "Update on Empirically Validated Therapies II," *Clinical Psychologist* 51 (1998): 3–16.

14. D. L. Allumbaugh and W. T. Hoyt, "Effectiveness of Grief Therapy: A Meta-Analysis," *Journal of Counseling Psychology* 46 (1999): 370–380; J. M. Currier, J. M. Holland, and R. A. Neimeyer, "The Effectiveness of Bereavement Interventions with Children: A Meta-Analytic Review of Controlled Outcome Research," *Journal of Clinical Child and Adolescent Psychology* 36, no. 2 (2007): 253–259; J. M. Currier, R. A. Neimeyer, and J. S. Berman, "The Effectiveness of Psychotherapeutic Interventions for the Bereaved: A Comprehensive Quantitative Review," *Psychological Bulletin* 134 (2009): 648–661; B. V. Fortner, *The Effectiveness of Grief Counseling and Therapy: A Quantitative Review* (Memphis, TN: University of Memphis, 1999); J. R. Jordan and R. A. Neimeyer, "Does Grief Counseling Work?" *Death Studies* 27 (2003): 765–786; and P. M. Kato and T. Mann, "A Synthesis of Psychological Interventions for the Bereaved," *Clinical Psychology Review* 19 (1999): 275–296.

15. Scott O. Lilienfeld, "Psychological Treatments That Cause Harm," *Perspectives on Psychological Science* 2 (2007): 53–70.

16. G. S. Everly and S. H. Boyle, "Critical Incident Stress Debriefing (CISD): A Meta-Analysis," *International Journal of Emergency Mental Health* 1 (1999): 165–168.

17. J. T. Mitchell, "When Disaster Strikes: The Critical Incident Stress Debriefing Process," *Journal of Emergency Medical Services* 8 (1983): 36–39.

18. R. J. McNally, R. A. Bryant, and A. Ehlers, "Does Early Psychological Intervention Promote Recovery from Posttraumatic Stress?" *Psychological Science in the Public Interest* 4 (2003): 45–79.

19. R. A. Mayou, A. Ehlers, and M. Hobbs, "Psychological Debriefing for Road Traffic Accident Victims," *British Journal of Psychiatry* 176 (2000): 589–593.

20. World Health Organization, "Single Session Debriefing: Not Recommended," February 7, 2005; see http://www.helid.desastres.net/ and then search for the article title. Questions about this article may be directed to Dr. Mark van Ommeren, Department of Mental Health and Substance Abuse, World Health Organization, vanommeren@who.int.

21. The most efficacious treatment for PTSD is prolonged exposure therapy; see E. B. Foa et al., "A Comparison of Exposure Therapy, Stress Inoculation

Training, and Their Combination for Reducing Posttraumatic Stress Disorder in Female Assault Victims," *Journal of Consulting and Clinical Psychology* 67 (1999): 194–200. For a thoughtful discussion of PTSD, see R. J. McNally, "Progress and Controversy in the Study of Posttraumatic Stress Disorder," *Annual Review of Psychology* 54 (2003): 229–252.

22. H. Prigerson et al., "Prolonged Grief Disorder: Empirical Test of Consensus Criteria Proposed for DSM-V," *PLoS Medicine* (in press), and G. A. Bonanno et al., "Is There More to Complicated Grief than Depression and PTSD? A Test of Incremental Validity," *Journal of Abnormal Psychology* 116 (2007): 342–351.

23. Horowitz et al., "Diagnostic Criteria"; K. Shear et al., "Treatment of Complicated Grief: A Randomized Controlled Trial," *Journal of the American Medical Association* 293, no. 21 (2005): 2601–2608, and W. G. Lichtenthal, D. G. Cruess, and H. G. Prigerson, "A Case for Establishing Complicated Grief as a Distinct Mental Disorder in DSM-V," *Clinical Psychology Review* 24 (2004): 637–662.

24. P. A. Boelen et al., "Treatment of Complicated Grief: A Comparison Between Cognitive-Behavioral Therapy and Supportive Counseling," *Journal of Consulting and Clinical Psychology* 75, no. 2 (2007): 277–284, and K. Shear et al., "Treatment of Complicated Grief."

25. Boelen et al., "Treatment of Complicated Grief."

26. R. F. Bornstein, "Adaptive and Maladaptive Aspects of Dependency: An Integrative Review," *American Journal of Orthopsychiatry* 64 (1994): 622–635.

Chapter 8

1. G. A. Bonanno et al., "Resilience to Loss and Chronic Grief: A Prospective Study from Pre-Loss to 18 Months Post-Loss," *Journal of Personality and Social Psychology* 83 (2002): 1150–1164; C. G. Davis, S. Nolen-Hoeskema, and J. Larson, "Making Sense of Loss and Benefiting from the Experience: Two Construals of Meaning," *Journal of Personality and Social Psychology* 75 (1998): 561–574; and C. G. Davis et al., "Searching for Meaning in Loss: Are Clinical Assumptions Correct?" *Death Studies* 24 (2000): 497–540.

2. E. Becker, *The Denial of Death* (New York: Free Press, 1973).

3. T. Pyszczynski, J. Greenberg, and S. Solomon, "A Dual-Process Model of Defense Against Conscious and Unconscious Death-Related Thoughts: An Extension of Terror Management Theory," *Psychological Review* 106 (1999): 835–845.

4. J. Greenberg, S. Solomon, and T. Pyszczynski, "Terror Management Theory of Self-Esteem and Cultural World Views: Empirical Assessments and Conceptual Refinements," *Advances in Experimental Social Psychology* 29 (1997): 65.

5. For interesting discussions of ethnocentricism in beliefs about one's country, see T. Adorno et al., *The Authoritarian Personality* (New York: Harper, 1950). See also J. Hurwitz and M. Peffley, "How Are Foreign Policy Attitudes Structured? A Hierarchical Model," *American Political Science Review* 81 (1987): 1099–1120.

6. J. Greenberg et al., "Evidence for Terror Management Theory II: The Effects of Mortality Salience on Reactions to Those Who Threaten or Bolster the Cultural Worldview," *Journal of Personality and Social Psychology* 58, no. 2 (1990): 308.

7. L. Ross, D. Greene, and P. House, "The 'False Consensus Effect': An Ego-Centric Bias in Social Perception and Attribution Processes," *Journal of Experimental Social Psychology* 13 (1977): 279–301; C. E. Brown, "A False Consensus Bias in 1980 Presidential Preferences," *Journal of Social Psychology* 118 (1982): 137–138; and B. E. Whitley, Jr., "False Consensus on Sexual Behavior Among College Women: A Comparison of Four Theoretical Explanations," *Journal of Sex Research* 35 (1998): 206–214. For a review of the research on false consensus, see B. Mullen et al., "The False Consensus Effect: A Meta-Analysis of 115 Hypothesis Tests," *Journal of Experimental Social Psychology* 21 (1985): 262–283.

8. A. Rosenblatt et al., "Evidence for Terror Management Theory I: The Effects of Mortality Salience on Reactions to Those Who Violate or Uphold Cultural Values," *Journal of Personality and Social Psychology* 57, no. 4 (1989): 682.

9. The studies on the setting of bail for prostitutes and reward for heroes are described in Rosenblatt et al., ibid.

10. For reviews of the terror management research, see S. Solomon, J. Greenberg, and T. Pyszczynski, "Pride and Prejudice: Fear and Social Behavior," *Current Directions in Psychological Science* 9 (2000): 200–204, and J. L. Goldenberg, "The Body Stripped Down: An Existential Account of the Threat Posed by the Physical Body," *Current Directions in Psychological Science* 14 (2005): 224–228.

11. C. D. Navarrete et al., "Anxiety and Intergroup Bias: Terror Management or Coalition Psychology?" *Group Processes and Intergroup Relations* 7 (2004): 370–397.

12. J. Greenberg et al., "Proximal and Distal Defenses in Response to Reminders of One's Mortality: Evidence of a Temporal Sequence," *Personality and Social Psychology Bulletin* 26 (2000): 91–99.

13. A deeper awareness of death was induced when the students were asked to "consider their deepest emotions about their own death" and to imagine that they had been diagnosed with an advanced stage of cancer. Then they were asked to answer an additional series of provocative, open-ended questions about their own death, for example, "The one thing I fear most

about my own death is———," or "My scariest thoughts about death are——." Longer-term awareness of death was induced by having the students continue to think about death for three minutes by solving word puzzles that included death-associated words like *tomb, skull, corpse,* and *burial.* See J. Greenberg et al., "Role of Consciousness and Accessibility of Death-Related Thoughts in Mortality Salience Effects," *Journal of Personality and Social Psychology* 67 (1994): 627–637.

14. Greenberg et al., "Proximal and Distal Defenses."

15. Michael Luo, "Calming the Mind Among Bodies Laid Bare," *New York Times,* April 29, 2006.

16. Bruno J. Navarro, "Exhibition Opens Windows on the Human Body: Skinless Cadavers, Variety of Organs, on Display in New York Show," MSNBC, December 1, 2005. The show was entitled "Bodies: The Exhibition."

17. Luo, "Calming the Mind."

18. A. Martens, J. L. Goldenberg, and J. Greenberg, "A Terror Management Perspective on Ageism," *Journal of Social Issues* 61 (2005): 223–239. See also William D. McIntosh, "East Meets West: Parallels Between Zen Buddhism and Social Psychology," *International Journal for the Psychology of Religion* 7 (1997): 37–52.

19. K. Armstrong, *Buddha* (New York: Penguin Putnam, 2001).

20. Thich Nhat Hanh. *The Heart of the Buddha's Teaching: Transforming Suffering into Peace, Joy and Liberation* (New York: Broadway Books, 1999).

21. J. Goldstein and J. Kornfield, *Seeking the Heart of Wisdom: The Path of Insight Mediation* (Boston: Shambhala, 1987).

22. Ibid., 3.

23. Bhikkhu Bodhi, *The Connected Discourses of the Buddha: A New Translation of the Samyutta Nikāya*, vol. 2 (Somerville, MA: Wisdom Publications, 2000): 1209.

24. E. Sachs et al., "Entering Exile: Trauma, Mental Health, and Coping Among Tibetan Refugees Arriving in Dharamsala, India," *Journal of Traumatic Stress* 21, no. 2 (2008): 199–208.

25. H. H. The Dalai Lama, Foreword to R. Thurman, *The Tibetan Book of the Dead* (New York: Bantam, 1994): xvii.

26. Thich Nhat Hahn, *The Blooming of a Lotus: Guided Mediation Exercises for Healing and Transformation* (Boston: Beacon Press, 1993): 32.

27. Adorno et al., *Authoritarian Personality.*

28. S. Milgram, *Obedience to Authority: An Experimental View* (New York: HarperCollins, 1974).

29. J. Greenberg et al., "Evidence for Terror Management Theory II: The Effects of Mortality Salience on Reactions to Those Who Threaten or Bolster the Cultural Worldview," *Journal of Personality and Social Psychology* 58 (1990): 308–318.

30. A. Wisman and J. L. Goldenberg, "From Grave to the Cradle: Evidence That Mortality Salience Engenders a Desire for Offspring," *Journal of Personality and Social Psychology* 89 (2005): 46–61.

31. G. Hirschberger et al., "Gender Differences in the Willingness to Engage in Risky Behavior: A Terror Management Perspective," *Death Studies* 26 (2002): 117–141.

32. Frans de Waal. *The Ape and the Sushi Master* (New York: Basic Books, 2001): 10.

33. C. Hazen and P. R. Shaver, "Romantic Lover Conceptualized as an Attachment Process," *Journal of Personality and Social Psychology* 52 (1987): 511–524, and P. R. Shaver and C. Hazen, "Adult Romantic Attachment," in *Advances in Personal Relationships,* ed. D. Perlman & W. Jones, 29–70 (London: Kingsley, 1993).

34. R. C. Fraley and G. A. Bonanno, "Attachment and Loss: A Test of Three Competing Models on the Association Between Attachment-Related Avoidance and Adaptation to Bereavement," *Personality and Social Psychology Bulletin* 30 (2004): 878–890; M. Mikulincer and V. Florian, "Exploring Individual Differences in Reactions to Mortality Salience: Does Attachment Style Regulate Terror Management Mechanisms?" *Journal of Personality and Social Psychology* 79 (2000): 260–273; and V. Florian, M. Mikulincer, and G. Hirschberger, "The Anxiety Buffering Function of Close Relationships: Evidence That Relationship Commitment Acts as a Terror Management Mechanism," *Journal of Personality and Social Psychology* 82 (2002): 527–542.

35. F. Gonzalez-Crussi, *Day of the Dead and Other Mortal Reflections* (New York: Harcourt, Brace, 1993): 134.

36. R. Leakey, *The Origin of Humankind* (New York: Basic Books, 1994).

Chapter 9

1. C. S. Lewis, *A Grief Observed* (San Francisco: HarperSan Francisco, 1961): 34.

2. Ibid., 35–36.

3. K. Kim and S. Jacobs, "Pathologic Grief and Its Relationship to Other Psychiatric Disorders." *Journal of Affective Disorders* 21 (1991): 257–263, and A. Lazare, "Bereavement and Unresolved Grief," in *Outpatient Psychiatry: Diagnosis and Treatment,* 2nd ed., ed. A. Lazare, 381–397 (Baltimore, MD: Williams & Wilkins, 1989).

4. Lewis, *A Grief Observed,* 57.

5. S. R. Shuchter and S. Zisook, "The Course of Normal Grief," in *Handbook of Bereavement: Theory, Research, and Intervention,* ed. M. S. Stroebe, W. Stroebe, and R. O. Hansson, 23–43 (Cambridge, UK: Cambridge University Press, 1993).

6. D. Klass, P. R. Silverman, and S. L. Nickman, eds., *Continuing Bonds: New Understandings of Grief* (Bristol, PA: Taylor & Francis, 1996).

7. Shuchter and Zisook, "Course of Normal Grief," 34.

8. N. P. Field et al., "The Relation of Continuing Attachment to Adjustment During Bereavement," *Journal of Consulting and Clinical Psychology* 67 (1999): 212–218, and N. P. Field, B. Bao, and L. Paderna, "Continuing Bonds in Bereavement: An Attachment Theory Based Perspective," *Death Studies* 29 (2005): 277–299.

9. Field et al., "Continuing Bonds," and N. P. Field and M. Friedrichs, "Continuing Bonds in Coping with the Death of a Husband," *Death Studies* 28 (2004): 597–620.

10. N. P. Field, E. Gal-Oz, and G. A. Bonanno, "Continued Bonds and Adjustment 5 Years After the Death of a Spouse," *Journal of Consulting and Clinical Psychology* 71 (2003): 110–117.

Chapter 10

1. Deborah Solomon, "The Right Stuff: Questions for Christopher Buckley," *New York Times Magazine,* October 26, 2008, 16.

2. K. J. Flannelly et al., "Belief in Life After Death and Mental Health: Findings from a National Survey," *Journal of Nervous and Mental Disease* 194 (2006): 524–529.

3. K. A. Alvarado et al., "The Relation of Religious Variables to Death Depression and Death Anxiety," *Journal of Clinical Psychology* 51 (1995): 202–204.

4. S. R. Shuchter and S. Zisook, "The Course of Normal Grief," in *Handbook of Bereavement: Theory, Research, and Intervention,* ed. M. S. Stroebe, W. Stroebe, and R. O. Hansson (Cambridge, UK: Cambridge University Press, 1993).

5. Elaine Pagels, *The Origins of Satan: How Christians Demonized Jews, Pagans, and Heretics* (New York: Random House, 1995).

6. R. W. Hood Jr. et al., *The Psychology of Religion: An Empirical Approach,* 2nd ed. (New York: Guilford Press, 1996).

7. J. J. Exline, "Belief in Heaven and Hell Among Christians in the United States: Denominational Differences and Clinical Implications," *Omega: The Journal of Death and Dying* 47 (2003): 155–168, and J. A. Thorson and F. C. Powell, "Elements of Death Anxiety and Meanings of Death," *Journal of Clinical Psychology* 44 (1988): 691–701.

8. Pippa Norris and Ronald Inglehart, *Secular and Sacred: Religion and Politics Worldwide* (New York: Cambridge University Press, 2004).

9. David Van Biema, "Does Heaven Exist?" *Time,* March 27, 1997, 71–78.

10. Colleen McDannell and Bernhard Lang, *Heaven* (New Haven, CT: Yale University Press, 1988): 322–333.

11. Don DeLillo, *White Noise* (New York: Viking Penguin, 1984): 318–319. I am thankful to my colleague, Barry Farber, for pointing me to this passage.

12. R. Thurman, *The Tibetan Book of the Dead* (New York: Bantam Books, 1994): 23.

13. Paul Serges, *Reincarnation: A Critical Examination* (Amherst, NY: Prometheus Books, 1996).

14. *Biography—Dalai Lama: The Soul of Tibet,* A & E Home Video, April 2005.

15. Commentary by F. Fremantle and Chögyam Trungpa, in Chögyam Trungpa, *The Tibetan Book of the Dead* (Boston: Shambhala, 2003): 1–74.

16. Thurman, *Tibetan Book of the Dead*, 5–96.

17. Herbert Stroup, *Like a Great River: An Introduction to Hinduism* (New York: Harper & Row, 1972).

18. Ernest Valea, "Reincarnation: Its Meaning and Consequences," 2008, http://www.comparativereligion.com/reincarnation.html; R. C. Zaehner, *Hinduism* (Oxford, UK: Oxford University Press, 1966); and Robert Ernest Hume, *The Thirteen Principal Upanishads, Translated from the Sanskrit* (London: Oxford University Press, 1921).

19. Jean-Francois Revel and Matthieu Ricard, *The Monk and the Philosopher: A Father and Son Discuss the Meaning of Life* (New York: Schocken Books, 1998): 30.

20. Bhikkhu Ñāṇamoli and Bhikkhu Bodhi, *The Middle Length Discourses of the Buddha: A Translation of the Majjhima Nikāya* (Somerville, MA: Wisdom Publications, 1995): 92.

21. Fremantle and Trungpa, *The Tibetan Book of the Dead.*

22. Thich Nhat Hanh, *Heart of the Buddha's Teaching.*

23. Thurman, *Tibetan Book of the Dead,* 40.

24. Ibid., 41.

25. Bhikkhu Bodhi, *Connected Discourses* (1391).

26. William James, *Human Immortality: Two Supposed Objections to the Doctrine,* 2nd ed. (New York: Dover, 1896): 2.

27. Ibid., 12.

28. Ibid., 13.

29. Ibid., 23.

30. Ibid., 15.

31. Ibid., 40.

32. Ibid., 41.

33. Ibid., 42.

34. William Steig, *Amos and Boris* (New York: Farrar, Straus & Giroux, 1971).

35. Shelby A. Wolf, *Interpreting Literature with Children* (Mahwah, NJ: Erlbaum, 2004).

36. F. Gonzalez-Crussi, *Day of the Dead,* 71.

37. Octavio Paz, *The Labyrinth of Solitude* (New York: Grove Press, 1985): 57.

38. C. A. Corr, C. M. Nabe, and D. M. Corr, *Death and Dying, Life and Living* (Pacific Grove, CA: Brooks/Cole, 1994); R. A. Kalish and D. K. Reynolds, *Death and Ethnicity: A Psychocultural Study* (Farmingdale, NY: Baywood, 1981), and J. Moore, "The Death Culture of Mexico and Mexican Americans," in *Death and Dying: Views from Many Cultures,* ed. R. A. Kalish (Farmingdale, NY: Baywood, 1980): 72–91; and Kalish and Reynolds, *Death and Ethnicity.*

39. F. Gonzalez-Crussi, *Day of the Dead,* 37.

40. Ibid., 81.

41. Paul Westheim, *La Calavera* (Paris: Organization for Economic Cooperation and Development, 1983).

42. R. De Nebesky-Wojkowitz, *Oracles and Demons of Tibet* (New York: Gordon Press, 1977).

43. M. J. Herskovits, *Dahomey* (New York: Augustin, 1938): 166.

44. J. K. Okupona, "To Praise and Reprimand: Ancestors and Spirituality in African Society and Culture," in *Ancestors in Post-Contact Religion,* ed. S. J. Friesen, 49–66 (Cambridge, MA: Harvard University Press, 2001).

45. J. K. Opoku, *To Praise and Reprimand* (1989): 20, and. K. A. Dickson, *Theology in Africa* (London: Darton, Longman, &Todd, 1984): 196.

46. Opoku, *To Praise and Reprimand,* 20.

47. Kalish and Reynolds, *Death and Ethnicity,* and A. J. Marsella, "Depressive Experience and Disorder Across Cultures," in *Handbook of Cross-cultural Psychology: Psychopathology,* vol. 6, ed. H. C. Triandis and J. G. Draguns, 237–290 (Boston: Allyn & Bacon, 1979).

48. A. Laurie and R. A. Neimeyer, "African Americans in Bereavement: Grief as a Function of Ethnicity," *Omega* 57, no. 2 (2008): 173–193.

49. R. Kastenbaum, *Death, Society and Human Experience* (Boston: Allyn & Bacon, 1995).

50. F. Eggan, *Social Organization of Western Pueblos* (Chicago: University of Chicago Press, 1950): 110.

51. R. Price and S. Price, *Two Evenings in Saramaka* (Chicago: University of Chicago Press, 1991): 1, 3, 56–57.

52. This anecdote reported in Emily A. Ahern, *The Cult of the Dead in a Chinese Village* (Stanford, CA: Stanford University Press, 1973): 220–244.

53. Ibid., 230.

Chapter 11

1. J. Gernet, *A History of Chinese Civilization* (Cambridge, UK: Cambridge University Press, 1982).

2. William Theodore de Barry, Wing-Tsit Chan, and Burton Watson, *Sources of Chinese Tradition,* vol. 1 (New York: Columbia University Press, 1960).

3. Lu Yaw, "Providing for Life in the Other World: Han Ceramics in the Light of Recent Archaeological Discoveries," in *Spirit of Han: Ceramics for the After-Life*, ed. A. Lau, 10–17 (Singapore: Southeast Asian Ceramic Society, 1991), and Xiaoeng Yang, *The Golden Age of Chinese Archaeology: Celebrated Discoveries from the People's Republic of China* (New Haven, CT: Yale University Press, 1999).

4. L. E Butler, "The Role of the Visual Arts in Confucian Society," in *An Introduction to Chinese Culture Through the Family,* ed. H. Giskin and B. S. Walsh, 59–88 (New York: State University of New York Press, 2001).

5. J. L. Watson, "The Structure of Chinese Funerary Rites: Elementary Forms, Ritual Sequences, and the Primacy of Performance," in *Death Ritual in Late Imperial and Modern China,* ed. J. L. Watson and E. S. Rawski (Berkeley: University of California Press, 1988): 10.

6. Ibid., 3, 4.

7. R. Cave, *Chinese Paper Offerings* (Oxford, UK: Oxford University Press, 1998).

8. Ibid.

9. S. R. Teiser, *The Ghost Festival in Medieval China* (Princeton, NJ: Princeton University Press, 1988).

10. F. Fremantle and Chögyam Trungpa, commentary in Chögyam Trungpa, *The Tibetan Book of the Dead* (Boston: Shambhala, 2003): 1–74.

11. Teiser, *Ghost Festival.*

12. Ibid.

13. E. A. Ahern, *The Cult of the Dead in a Chinese Village* (Stanford, CA: Stanford University Press, 1973).

14. Ibid.

15. K. L. Braun and R. Nichols, "Death and Dying in Four Asian-American Cultures: A Descriptive Study," *Death Studies* 21 (1997): 327–359; R. Cave, *Chinese Paper Offerings;* and C. Ikels, *The Return of the God of Wealth* (Stanford, CA: Stanford University Press, 1996).

16. Heonik Kwon, *Ghosts of War in Vietnam* (Cambridge, UK: Cambridge University Press, 2008).

17. Jonathan Mirsky, "Vietnam: Dead Souls," *New York Review of Books,* November 20, 2008, 38–40.

18. Kwon, *Ghosts of War*.

19. G. A. Bonanno et al., "Grief Processing and Deliberate Grief Avoidance: A Prospective Comparison of Bereaved Spouses and Parents in the United States and People's Republic of China," *Journal of Consulting and Clinical Psychology* 73 (2005): 86–98; K. Lalande and G. A. Bonanno, "Culture and Continued Bonds During Bereavement: A Prospective Comparison in the United States and China," *Death Studies* 30 (2006): 303–324; and D. Pressman and G. A. Bonanno, "With Whom Do We Grieve? Social and Cultural Determinants of

Grief Processing in the United States and China," *Journal of Social and Personal Relationships* 24 (2007): 729–746.

20. Ahern, *Cult of the Dead.*

21. Ibid., 225.

22. Lalande and Bonanno, "Culture and Continued Bonds."

23. D. Klass, "Grief in an Eastern Culture: Japanese Ancestor Worship," in *Continued Bonds: New Understandings of Grief,* ed. D. Klass, P. R. Silverman, and S. L. Nickman, 59–71 (Washington, DC: Taylor & Francis, 1996).

24. M. S. Stroebe et al., "Broken Hearts or Broken Bonds," *American Psychologist* 47 (1992): 1205–1212.

25. Liao Yiwu, *The Corpse Walker* (New York: Pantheon, 2008): 10–11.

26. Ha Jin, *A Free Life* (New York: Pantheon, 2007): 189.

27. Cave, *Chinese Paper Offerings*, 55.

28. Watson, "Structure of Chinese Funerary Rites," 4.

29. Cave, *Chinese Paper Offerings*.

30. Ibid.

Chapter 12

1. K. Boerner, C. B. Wortman, and G. A. Bonanno, "Resilient or At Risk? A Four-Year Study of Older Adults Who Initially Showed High or Low Distress Following Conjugal Loss," *Journal of Gerontology: Psychological Science* 60B (2005): P67–P73.

2. A. D. Mancini, G. A. Bonanno, and A. E. Clark, "Stepping Off the Hedonic Treadmill: Latent Class Analyses of Individual Differences in Response to Major Life Events," unpublished manuscript, 2008.

3. Quoted in John Colapinto, "When I'm Sixty-Four," in column "Onward and Upwards with the Arts," *New Yorker,* June 4, 2007, 67.

4. K. B. Carnelley et al., "The Time Course of Grief Reactions to Spousal Loss: Evidence from a National Probability Sample," *Journal of Personality and Social Psychology* 91 (2006): 476–492.

5. Ruth Malkinson and Liora Bar-tur, "The Aging of Grief: Parents' Grieving of Israeli Soldiers," *Journal of Loss and Trauma* 5 (2000): 247–261.

Index